HAVE MERCY!

HAVE MERCY!

Confessions of the Original Rock 'n' Roll Animal

WOLFMAN JACK

With Byron Laursen

WARNER BOOKS

A Time Warner Company

Warner Books, Inc., 1271 Avenue of the Americas, New York, NY 10020

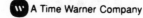 A Time Warner Company

Printed in the United States of America
First Printing: June 1995
10 9 8 7 6 5 4 3 2 1

Library of Congress Cataloging-in-Publication Data

Wolfman Jack, 1938–
  Have mercy! : Confessions of the original rock 'n' roll animal /
Wolfman Jack with Byron Laursen.
    p.   cm.
  ISBN 0-446-51742-9
  1. Wolfman Jack, 1938- . 2. Disc jockeys—United States—
Biography. I. Laursen, Byron.
ML429.W64A3   1995
781.66'092—dc20
[B]   94-48458

Book design by Giorgetta Bell McRee

You can't have a good life without a lot of people helping you out, catching you when you fall, keeping you tuned in to what really matters in your soul. One particular person has done all those great things every day, ever since I met her. That's the Wolfwoman, Lou Lamb Smith, my wife for many years and for always. Take a bow, darling. You're my everything.

Acknowledgments

So many great folks have been part of my life and have given of their talents to the ever-changing slice of carnival that has been *The Wolfman Jack Show*. I'd need another whole book just to praise their names and thank them as much as they deserve. There are many more influential and helpful people I want to thank whom I never met, yet they influenced me big-time with their artistry. I'm talking about all the great musicians and jocks whose magic pulled me in the direction of radio.

Eric and Maureen Lasher are the very smart agents who convinced Warner Books how cool it would be to publish my story. Byron Laursen is the talented and devoted writer who, month by month, brought the story together and made all the impulsive chaos of my life work out on the page. Mauro Di Preta is the very bright, capable, and friendly editor who took the manuscript in hand at Warner, came up with some key suggestions, and helped get it in great shape for you.

As you'll learn in the chapters Byron wove together, my family is of paramount importance to me. Having such a crazy character as me in their midst has required a lot of love and understanding. They've come through like champs.

Then there are all the unforgettable people who gave me breaks and helped polish my performance along the way. You'll be meeting them in these pages, too.

Special recognition is due to Lonnie Napier: my right arm, work partner, musical mainstay, road buddy, and ever-ready friend for many years.

Many of the photos you'll see inside came from a super-talented guy named Jeff Dunas. He started his career as a teenager, hanging around the Wolfman's lair, taking pictures of famous visitors to my radio studio, then went on to be one of the main guys, worldwide, in erotic photography.

Come to think of it, *he* should probably write a book someday. With lots more of his pictures.

Somebody who already did write a terrific book is Art Fein. *Musical History Tour,* his collection of L.A.'s hot spots of rock 'n' roll history, was quite a memory-stirrer.

Big thanks will always be due to George Lucas, who made my voice one of the stars of his first big hit movie. And even put my face in there, too. Burt Sugarman gave me close to a decade of fun on *The Midnight Special.* Don Imus pressured the executives at WNBC to track me down and bring me to the New York airwaves, giving a local boy a chance to return in triumph. Burton Cummings of the Guess Who wrote a hit song featuring my name and voice, then generously took me on the road to promote it. Don Kelley managed my career at some crucial early turns, and he opened up his files to help make this book possible. "Mo Burton," a rich, secretive friend who doesn't want his real name published, taught me—or at least tried to teach me—how to succeed in the radio business jungle. Bob Wilson, then of KDAY,

The man is a legend! I've waited for years for him to tell his fabulous story. Wolfman Jack is one of the most colorful personalities to ever emerge from the world of radio—his true life story is just as much fun as the images he conjures up in your mind when you hear his unmistakable Wolfman howl soaring out over the airwaves.

—DICK CLARK

Introduction

Folks, I'm real nervous about getting this book *right*. I've ranted and raved, screamed, shouted, and even crooned at you all through microphones jacked into the pumped-up, megawatt transmitter towers of the world's biggest radio stations. I've danced, sung, and clowned in front of hundreds of nightclub and Vegas showroom crowds, and before the blissed-out faces of ocean-sized, bigger'n-Woodstock festival audiences. Not to mention my thousands of hours of sweaty, valuable experience in front of television and movie cameras.

But one thing that I'd never, ever done before—which has made me more scared than the most nervous virgin you ever met—was to sit down in a quiet place in front of blank paper and try to make sense of my life.

A great musical pal of mine, a Texas rhythm and blues man by the name of Delbert McClinton, once wrote a song that said, "It ain't what you eat, but the way how you chew it."

Well, I ate up all kinds of wild experiences so far in this crazy life of mine. I've spent my time living for music and other sensual thrills, instead of doing the sensible things that everybody tells you you're supposed to do. Some of my experiences, I had to chew on for a long time before I knew what they were all about. But once I got started with the writing of it, I realized there could be only one name for this book.

"Have Mercy!" is something I've said more than a million times in my life—yelling it over the final notes of a classic rhythm and blues tune, whispering it under my breath at the first bite of a juicy T-bone steak, moaning it softly to my sweet Wolfwoman in a moment of bedroom ecstasy.

"Have Mercy!" It's a simple expression of amazement, and gratitude for all the stimulating satisfactions that come from being alive.

I needed a title, and those two words just popped into my head. I liked them there. Whenever inspiration comes along, it's best to just latch on to it. Explanations will reveal themselves later on. Eventually, I realized that there are several reasons why "Have Mercy!" is perfect.

First of all, in these pages I'm trying to pull together more than half a century of living—some of it very fast living, indeed. By and large, I remember what happened. And I definitely remember what it all *felt* like. Sometimes I remember things even better than I really want to, if you know what I mean. But I'd already seen a lot of water pass beneath a great many bridges, and burned several of those bridges behind me, too, before I ever dreamed that there'd come a time to put my life down on paper. So it has been hard to pin some things down, or to recall exactly who was there in the room with me, and whether we went out for barbecue afterward, haunted a funky, smoky nightclub until closing time, or hopped the red-eye to Las Vegas.

I've asked a lot of my old friends to help me recall the days gone by, when we all dipped into the electricity of the moment. When rhythm and blues made its transition into rock 'n' roll, and rock 'n' roll into the music that suddenly shook up the whole world. Some of my old pals were a little worried: "I dunno, Wolf. It's been a long time, but they still might press charges, y'know?"

Thankfully, some of the many reprobates I've known were willing to open up their minds and their hearts and help me recall what a long, strange, and *exhilarating* trip it's been.

Even so, the story line may run through a patch of fog here and there. So please have a little mercy on me, 'cause I've tapped those old memory banks as deeply as I can. And I promise that some of these memories will amaze you.

Now, you might get shocked here and there by some of the stuff I've been into during this life. I believe that I've got a good heart. I even think there's actually something pure about what has motivated me along the way. If that wasn't true, I wouldn't have stayed with this Wolfman trip as long as I have, all the way since rock 'n' roll was just a gleam in the eyes of sexy Miss Rhythm and restless Mister Blues. But it hasn't been a choirboy's life. It hasn't been my nature to let many chances for pleasure pass me by. As Oscar Wilde—or some other wild cat— once said, "I can resist anything except temptation." That's me all over, baby. The Wolfman is a sensualist: I like my sugar sweet. If someone was to nominate me for the Supreme Court it would be a shame, because with my two-toned wolfish goatee and all I'd probably look great in those dignified robes. But I would never get past the preliminary phase, where they check your closet for skeletons. 'Cause I've got enough bones kicking around in there to build my own dinosaur.

Please don't misunderstand, though—I've always been good, as good as I can, to the people around me. And I have a strong sense of religious faith. In fact, as you'll learn in the pages ahead, at one time in my life the proper way to address me was as "The Right Reverend Bishop Wolfman Jack." That's right! Right Reverend Bishop! You can almost see those blue and purple rays of heavenly light radiating from my countenance.

But—as far as certain of life's rules, regulations, and standards of conduct go—I'll admit there have been times when I have done what I shouldn't ought to have.

Pretty soon in these pages you'll see me transporting marijuana from town to town for shady nightclub operators, and handling client connections for ladies who put bread on their table by laying booty on the mattress. And you'll see me generally going overboard in a number of foolish ways, including the pursuit of business opportunities in a slightly slicker way than the law allows.

When the curtain is lifted on these dark deeds, please have a little mercy on me, and try not to pass judgment until you've taken in the whole picture.

But there's an even more important reason for the name of this book.

"Have Mercy!" is a phrase that I picked up on a long time ago. I first heard it spoken by the inspirational people who played black and black-styled music on the radio. I'm a guy who was born white, but soon got captivated heart and soul by black American culture. That culture, especially the musical and verbal sides of it, has made all the difference in my life. "Have Mercy!" stands for the vibrancy and all-out expressiveness of African-American culture: how it points people toward the happy-go-lucky,

good-times side of life; how it creates music that is sexy,
funny, crazy, and wise all at the same time; how that
music has the power to even make you feel *good* about
feeling *bad*.

At first, I was just another one among the countless
legions of white kids who got amazed and irreversibly
bopped on the head by the provocative, pulsating, and
wonderful music that African-American culture has given
us all. The deep and ultimately joyous sounds of Ray
Charles, Billy Eckstine, Ike and Tina Turner, "Good
Rockin' " Roy Brown, Wynonie Harris, Big Joe Turner,
Freddie King, Sister Rosetta Tharpe, Otis Redding, Roscoe
Gordon, Fenton Robinson, Louis Armstrong, Louis Jordan, B.B. King, Chuck Berry, Muddy Waters . . . the list
goes on forever. I keyed in to their art, drew pleasure
from it, and used it in my attempts to find a cool world
to live in—away from the morose hang-ups of "real life."
Because in my philosophy, nothing is more unreal than
being unhappy.

Eventually, that great music wasn't just something I
used, it was something I merged with and even served
a little bit—by introducing lots of dark-skinned artists to
millions of pale-skinned listeners via some of the most
powerful radio stations that ever sent signals around
Planet Earth.

Of course, I didn't perform that service because I'm a
noble guy, or even a crusader. I did it because the music
got me so excited—and I knew that kind of excitement
could rock the radio world just as powerfully as it reso-
nated in my own soul.

As one result, some great black artists got a little further
into the mainstream than they might've, maybe a little
sooner than they might've.

As another result, their music lifted me beyond being

a bummed-out little teenage boy named Bob Smith who was going through nasty times in Brooklyn, to a fresh incarnation by the name of Wolfman Jack—who has known happy times in several corners of the world.

The one thing I've learned, getting out to all those foreign and domestic locales, is that people in every country of the "civilized" world wish—either secretly or openly—that they had the expressiveness, the flair, the I'm-so-glad-to-be-me spirit that black folks have made a part of American life.

I stood in a club one hot summer night in a faraway land, several years back, watching a crowd of local teenagers tearing it up. They were all doing their best boogaloo while a DJ played Motown sides nonstop. The dancing looked pretty good at first. But if you watched for just a few minutes, you realized that those dancers were repeating precisely the same steps over and over again. Those kids had studied *American Bandstand* and *Soul Train* programs like they were Sacred Scripture. They had copied the form to perfection. But they couldn't capture the spirit. They were dying to have soul.

And they're not the only ones.

The whole world is dying to have soul.

If there's any one thing I can promise that you'll get out of reading this book—besides my backstage glimpses of famous people, tales of funny goings-on, and insights into the interwoven histories of radio and of rock 'n' roll—it's the straight truth about how to have soul.

All right, baby. Now let's get the story rolling.

Turn it up! Turn it up! A little bit higher—Radio!
Turn it up! Just enough
So you know
It's got soul.

—VAN MORRISON

Chapter One

You have to respect what bullets can do.

It was 1965, and I had just moved back into the United States from Mexico after a wild eight-month sojourn in which *The Wolfman Jack Show* had been born. The reasons why we decided to move north of the border and east of the Pecos, I'll tell you about a couple of chapters down the line. Anyway, my wife, Lou, and I gathered up our two babies—Joy and Tod—and headed back to our nice three-bedroom home in peace-loving Shreveport, Louisiana. That's the town where I had recently been on the air as "Big Smith with the Records," spinning what folks in those parts referred to as "both kinds of music—country *and* western."

The Wolfman Jack Show continued on XERF, the megawatt Mexican border blaster where it had initially emerged. We taped the show in a Shreveport studio and mailed it down to XERF, about ten miles outside Ciudad Acuña, a frontier-style town in the state of Coahuila, across the Rio Grande from Del Rio, Texas, maybe four hundred miles south and east of El Paso.

At that time, segregation was still a sore fact of life in the Shreveport area, which is up in the northwestern part of Louisiana. Culturally, things there are more similar to Texas or Arkansas than they are to the Creole atmosphere of New Orleans or the Cajun flavor of the bayou country.

Northwestern Louisiana is mainly farming country, but it also produces a lot of oil and natural gas. Just a few years before my arrival in Shreveport, most of the oil companies had cut out for the brighter lights of Houston. The local economy was hurting, quite a few people were out of work—which might explain why some of them vented their anger one night at a nightclub because people of different races were having fun together.

People around Shreveport already knew me from my days of clanging a cowbell and playing all their favorite Ferlin Husky, Hank Williams, and Cowboy Copas tunes. But ever since launching *The Wolfman Jack Show*, with that super-powered XERF signal coming in from Mexico as clear as a bell, I had become one of the biggest fishes in that small pond, getting a little taste of how it feels to be famous.

Across the Red River, east of Shreveport, is the town of Bossier City, which has a little more of a wide-open feel. The Bossier City strip is just one nightclub after another, each trying to outdo all the others with big, wild neon signs, some of them about twice the size of the buildings they're bolted to.

I had become friendly with one of the club owners along the Bossier City strip, a really nice guy by the name of Gus Theodosis. Gus had wavy black hair and a nose that looked like it had two knuckles in the middle. He was the owner of the Peppermint Lounge, one of the flashiest places in the whole area. He'd named the club after that place in New York where the house band, Joey Dee and the Starlighters, had a No.1 hit record in 1961 called "Peppermint Twist—Part I."

Besides having one of the tallest, most eye-catching neon signs in the area, Gus's place also had one of the Bossier strip's biggest stages. I hung out there a few nights and got to know the guys in his house band. They played some pretty good southern-style blues 'n' boogie music, which I dug. Sometimes I sat in with them after hours and jammed on vocals, just for fun.

I love to sing. It may not surprise you to hear that almost every disc jockey would love to be a singer. But the crazy thing I've learned over the years—from James Brown, Johnny Otis, and others—is that there are lots of famous singers who also want to be disc jockeys. It's all in the same field. Somebody who's stoked by music just loves trying to get other people on the same wavelength. Singing, blowing a horn, or spinning a record over the air—it's all just different ways of turning other people on.

One night, Gus listened to me carrying on with the guys in his band and all in a flash he experienced a big moneymaking idea. "Wolf," he said, waving a glowing cigar in the air, "why don't you and these fellas record an album? You can do it live, onstage, right here at the club. Hardly anybody knows what you look like. People would pay a whole lot of money just to get in and see. We could sell your record by mail order over XERF: *Wolfman Jack—Live at the Peppermint Lounge*. It's a natural!"

Well, it sounded like a great idea, but I had a big problem. How should I look?

I wanted to prevent people from getting too familiar with my everyday appearance. As it was, I was able to be

Wolfman Jack one minute, and Bob Smith, hardworking radio businessman, the next. There were a lot of advantages to that setup.

Because of my voice, everybody who heard me on the radio assumed that I was black. But I didn't want to do a blackface act. That was out of the question. So I decided to look like something that couldn't be figured out. Right at that time, the Beatles were the newest thing. A local department store was selling mop-top wigs for people who wanted to look groovy on weekends but had to show up at the job on Monday morning looking straight. Lou went out and got me one, then hacked it up with scissors so it looked all raggedy and wolflike. I got a cape and fake fingernails and a whole bunch of dark makeup and a phony beard and I glued all that stuff on my face.

Before long I was looking at this guy in my dressing-room mirror who seemed like he might be the offspring of a Greek Mexican from Nairobi and the Portuguese-French woman he met one carefree night in a Bangkok backstreet. Nobody could tell what the hell I was—and I couldn't either, because I had to swallow more than half a bottle of whiskey before I collected enough courage to climb up on a stage in front of a live audience for the very first time in my life.

I was used to being a faceless voice on the airwaves, operating behind the safety of a big steel microphone and a fortress of tape machines and dials in a dark, cozy broadcast studio. Coming face-to-face with an audience scared the shit right out of me.

Frankly, to this day it still does. But I get off on it anyway.

That night at Gus's place, I noticed that being scared also got my juices flowing, which is another thing that still happens to me every time.

I was spreading glue on my chin and reaching for a fake goatee to plant there when Gus came barging into my dressing room. "The place is packed to the rafters!" he said. "You're gonna kill 'em!"

Overlubricated as I was, I went out and slugged my way through it. The band did a great job; I hit as many notes in the right places as I could. Maybe 50 percent of them. Between tunes I prowled around the stage and spouted many, many profanities. That was my whole personal appearance act—and would be for years to come.

Fortunately, everybody in the Peppermint Lounge seemed to love it.

We did two sets, getting a little more chaotic the second time through. The record we cut that night was pretty embarrassing, even though it eventually sold a few thousand copies by mail order, the very first of many releases yet to come on the newly formed Bread Records label.

I was very happy to cash all the checks that came in, but I still cringe whenever I hear that Peppermint Lounge album. Every now and then, some DJ who's interviewing me on the air will say, "I've got a copy of your first album right here," and I always have to plead with them, "Please, man, do *not* play that thing!"

Gus's place held several hundred customers. Every one of them paid $25 a head for the show, so we made out like bandits. The cash in my hands after the show did even more to cure my stage fright than the whiskey I had downed beforehand. Gus was feeling so inspired that he offered me a small fortune to come back and do it again two more nights in a row. I couldn't pass that up.

Gus came originally from New York. He knew that

there were plenty of folks in that part of Louisiana who didn't think blacks and whites should be in the same room at the same time, digging the same show. But the way Gus figured it, anybody who came to his door with the right money, it didn't matter to him if their folks came from Africa, China, or Sweden. First come first served, he'd let them in and give them the best table available, no problem. If there was money in the hand, that hand could be any color it wanted to be.

It was other people who had the problem. On the second night, after the final set, everybody who walked out of the Peppermint Lounge got a big surprise. Right across the street, standing about nine feet tall, was a flaming Ku Klux Klan cross lighting up the Bossier City strip, as if to say, "We are *seriously* unhappy with you folks for commingling the different races. We know for a fact that God don't like it, and we've showed up to take care of His business."

Personally, I've never understood where bigoted people got the idea God is just as small-minded as they are. I never tumbled to the notion that the Lord wants His crosses burned, or any of His people terrorized. I think He accepts us in all styles, sizes, and colors—because that's how we come.

Anyway, Gus stuck his head out the door to see what all the commotion was. "Oh yeah," he said, "those sonsabitches have been calling up all afternoon. They've been saying they were gonna kill the both of us."

This news put my nerves on edge.

Lou and I took several looks around before we got into our Cadillac and headed home. I was sweating bullets. I kept checking the rearview mirror, trying to be sure we weren't being followed. We looped through the streets for maybe half an hour, taking sudden turns every now and then in case any local sheetheads were on our trail.

When we finally pulled up in front of our house, it was just in time to see a couple of guys touch a match to another big cross, which was stuck in our front lawn and wrapped in gasoline-soaked rags. As the flames licked their way up to the top, the Klan guys scrambled off, jumped into the back of a waiting pickup truck, and peeled away.

Ever since I was a kid, the only thing I had ever wanted in life was to be a cool rhythm and blues disc jockey. It had been my secret dream, the driving wheel behind nearly everything I had done for about as long as I could remember.

I watched the firelight of that cross throw reflections off the picture window that looked in on our living room, realizing that even though I was only twenty-five, my dream had already come true, in ultra-deluxe form. I had spent time with people like Gary "U.S." Bonds and Soul Brother Number One, James Brown, which is about as cool as things can get for a white guy. I didn't know it then, but I also had a whole lot of great times yet to come: friendship with Elvis; soul-to-soul talks through the night with John Lennon; eight years on *The Midnight Special*, working with folks like Chuck Berry, Ray Charles, Aretha Franklin, the Beach Boys, the Eagles, and practically everyone who was high on the charts throughout the 1970s and 1980s; plus reigning for one intense, hyperinsane year as the number one nighttime DJ in New York City; plus appearing in *American Graffiti* for George Lucas, with Harrison Ford, Richard Dreyfuss, Ron Howard, and all those other brilliant newcomers; not to mention playing a big, unruly, post–Woodstock rock festival where a kid got born right in front of the stage and his folks named him Wolfman Johnson;

or sharing smoky BBQ ribs with Bo Diddley as he cooked them up on a backstage hot plate . . . a million different kinds of fun that still lay before me.

But as those crucifix flames threw red light across my wife's face, I thought about our two kids inside with nobody but a teenage baby-sitter to protect them. The panic hit me hard. I started remembering some of the scrapes we'd just left behind in Mexico—how that bullet had come out of nowhere and subtracted a layer and a half of skin off the tip of my nose, how a band of pistoleros circling the XERF building on horseback like crazy extras in a Sam Peckinpah movie had rained bullets on my men inside the radio station. Putting *The Wolfman Jack Show* on the air had involved stepping on some toes. Several of those toes were connected to the feet of some hellaciously vicious people. Now, thanks to some local racists, I was getting the clear message that there were plenty of vicious people to go around, no matter what country you might be in.

When I was an eager kid starting out in the radio business, I knew that the pay was low and the hours were long. I knew that you had to love it so much that nothing else mattered. But I didn't know there were so many ways that being a disc jockey could get hazardous to your health.

I'm glad I'm still here to tell you about it, because it's been a great life.

I wonder if you can imagine what it feels like: sitting in a dark studio and riffing your head off, saying anything sly, suggestive or funny that comes to mind, playing your favorite music while 250,000 watts of radio power kick the signal from the transmitter tower all the way up to the ionosphere, where it can ricochet to Australia, Russia, and other points unknown.

Imagine: seeing in your mind's eye, having that kind of fun while people of every type get all stimulated and happy by what you do.

Chances are you've never experienced a feeling like that. I'm going to do my best to share it with you.

Chapter Two

You know, sometimes when I catch a look at my own face in the mirror, I start to thinking that I must've been around for a few lifetimes before this one.

One thing's for sure: Back when I was floating out there in the stardust of preconception land, looking over the options for where to get born, I picked out a time and place that almost guaranteed I would grow up to be somebody *unusual*.

I came along in 1938, as the second child in a family of good-hearted, talented, sweet people. Robert Weston Smith was the name they gave me, but everybody just called me Bobby.

The Smith family lived in Manhattan then, at 680 West End Avenue, in a big, stylish apartment with a broad terrace overlooking the city.

My old man, Weston Smith, had gotten pretty close to being a millionaire—on paper, anyway. Unfortunately, the stock market crash of 1929 came along and most of that fortune evaporated. By the time I arrived, Weston had gone through years of struggle, attempting to reestablish the family's finances.

He was a very driven guy, with a jones to get back on top, to renew his application to the Millionaires Club, and he was willing to work twenty-four hours a day for that membership card if necessary.

Getting into a money cramp is real abrasive to the human spirit. All their financial struggles and all Weston's obsessive working gradually caused things to go a little sideways between my parents. It eventually caused them to split up and remarry with people that weren't as right for them as they were for each other. Problems in their new marriages set me up for a lot of treacherous conflict trips with the spouses they had each chosen.

That conflict ultimately turned me, by the early 1950s, into the kind of kid that people were then beginning to call a "juvenile delinquent." It's what made me grow up to be someone who's always going to be standing on the outside looking in. That's why one day there came to be a Big Smith with the Records, a Daddy Jules, a Wolfman Jack, and all of the other bigger-than-life identities I've tried on for size at one time or another.

I hope this inspires anybody out there who knows what it's like to feel unhappy. 'Cause I don't want to bum you out with my childhood pain. I just want to show you how I got past it, in time, with a three-part formula that I swear can work for *anybody*. It's a combination of soul-stirring music, renewed family love, and going headlong after a dream. This medicine is guaranteed, so try it today. You've got nothing to lose but your heartaches, baby.

Even though there's trouble coming up in my story line, there was also a sunny side to my young life.

My mother, Rosamund, is still one of the sweetest

people who ever came along. In fact, that was always her problem—being a little too open-hearted, sympathetic, and trusting.

My dad passed on almost twenty years ago. He was an amazing cat—a smart businessman, a talented writer, and a bona fide magician. He not only taught Sunday School, he trained other Sunday School teachers as well.

Weston's folks had come over from England. His old man, my grandfather, taught architectural drawing at Pratt Institute in Brooklyn. He and my grandmother also spent many of their summers running a camp, funded by Eddie Cantor, for underprivileged city kids. So my old man's folks had lots of brains and lots of heart.

Before I was born, when the money situation was flush, the family lived in some very fancy settings. My older sister, Joan, remembers a great Manhattan penthouse in a building called London Terrace, over on 25th Street. Before that, they lived in a big mansion in White Plains, New York, near the Connecticut state line. Weston drove to work every day in a Stutz Bearcat.

It takes an old-timer to know this, but Stutz Bearcats were just about the hottest, most stylish cars of their day. They had big, swooping fenders, long-legged straight-8 engines, and special little doors in the side to stash your golf bag on the way to the country club. A primo condition Stutz is worth more than a hundred grand nowadays, easy.

After the Crash, Weston worked for a long time as a shoe salesman. Ironically, he and Rosamund didn't have their problems when they were way down financially. It was when things got slightly better that Weston really turned into a work fiend, trying to make sure that his new success would last.

The way I see it, when that happened my mother started to feel neglected.

Joan was already ten years old when I was born. This difference in age was important, because when our lives got rough, she became like a second mother to me. No question, I wouldn't have made it through without having her in my corner.

Someone else also kept my world together. That was Francis Gregory. She was a black woman, originally from the Deep South, who had been working as a maid for our family since Joan was one year old. But she was also a whole lot more than that. She was *family*—more like an active, ever-present grandmother than a servant. She was in love with all of us, especially with Rosamund and Joan. When my sister was too little to say "Francis" right, it came out as "Tantan." From then on, Francis insisted that everyone had to call her by that name, like it was a special gift Joan had given her.

Tantan had raised a son of her own in Harlem, but he was by then all grown up and out on his own, so she sort of started all over with a new, young family. Her son painted houses and washed windows for a living. Sometimes he'd visit on a Saturday and we'd get to hear him sing. Man, he had a great voice. Real smooth. Everybody called him "Bing," because he sounded like a black Bing Crosby.

Tantan was pure love and devotion. I wish I could put my arms around her and hug her right now. Once, when my father ran into tough times, he had to tell her that there just wasn't any money for her salary. She said never mind that, she didn't intend to go. She stuck with us until he got back on his feet again, helping the family for free, because staying together with us was the most natural thing for her to do.

With Tantan always around, and with some of the talented, terrific people of all colors who visited our folks in Manhattan, I grew up in a real great atmosphere for learning to accept folks for who they were. I feel sorry for anybody who missed out on getting that point of view when they grew up.

By the time I was big enough to be walking and talking, Weston was moving up in the world again. He'd gotten a job at a magazine called *Financial World*. He wrote a lot of important stories for them, and for the *Wall Street Journal*. He edited and did lots of other things, until they eventually boosted him to vice president. He came up with the idea that *Financial World* should give annual awards for companies that had outstanding business achievements. It created huge publicity for the magazine. They were the Golden Globe Awards. Eventually, the magazine went out of business, and the Golden Globes became a film industry award. Anyway, while Weston was overseeing them, we got to meet the celebrities who came to host the ceremony. Milton Berle one year, Ernie Kovacs another, people like that.

Joan remembers the family's happy years better than I do. She was the right age to really drink them in. While I was still a little kid, she became grown-up enough, and beautiful enough, to serve as a model and hostess at the Golden Globe Awards. She studied French and Latin at St. Agnes Chapel School, a private Episcopalian school, sang in the choir, and eventually taught Sunday School.

When she won the title of "Miss Stardust" in a beauty contest, the paper ran a picture of my sister reading a book to a bunch of Sunday School kids, all looking up into her eyes. Her prize included a modeling contract.

Weston kept a huge scrapbook of all the things she won and all the magazine covers and advertisements she posed for in her modeling career. Unfortunately, most of that stuff got lost in a fire later on. Joan wasn't concerned. By that time she had become totally involved in raising her own family. In 1948 she got married to Emile Achee, a midshipman just graduated from the Naval Academy in Annapolis, and she let the modeling career go.

Somehow, a few great photographs have gotten saved—Joan wearing a regal crown of eggs, as "Miss Good Egg of 1947"; in a red sweater, fishing a mountain stream on the cover of *Pic*, "The Magazine Men Prefer"; standing on an airplane wing with William Holden to publicize a New York air show; posed alongside Edgar Bergen and Charlie McCarthy; reigning as "Pretzel Queen" of Philadelphia, draped inside an eight-foot-tall pretzel; as "Miss Nassau"; as a girl-next-door type in a Pepsodent ad; and another one illustrating a feature story in *Vital Detective Cases*, "The Perfumed Death of the Hollywood Extra."

One of her photos got Joan a little more exposure than she really wanted. One day she did a series of poses, in all different kinds of outfits, for a woman photographer in Manhattan. In one of them she was leaning against a wall in a filmy nightgown.

Before there was such a thing as *Hustler*, *Penthouse*, or *Playboy*, *Esquire* was the home of cheesecake shots. The photographer ran down to *Esquire*—without telling Joan—and sold them the nightgown pose. Which they ran, full-page, in their next issue. If you strain your eyes at that particular picture real hard, you might begin to see a little rosy nipple sunrise coming over the horizon.

That was pretty racy stuff in the late 1940s, I'll tell you. So it wasn't too cool when her husband-to-be saw that picture for the first time—pasted over a sailor's bunk.

Joan always had lots of dates in high school and a big circle of friends. When we moved out to Long Island and got a house with a garage, Dad turned it into an after-school dance hall for her and her crowd. He got one of those classic 78 RPM Wurlitzer jukeboxes that had fat tubes on each side, with endless multicolor bubbles rising in the tubes as the records played.

Whenever Joan and her friends got together in the afternoons, I was in charge of punching numbers on the jukebox. I loved watching all of the teenagers dance and have fun, so I figured out which tunes really got them moving and punched those ones up just to see the energy level in the room rise. I saw that I could build a mood slowly, through a good sequence of songs, and eventually bring the whole room to a real dynamic peak. This was a tremendous kick.

I loved having a role to play in all this social activity, being somebody who could boost the party atmosphere. I guess that was my first disc jockey gig. A ten-year-old kid is hungry for an identity, and I had begun to find mine at those garage dance parties.

Those were the best years. Nobody in that teenage crowd was getting into trouble because they were already having so much fun. All their energy went into dancing.

Those times are always in the back of my mind whenever I do a live show. If people have as much fun at the gigs I emcee nowadays as we all had in those jukebox dances in the family garage, then I'm satisfied. I still love that role of juicing up the party. When you get down to basics, that's my job description today: Life of the Party.

Everyone said, "Bobby, you have the coolest parents in the world." Our mom was just as good-looking as her daughter, and the boys would always be asking her to dance.

Weston would also entertain all the kids with his magic act. He had real good sleight of hand. Nobody could ever see how he pulled the tricks off. He even belonged to the Magicians Union.

Looking back, I believe I got a lot of showmanship instincts from my old man. He billed himself as "Kandu the Magician" and he set me up with my own little junior magician outfit, complete with a kiddie-size Hindu turban and a jewel in the middle of my forehead. I was Kandu's trusty assistant, "No-Kandu." Joan was always helping out in the act, too, as Princess something-or-other.

Every year there was a church fund-raiser carnival, and Weston would get out his cape, his magic wand, and his top hat that could squash down and pop back up. He would say, "Now I'm really going to surprise you," and he'd break eggs right into the hat. He'd pour in milk and sugar and all the kids would go "Oooh!" Then he'd stir it all up with his magic wand, drape his cape over the top, and say, "Abracadabra, Please and Thank You!" Out of the top hat he'd pull a white bunny. The kids would get all excited and scream.

He loved to make kids laugh. That was what really made him happiest.

My mother's side of the family gave me some inspiration, too. Uncle Tony, Rosamund's big brother, lived in upstate New York. He was a very successful salesman for a company that made calendars and other promotional items for businesses. Whenever we visited, he took me along on his day's travels, riding in his big Packard sedan. "There are two hundred horses pulling this car," he would say, pointing out across the hood. "Look out there. Can you see them pulling us along?" I got to thinking that I really could *see* those horses. Uncle Tony taught me that it was a lot of fun to stretch out your imagination.

As we were driving around town, he'd say, "I'm looking for somebody." By late afternoon, he'd say, "I think that's who we're looking for." He'd pull over and walk up to some guy who looked like he was down on his luck. Uncle Tony would talk to him for a while, then shake hands and give him some money. When he got back behind the wheel he'd say, "Didn't that feel good?" So he gave me two gifts—a sense of wonder and a sense of how you can make yourself feel good by generating some happiness around you.

Uncle Tony passed away just a couple of years ago. When we went up to his house to sort things out, we found that it was full of valuables that other people had given him—swords from the Civil War, antique furniture, all kinds of fine stuff. Just because he was the nicest person anybody knew. You would've loved the guy, too.

I wish that great family scene of my early years could have lasted forever. What happened instead is that my folks got involved with another couple, Marge and Gordon Parker, who lived about ten minutes' drive away. They threw lots of parties at their home, where there was lots of drinking. And out of that freewheeling social circle came some different-shaped relationships.

You have to remember that back in those days, people tended to see heavy drinking as a sophisticated thing. But the scene at the Parkers' was pretty much out to the limit. Joan used to baby-sit for some neighbors who ran with the same crowd, and one day the lady told her, "I'm not going to Marge and Gordon's house anymore. They put out too much liquor. I don't like the atmosphere."

The atmosphere definitely did have something wrong with it. The Parkers hated each other, and booze was about the only way they had of getting along. Unfortunately, their marriage was getting to a point where being swacked wasn't enough anymore. Marge did a lot of running around with different men. In fact, as soon as the Parkers met my parents, Marge started calling my mom and asking her to lunch. But when they went out, it became obvious right away that Marge was intent on hooking up with some boyfriend. Inviting my mom along was just a way of covering her tracks.

Gordon was a very tall, handsome guy. He had gone to Princeton, but only for a little while, because he came down with polio, which left him with a permanent limp. So between being a dropout, having an affliction, and being married to someone who he couldn't get along with, there was always something in his life to keep him from feeling good.

Gordon started coming around to our house, to ask my mother if she knew what Marge was doing. So my mom kind of got caught in the middle of their strife.

My mother felt really sorry for him. Time after time, she listened to his problems and gave him sympathy. After a while she started to feel attracted to the guy. Which undoubtedly had been his plan from the very start. Helping Gordon must've made her feel needed. And that's when the trouble really started.

My sister and I started noticing, when we came home from school, that Gordon's big red car was parked out in front of our house pretty often. He was a successful salesman and he got to set his own hours, so it was easy for him to come by our place. Tantan was there, so there couldn't have been any off-color action taking place, but to my sister and me it was very creepy to see him there all the time.

Joan would ask our mom, "Why is Mr. Parker's car here again?"

"He's having a real rough time," she said. "He just has to talk to me. He's very unhappy."

On Joan's fifteenth birthday she spent the afternoon at the beach with her friends. When they dropped her off, there was Gordon Parker's red car again.

"Oh, happy birthday," my mother said when she came in the house. "We've got lots of surprises for you."

Mom went into the kitchen to bring out Joan's birthday cake. Meanwhile, Gordon took Joan aside and said, "Listen, I've got something to tell you, and I want you to be the first to know."

"What?"

"Since it's your birthday, I feel you're old enough to understand. I happen to love your mother. I'm going to marry her and I'm going to make her very happy."

"I don't want my mother to marry anyone else!"

"Well, your mother and father aren't very happy."

"Yes they are!"

"No they're not. But I'm going to devote the rest of my life to making her happy."

Joan tore up the stairs to Tantan's room and the two of them hugged and comforted each other for the rest of the evening. They didn't tell me about what was going on because they figured that at age five I was too young a kid to get a handle on the situation.

In the days to come, Tantan was just as grief-stricken as the rest of us. She really began to get old then. Her appearance changed a little from week to week—more gray hair, a posture like she was carrying a heavy load, a sorrowful look in her eyes.

I guess I started getting old then, too, in my own way.

Chapter Three

Like I admitted before, sometimes my recall of details gets hazy.

The first few months after my parents' divorce really remain a blur. It just isn't possible now, half a century later, to know if the memories in my head are what a five-year-old Bob Smith actually saw, things that relatives told me later, or just images that confusion and hurt caused me to invent.

For example, I believe that my sister and I were sent off to an orphanage for about six months.

But Joan doesn't remember things that way. "No, Bob," she tells me, "you just feel that way because the most important person in your life was suddenly taken away from you. With your mother gone, you felt like you were completely abandoned."

Maybe she's right. After all, she was about fifteen when it all happened. But why do my memories seem so real? I recall being hovered over by people I didn't recognize, complete strangers, and living for months in an institutional atmosphere of silence and distance. Were those people my grandparents, aunts and uncles, or were they matrons and attendants?

I'll never know for sure; I only know what it felt like to be totally frightened, shaken all the way down to the ground, as though everything in my life stopped. I was crushed. Everyone around me was crushed. That was the tone of my emotional existence.

One thing I am sure of: from here until I grew up enough to leave home was a very tough stretch, but it was also the time that set my course in life. It started my grooming, my apprenticeship, to be in the happiness business. It knocked me upside the head, but in some ways it made me stronger.

First off, I started thinking that the way to survive was to make sure that people liked me. I taught myself to tune in to another person's wavelength, figure out what they were looking for, and try to project that thing back at them. I became a little salesman for myself, just like later on I would become a salesman for rhythm and blues music, for rock 'n' roll, for sugarcoated aspirin pills that claimed to make folks feel younger and sexier, for oldies record packages, genuine Wolfman Jack roach clips, all the hundreds of things I've pushed and promoted in my life.

My salesmanship came out of wanting to prevent rejection. I became a junkie for approval and recognition.

Most of all, I had to learn to think fast. Which, believe me, becomes a hell of a useful skill later in life if you find yourself standing in front of a live microphone.

Whatever my natural abilities were, whatever things I could do or say to make an impact, I learned to instantly put it all out on the line.

All kids do stuff for attention, but I took it even further. I analyzed how my act was working, and honed it. That was the only thing that gave me a sense of control.

Put those dynamics together in the mind of an impressionable, talented child, and you're halfway down the road to creating an entertainer—or a mental case. Or a charming combination of the two. If you could scratch any show business person deep enough, you'd probably find a scared little kid inside there pleading, "Hey, hey, look what I can do. Do you love me now?"

That's why I like being Wolfman Jack. Bob Smith from Brooklyn is a guy who sometimes gets hung with problems and fears. Wolfman Jack is a happy-go-lucky guy who knows how to enjoy a party. The challenge of my life has been letting more and more of Bob Smith go, becoming the Wolfman on an almost full-time basis, while still taking care of business.

It's a pretty good trick, I don't mind telling you.

Anyway, through all the confusion of the family's upheaval, Tantan was still there, being wonderful. So was Joan. They seemed to be the only people in my life who hadn't gone screwy. On Sunday mornings, Tantan would be dressed in a long, soft, flannel nightgown. She would invite Joan and me to cuddle up next to her in an easy chair while the radio on her bedside table played black spirituals. Gorgeous music, full of suffering and grandeur and hope. There was just as much feeling of comfort in her presence as there was in the music.

Apart from Tantan and Joan, everyone else in my life was like machinery that had no instruction manual. You didn't know where the buttons were, or whether it would be dangerous to give them a push once you'd found them.

At first, my parents were only separated. My mother went to live with relatives in New Jersey so she could think everything out. But before long, divorce proceedings were in the works.

My father became more of a workaholic than ever.

Hanging on to his job became the big thing. If that blew up he'd have really been lost. He came home from the office late and disappeared into his room practically all the time. Sometimes we'd hear his typewriter clicking and clacking, sometimes we'd hear sentimental records being played. There was one song he played over and over again—"Oh! How I Miss You Tonight."

With Gordon now out of her life, Marge started coming over, bringing gifts for me and Joan, trying to "cheer up" my father.

I guess he needed it bad. A year after the split-up, everything went through another radical change. Joan and I came home from school to find Tantan all upset. She took me upstairs to give me a bath, then she spoke privately with Joan. "I didn't want Bobby to hear us. I have something really terrible to tell you: your mother called a few hours ago. She said that things with Gordon weren't working out. She wanted to know if there was a chance she could come back to Weston. I had to tell her it was too late."

"Tantan, what do you mean?"

"Your father went down to the courthouse and married Marge this morning."

The next morning I woke up early and went to jump in bed with my father. There was Marge by his side. It seemed crazy and wrong. I was horrified and I started to cry. I ran off to find Joan. She held me and we both cried a long time.

After a while, I started feeling more furious than hurt. That's the way I kept feeling for a long time, especially after my mother went ahead and married Gordon. Now the cycle was complete. Two couples had split and, over the course of about a year, changed partners.

Ultimately, an arrangement was worked out where I

lived with my mother and her new husband in the summer and my father and his new wife during the school year.

Each half of the arrangement had its own problems. Gordon would sometimes get into drunken rages and slap my mother around. All Joan and I could do was hide until these scenes blew over. Rosamund didn't want to talk about it, almost as if taking a beating was her form of penance.

In the meantime, the breakup of our family eventually made Tantan heartsick with grief. She had to let go and move on. It wasn't the same gig she had signed on for, after all. Her first love was my mother. Unfortunately, none of us ever saw Tantan again. If there is a heaven, and I somehow sneak my way past the guy watching the front door, I expect to find her there.

When I was about seven, Marge and Weston had a kid of their own—Stewart. He was the only person Marge never yelled at.

Stewart grew to be a pale, fragile child. Marge was always looking for ways to make him more healthy. A doctor put her on to the idea that she should buy prime beef and squeeze all the juices out, to give Stewart a dose of vital energy. Of course, it didn't have much effect. In fact, all her overprotectiveness did was to turn Stewart into a creepy kid.

It wasn't his fault. Years later, when he grew up enough to become his own person, he checked himself into a military school—against Marge's wishes—and totally turned himself around.

But for the time being, he was the prize pup and I was the mangy dog of the family. One night he crawled under the dinner table and bit my leg, real hard. It hurt real bad. I yelled and kicked my leg free. Stewart's lip got bruised, so he started crying and I ended up being the one who got punished.

Almost every family dinner ended with either Joan or me getting sent to our room because of something we did wrong. We would go upstairs and listen to the radio until bedtime.

I acquired another half-brother around this time, when Gordon and Rosamund had a kid. This one, Gary, grew up to become one of my best friends in life. When he got in fights around the neighborhood, I'd go out and chase off the kids who were threatening to beat him up. When our parents went through their violent quarrels, I'd take Gary into the bedroom and hold him in my arms. He was always my shadow, tagging along through the whole summer.

Meanwhile, Joan was growing into a beautiful teen-ager, coming of age, getting ready to spread her wings and fly. Pretty soon she had her modeling career, and then a husband and children of her own to look after. When that happened, I was more or less on my own. Gary was my buddy, but he was too small to be a protector. He *needed* a protector.

Marge came out of a rich but very strange family. When she was younger, she had run off and gotten married to the family chauffeur. Her mother didn't approve, so she tracked the two of them down and somehow got rid of the guy. Marge never forgave her mother, and yet she grew up to become the same kind of overbearing, manip-ulative person. With a mean streak a mile wide.

Marge's mother lived with an unmarried sister in upstate New York during the summer, where they owned a hotel with several cottages on the grounds. The rest of the year, they lived in a huge Victorian place in Brook-lyn with at least twenty-five cats. A concentrated whiff of feline piss slammed you in both nostrils when you stepped up to the front door. One of her favorites was a jet-black cat called Satan. He always sat on a big square satin pillow, staring. Very spooky.

Marge's unmarried sister lived nearby with some fifty cats of her own. Between them all, the family had a standing weekly order at the local butcher shop for enough meat to feed a couple of families.

Marge was into cats almost as heavy. She always had somewhere between five and a dozen of them living with us. Joan and I wanted dogs, but whenever we got one, something bad would happen. One time Marge "accidentally" backed her car over a dog of Joan's. Later, when I was in my early teens, after school I found a dog out on the street and took him in. I named him Rags. He was truly my best friend at that point in my life. Every morning when I left, Marge locked him in an upstairs bathroom so he wouldn't agitate her cats. Naturally, out of loneliness, he would start to bark. She would go in there with a belt and beat him, then lock him up again. When I got home from school and opened the door, the dog would be so happy to see me, he'd jump up and lick my face.

Of course, he had no choice all day but to shit all over the bathroom floor, and it would be my job to clean it up.

One day when I got home I found Rags lying there stone cold. His tongue had turned purple and there was froth all around his mouth. She'd poisoned him right after I left the house. When Weston got home that evening, she admitted that she'd done it. She called it "putting him to sleep" because she couldn't stand the barking.

I have to explain that Weston was a unique character. It's like he wasn't able to see bad in anybody. Dealing with Marge wore him down, though, I think, to the point that it eventually took away his soul. I tried to let him know how bad things were for me, but I couldn't get the message through. It was just something he didn't want to hear.

I don't want you to think that my whole childhood was terrible, though. One day, long before my teens, something unexpected came along to make me real happy: a very early introduction into the wonders of maleness and femaleness.

The first summer I spent with my mother, she took me to live for a while with Aunt Sally.

She wasn't really my aunt—just someone who had been my mother's close friend since childhood. Sally's husband, Chris, had just passed away, so Rosamund went down to help out for a few weeks.

Aunt Sally lived in a big plantation-type country home outside Annapolis, Maryland, with horses and long, white, wooden fences. I got to play with all the black kids whose parents worked on the nearby farms and I had a great time.

The only strange part was walking through Aunt Sally's living room. She kept Uncle Chris there in his casket for several days. In the morning she would get herself a cup of coffee and go sit beside him and have a long chat.

I hope it was good for both of them.

There was another strange thing that went on, but it felt awfully nice. It happened on the afternoons that Aunt Sally and my mother left me for the day with a baby-sitter in Annapolis.

I don't remember her name. Let's say it was Maria. She was a dark-haired girl, probably Italian, about twenty years old, a little on the hefty side, real generously endowed in the boobies department.

Maria would put out some toy cars and trucks for me

to play with while she took care of cleaning and ironing. Then, around mid-afternoon, she would tell me it was time for "our secret." That was when she would take me upstairs and pull back the covers on her bed, then take off her clothes and mine.

I don't want to incite any baby-sitters out there into deviant behavior, but I have to admit that "our secret" was the most fantastic experience I'd ever had up to that point in my young life. Maria rubbed her tremendous breasts all over me, like massage mittens. Front and back, head to toe, like a soft avalanche of nipple and tittie that covered every inch of my body. Then she would cuddle me up to her chest and start kissing me softly while she dipped a hand down between her legs and brought herself to a nice, wet climax.

Afterward she told me, "This is something we don't tell anybody about it."

I must have decided to honor the agreement, because my mother brought me back there several more times. Whenever I was dropped off at Maria's, I'd run right up to her and snuggle right in between that soft, friendly pair.

"Little Bobby really likes you, doesn't he?"

"Oh, yeah. We get along fine."

I hope Maria eventually found someone her own size to play with. I did. And I didn't tell anybody about "our secret" for a long, long time.

Around the age of eight, I came down with a case of mononucleosis. For almost a year, I couldn't do much of anything except listen to the radio. In those days, there was a greater variety of programs—comedians like Abbott and Costello or Jack Benny doing long sketches, crime fighters like the Shadow or the Green Hornet in half-hour dramas. You could really get absorbed in radio broadcasts, and I definitely did, all through that long convalescence. I loved how the words and the sounds brought pictures into my mind. Nowadays they talk about "interactive" media. If you let your imagination flow, radio can be *plenty* interactive.

Years later, as I got acquainted with show business people, I found out that many of them were sick in bed for a long spell when they were kids. It seems to develop real vivid imaginations. It happened to John Milius, Francis Coppola, and Martin Scorsese, and a lot of other filmmakers.

In a certain way, a disc jockey is like a filmmaker. Radio creates movies that go on in your own mind. It leads you to visualize different scenes and get captivated by moods. Part of the "movie" is a relationship with someone—the DJ, the announcer—that you never meet and you never know, but they're part of your life anyway.

My upbringing had a big religious element. Both my father and my sister taught Episcopalian Sunday School. By age nine I was an acolyte—which is like being an altar boy. I assisted a priest named Father Parks.

When you cleaned up after Parks, you never had to worry about having to throw away any unused wine from the chalice. He drained the big cup dry every time.

One time I was all alone with him in the room behind the altar. "Bobby," he said, "I want you to come over here and stand on this table."

It didn't make a lot of sense to me. The table was exactly in the middle of the room. There wasn't any cupboard you could reach from it. There wasn't any light fixture above that might need a bulb changed. But I did as I was told and climbed on up.

As soon as I was standing on the table, Father Parks unsnapped my corduroy pants and tried to tug them and my drawers down, pressing his face right up by my private parts for a boozy kiss. I jumped off that table and ran off, pulling my pants back up while I tried to stay out of his reach. I circled the table until I built enough of a lead, then made a dash for the door.

I went home and told my father what had happened. For some reason, I just couldn't make him believe me. At first, he seemed to think I was making some kind of badly conceived joke. The more I tried to tell him, the more he made it clear that he didn't want to hear this kind of stuff. Weston was just like that.

The thing is, I bet a lot of other boys got grabbed at in the back room of that church. Some of them probably didn't get away.

I never went back to church. In fact, I haven't been inside a church again since that day.

A long time later, when I was about fourteen, Weston came back one afternoon from teaching Sunday School and said, "I just heard the most incredible thing. They've gotten rid of Father Parks. He had a drinking problem, they said."

It was like he had never even considered the possibility before.

By that time we were living on Prospect Park West in Brooklyn. It was kind of a white-bread neighborhood, but there was plenty of trouble to be found if you knew where to look.

This was the very early 1950s, pre-*Blackboard Jungle*. I fell in with a guy named Lenny, and he got me in with his gang. The Tigers. Mostly Italian and Irish kids.

One night we went into Prospect Park, which was mostly a peaceful place in those days, to get it on with another gang. I was a newly inducted member, didn't even have my jacket yet. There were eight of us. We were walking along, passing a quart bottle of Rheingold beer between us and taking swigs. We were a real bad-ass group. Legends in our own minds. One guy had a baseball bat, another had a wooden tennis racket. I didn't have anything but a couple of pint-size fists. It was all I could do to keep a front up and not soil my drawers. But everybody else was acting real macho. I was so scared of what they'd say if I backed down, I didn't think ahead to what could happen when we connected with the other gang. So I joined in the chorus:

"We gonna beat the shit out of these guys."

"Yeah, we gonna kick their fuckin' ass."

I was going to Manual Training High School in Brooklyn then. It was a real dump of a school around the corner from Sixth Avenue and Fourth Street. The main reason I'd joined the Tigers is because they were the guys around school who'd perfected a "nothin'-can-touch-me" atti-tude. If you could look like you were cold and mean and you didn't care what the hell happened to you, there was less chance of somebody messing with you. The Tigers had the aura that I wanted, so I fell in and tried to cultivate my cool.

The big reason the Tigers were going to war that night was that Frank DellaCroce, the leader of the other gang, had stolen a girl who used to be the main squeeze of one of our gang members. That was a real no-no, a heavy code-of-honor type of thing.

Of course, the girl was probably just bored and ready for a new brand of thrills. But nobody stopped to think of that.

We passed under the street lamp at the entrance and walked deeper into the park. Finally we met up with the ten guys who were waiting for us. They called themselves the Falcons.

DellaCroce stepped forward and said something like, "I hear you fellas was looking for me."

"Yeah. We thought you might like the opportunity to kiss our dicks."

We jumped into each other. Before I knew it, my arms were swinging and I was hitting at anything and everything I could reach. My heart was pumping something fierce. It was like the whole world had closed down to one little area, just my body and whatever I could reach out and hit. Then, suddenly, someone took a side-arm swing with a beer bottle and hit me smack across the face. I never saw it coming. The bottle broke, half of a front tooth fell out, and I dropped to the pavement, completely out cold.

The next thing I remember is being dragged out of Prospect Park by my buddies. I don't know what ultimately happened to DellaCroce and the Falcons that night, but three of us Tigers ended up at the emergency room. Two guys with broken arms and me, sporting a three-stitch split across my chin and a busted tooth with its nerve exposed to the open air. The pain was enormous. I'd have been better off to stay unconscious until the doctors got the job done.

Of course, my folks were real upset about my sudden dentistry needs. They were always concerned with me hanging around with the wrong element around the block, and complaining about my friends, but I had found my missing sense of family in the gang thing. Just like all these young kids are doing now.

If you don't find where you belong at home, you go looking for it in other places. Sometimes you meet up with bad people who suck you in, but at least they give you an identity and a reason for being.

One of my buddies from the gang was a guy named

Richie Caggiano. He was lean and good-looking, with dark eyes and dark hair and a real bad-boy attitude. The girls were pretty crazy about him. Richie came from a home life that was a lot more messed up than mine, plus his family was real poor, too. I think he told me once that he was being raised by his grandmother, but none of us in the gang ever really knew much about each other's home life. It would've been uncool to ask for details. Still, Richie and I felt like we had a lot in common. We were both good-looking kids, and we both had the attitude that nobody at home wanted us around.

One night, five or six of us went walking into the local bus station to play the pinball machines—a nickel a game—and see who else might be hanging out. We discovered that evening that Richie's sex appeal worked both ways.

An older guy wearing a light brown suit and a cream-colored hat stood off to one side and watched us the whole time we played pinball. We just figured he wanted to learn our master techniques for how much you could jiggle the machine without lighting up the TILT sign, and how to catch the ball with the flipper bars and set it up for a slapshot at the bonus targets. Or the cool way that, when the game was lost, we'd pick the machine up about two inches off the ground and let it drop.

Anyway, when Richie went out the door, the older guy followed right behind him. Everybody thought this was pretty funny. We trailed behind.

Because of my experience with Father Parks, I had a pretty nasty outlook about homosexuals. The whole gang trip was about proving how big and tough a man you were, so everybody else spoke and acted the same way.

About a block and a half away from the station, the

guy got up the nerve to step up behind Richie and tap his shoulder. Richie spun around in a crouch and reached inside his black leather jacket like he had a knife or something in there. Just then, the rest of us closed in.

"Hey, man! Whatchoo doin'?"

"Yeah, you think he was gonna give you a blow job or somethin'?"

"Maybe you wanted to give *him* a blow job?"

And the guy went white. Maybe he had a job and a family. But right at that moment he probably started flashing that his compulsion to cruise for tough boys was about to put him in the hospital. He pulled out his wallet and laid a five-dollar bill on each one of us.

Richie said, "I'm the one you were trying to mess with. You better give me ten, man, and then get the fuck out of here."

The guy couldn't have been more agreeable. Compared to getting wailed on by six street punks, $35 was a bargain.

I can't speak for the other guys, but I wouldn't have actually done anything to him. It was just fun seeing him squirm. That made us feel powerful. From then on, anytime we needed money we used to send Richie through the bus station on purpose. It was amazing how often some middle-aged guy with puppy dog eyes would come out following him. We never actually rolled any of those guys, but we always convinced them that they were two inches away from serious pain. And we always collected instant cash.

It was a funny feeling: kind of like we were vigilantes, cleaning up the neighborhood by making these guys move on, but at the same time doing something evil, too. That was an interesting mix of emotions.

For all I know, our "victims" got their money's worth in walk-on-the-wild-side thrills, and a hell of a story to tell their friends, too.

Actually, Richie and I had more fun and made better money when we hustled people at the bowling alleys. He could rack up a score of 250 or better almost every time. We also picked up change by hanging around supermarkets and helping people load their groceries.

Weston was by now making enough money, and Marge had her rich family as backup, so I didn't actually need these jobs and scams. The truth was, I liked getting my own money. Not feeling any obligation to my stepmother, my father, or anybody else. But it was more than just the independence; it was the thrill of hustling, too.

Richie and most of the others in the Tigers truly didn't have any money. They had it tough. I preferred getting on a parallel track with their lives instead of living middle-class, like I could've.

One other kid in our group was the same way. Charles was a black kid whose father worked on Wall Street. He went to a private school, but he started hanging out with us because he wasn't accepted by either the WASP snobs in the school or the other black kids in the neighborhood. Just like me, Charles fit in best with the misfits.

We were sort of our own core group within the Tigers, and eventually we drifted apart from the gang and just hung out as our own unit. Richie and I were more or less the leaders. Charles tagged along. So did my friend Lenny and a guy we called Klepto.

Some guys resist getting hung with a nickname, like it'll bring down their dignity. Klepto was married to his nickname. It was the essence of his being. He was the biggest of us all, over six feet tall. He was awkward and ugly, too, with acne, a bobbing Adam's apple, and the kind of face that you might say "only a mother could love." Although his mother didn't seem to.

Klepto looked like he was totally dumb and harmless, and yet there was something menacing about him at the same time. He was too young to be so big. Store clerks usually looked the other way when he prowled the aisles. He was the most successful shoplifter I ever knew.

Klepto had a very big impact on my career as a DJ. Thanks to the very talents that earned him his nickname, I acquired a library of the hippest records of the early 1950s. Klepto laid the foundation of my collection. I eventually carried those sides with me to every corner of the United States, and parts of Mexico, and broadcast them worldwide. So I'd like to raise a toast here to Klepto, and his fantastic sticky fingers. He wasn't overly bright in school, but when it came to stealing records, he was the closest thing to a genius.

In those days, record stores had listening booths. The 45 RPM records were in bins, with the Top 10 arranged in front. You'd pick out the ones you were interested in, then take them into a soundproof booth and give them a listen before buying. Of course, lots of times kids came in and just listened and then put records back without buying any. The storekeepers tolerated us, believing that we would be back later when we got our allowances.

Klepto would pick out a bunch of 45s and stick his finger through the hole in the middle and spin them around, like he had a nervous habit. Which made him even less appealing to look at. He seemed so goofy and lost in his own world that nobody paid much attention when he walked into the listening booth with a whole lot of records and came back out later with a slightly skinnier stack. He had this cheap oversize gray wool jacket that smelled like a collie dog whenever it got rained on, which was just one more aspect of his appearance that bordered on the repulsive. He'd walk out of the store with half a dozen records stuck in that coat's inside pockets, or skillfully trapped under his armpits. And he'd give them to me, because I owned a record player and he didn't.

That's how I ended up owning a couple of boxes full of Louis Prima, Gatemouth Brown, T-Bone Walker, and Johnny "Guitar" Watson records.

Albums we had to buy. They were too big to hide under Klepto's smelly coat.

Anyway, whenever Klepto brought a fresh shipment in, they went straight down into the basement of the brownstone apartment where my family lived. The building had an old coal bin that they didn't need anymore because the heating system had been converted to an oil furnace. My buddies and I cleaned out the space with rags and kerosene and created ourselves a meeting place.

One Christmas my father bought me a fancy radio, a transoceanic model. That became the hot ticket in our coal bin get-togethers. It was really exciting to pull in signals from all over the globe. My half-brother, Stewart, who already had his own record player and tape recorder, got brand-new ones that same Christmas. I took the old ones down to the coal bin. The core group would get together down there in the evenings and we'd play the records Klepto had stolen, and listen to all the crazy outside stuff we could find on the radio dial.

Pretty soon, we became aware of some frantic, hip-talking disc jockeys. These guys just knocked us out. They were a lot cooler than even the toughest hood in the toughest street gang around. They had such command, just by being quick-mouthed and entertaining, that they took control of the room. Once they got you hooked, you couldn't stop listening. It was so powerful. And they didn't have to get into fights, or pimp, hustle, or steal, like the older guys we were used to seeing on the streets.

All of us wanted to be like these disc jockeys. We dug them so much, we started taping shows in order to memorize their patter. It was just something we did because it gave us a kick. I guess I got into it heavier than anybody else, because pretty soon the other guys, when we were walking down the street in the daytime, would ask me to repeat the bits and imitate the voices.

Without knowing it, I was prepping myself a little bit more for a career in radio.

One time I saw Magic Johnson interviewed during an NBA All-Star game. He talked about how, as a little kid, he would go out on the neighborhood blacktop court all alone and pretend to be Wilt Chamberlain for a while, shooting hook shots and finger rolls. Then he'd dribble to the other end and be Dave Bing, spotting up for jump shots from the wing. Then a different guy with a different shot. He'd imitate all his heroes, just for fun. Ultimately, learning all their moves made Magic a star in his own right.

It was the same thing for me in that coal bin. I didn't know what a studio was supposed to look like, but somehow I ended up making one and working in it. I didn't know how a person became a disc jockey, but I memorized whatever the cool jocks said on the air.

I wasn't a particularly industrious teenager. In fact, none of my teachers considered me to be very promising material. And by the way I was scuffling with the school routine, my folks were starting to think I'd never amount to anything. But I wanted an alternate world to live in, someplace more to my own liking. Radio and records gave me a cool world to belong to, so I plunged in, the way a guy would plunge into a river if his jockey shorts caught fire.

One of the coolest of my new role models was a guy on WDIA who called himself Jocko Henderson. He opened his show with "Hey Mommio, hey Daddio, this is your spaceman—Jocko! Three, two, one—blast-off time!" And then this great, rhythmic, devastatin', hip-shakin' music would coming roaring out of the speaker. Jocko was pure excitement.

Those were the days when folks like Patti Page, Teresa Brewer, Perry Como, and the Four Freshmen owned the top chart positions in popular music, with tunes that were all polite and restrained—"I love you, cherish all the stars above you, want your charms here in my arms" and all that unreal stuff that we didn't relate to at all. For our tastes, it was the Clovers singing "Down in the alley, just you and me, we're goin' ballin' 'til half past three." Or Goree Carter singing, "I'll send you if you'll let me, and it won't take me all night long." Now, that was *about* something!

We were teenagers, wanting to get the real perspective on what our hormone surges were all about, so we were enormously tickled by the sly messages and sexy feels of those rhythm and blues tunes. The whole aura was like you were into something forbidden, like looking at naked girls and all their sweet, mysterious private parts in a nudist camp magazine or something.

Another of the crazy jockeys we picked up on was John R. from WLAC in Nashville, Tennessee. The first thing you'd hear was a chorus chanting: "Hey, John R., whatcha gonna do? C'mon, John R., man, and play me some rhythm and blues."

Then John Richbourg, a white guy who did a real

warm-toned black accent, would crack open his mike.
John had the vocal quality that radio people call "a big
set of balls." Which means that his voice was deep, full,
and rich—the kind of voice that men want to have and
women want to hear.

"Yeah! It's big John R., the blues man! Whoa. Have
mercy, honey, have mercy, have mercy. John R., way
down south in the middle of Dixie. I'm gonna spread a
little joy. You stand still now and take it like a man, you
hear me?"

Oh, yeah. We heard him.

This Nashville station had a signal strong enough to
reach Brooklyn because they had appealed to the FCC
with the idea that black people in some rural areas around
the South didn't have any stations in their own area with
the kind of programming that they wanted to hear. So
WLAC got permission to have one of the most powerful
signals in the country, so long as they carried rhythm
and blues.

They were doing this soul broadcasting out of Nashville, hometown of the Grand Ole Opry, the heartland of
hillbilly. And there we were in Brooklyn, tape-recording it
off the air to play back later and practice saying all the
hip, black-styled phrases. We were a stone's throw from
Harlem, Bed-Stuy, Hell's Kitchen, and all those bad-ass
New York, Bronx, Queens, and Brooklyn neighborhoods,
but we were getting our lessons in cool from some white
guy broadcasting out of Tennessee.

George Carlin grew up in Morningside Heights, which
is adjacent to Harlem, at exactly the same time that I was
coming of age over on the other side of the Brooklyn
Bridge. I heard him talk about it on TV one night, and
it was like he and I went through almost exactly the
same thing. His trip was to hang out around a club called

the Baby Grand, where two black DJs named Willie and Ray did a show nightly over WHOM, playing songs like "Sixty Minute Man" and "One Mint Julep."

George and his buddies, who were one hundred percent Irish, started dressing like the uptown black characters who lived two blocks away in Harlem—wing-tip shoes and four-button charcoal suits, carrying tightly rolled black umbrellas—even on a sunshiny day. George described his motivation like this: "The black people, even though they'd been denied their freedom in the worst way possible, had more freedom in them than the people who had enslaved them. They had freedom with their bodies, freedom to speak and move beautifully. They had an ease with each other that white guys didn't have."

We didn't have anybody in our little gang who could put it into words the beautiful way George Carlin can, but me and my buddies were feeling the same things. We were seeing another universe, a very attractive one, and we wanted like crazy to go there.

Of course, we also got hooked on Dr. Jive out of Harlem, and Symphony Sid Torin out of Buffalo, who used to play some extremely far-out Afro-Cuban jazz. But John R. always remained a major touchstone.

"All right, looky here now. I got some fine things lined up for you and we gonna get 'em started in a minute, but I gotta tell you it's all brought to you through the courtesy of the Carnation people. They're the people that got that milk in the cans. They get it from contented cows, you know what I mean? We use it to whiten up our coffee and to cook pies and all that jazz. In the meantime, I got Fenton Robinson here. Look out, now."

Then some incredible-sounding blues guitar would hit us between the eyes, and that was the real payoff. Music that came right off the street and got you where you lived. Fenton Robinson's stuff was some of the most sophisticated on the John R. show. Other artists were a lot more raunchy. There was one song, though I don't remember who sang it, about "I love to dip my dipper into somebody else's dippings, 'cause the dippings is neater and the sugar is sweeter." We didn't need a sex education course to get the general idea. In fact, those records were sort of our Sex Ed, and our overview on what kind of stuff went on between grown-up men and women.

Whatever the lyrics didn't say, the thumping bass notes and the punching brass fills in between each verse gave you the rest of the message.

"The man gonna get to you here. Look out, he got a wild guitar, and he can *sing*. Look out, now, Fenton Robinson and 'The Getaway.'" Then Fenton would play nasty guitar licks and sing about how he'd been in Chicago too long, so he has to make a getaway, on down to Florida where the sun shines every day, and he can take his woman, Ella Mae, and go out in the sand and play.

And Klepto, Lenny, or somebody else down in that coal bin would say, "I bet they ain't gonna build sand castles," and we'd all laugh like we knew the score.

Before the song was over, John R. would be right back on the mike: "The man's wild, honey, I'll tell you right now. All right now, you know about Ella Washington, don't you? She met this cat on the street and she dug him, but he ain't got no bread."

Ella Washington, who had a voice real similar to Bonnie Raitt's, would sing about how her love was so strong that she knew she'd make that man give up his evil ways. The song would only be halfway done when John R.

would break in: "Not only is the cat broke, but he's mighty bad, too, you know. He's a low-down, no-good dog. But she don't care, 'cause he got something she wants, you hear me?"

Nowadays, radio stations compete with each other over how much music they'll play without any commercials, talk, or any other kind of interruptions. But when I was coming up, the trip was to be more of a master of ceremonies. DJs would play just enough of a record to give the flavor, titillate the audience and set the mood, then they'd step in with their own patented brand of rapping. The first priority was to create a party mood. Spinning the sides came in a very close second.

Part of this was economics. If a station didn't get much money for their ad time, they had to jam in as many ads as possible. That meant cutting the records short. But they had to do it artfully, so it didn't feel like a letdown. A disc jockey had to be a hell of a verbal performer. And those were the people I imitated. To me, they were the epitome of coolness.

Dr. Jive used to broadcast from midnight to three in the morning, out of a Harlem nightclub called Small's Paradise. By that time of night, I was usually alone in the coal bin. My folks knew where I was, so they didn't worry. When it got late they went to bed, knowing I'd come up the stairs sooner or later.

One night, Dr. Jive said he was totally gone on a brand-new record by a cat named Louis Prima, and he was going to play it for us. It was the album with a medley of "Just a Gigolo" and "I Ain't Got Nobody," the same one that David Lee Roth covered for a Top 20 hit in 1985. Well, Dr. Jive liked Prima's cut so much that he played it over and over again, back to back, for three hours straight. And it worked! I listened all the way to sign-off, and I bet that half the population of Harlem did the same.

Today, with all the tight playlists and demographic research that dictate what's on radio, the station owner would have Dr. Jive airlifted to Tierra del Fuego in a straitjacket within half an hour. Which is exactly why radio isn't as much fun today. Too many rules. That's why people nowadays are in so heavily to the "shock jocks." Howard Stern and those other guys might be crude, but at least they have some kind of definable personality. They aren't bland.

Anyway, by the time three in the morning rolled around and Dr. Jive said good night, I was crazy to have my own Louis Prima record.

Klepto went with me to the store. He found the record in the bins. He turned to me with a puzzled expression and said, "Are you sure this is the one you wanted? This guy's *white*."

Not only white, but Italian, too. I was stunned. He'd just dominated three hours of airtime on a black station featuring a black jock at a black club.

This opened my eyes to a big possibility: maybe soul was more about attitude, more about spirit, than it was about color of skin.

It also proved that black people will get behind a performer, no matter what color, if that performer's got the feeling right.

These ideas stayed with me.

Now, try to look up Louis Prima in a book about the history of rock 'n' roll. Chances are you won't find him. But he was definitely one of the guys who set the table for what was to come. Even though Louis is long gone now, luckily a lot of his band is still together. They're working Las Vegas to this day, as Sam Butera and the

Witnesses, and they just might be the greatest rock 'n' roll band in existence.

While I was getting my spirits lifted by all these new-found musical heroes, sister Joan was getting a family started. A distant cousin of ours was a midshipman at Annapolis. He showed a photograph of Joan as "Miss Aviation of 1947" to Emile Achee, a midshipman whose family had roots among Louisiana Cajuns. That was the start of their romance.

Emile was a halfback on the Navy Junior Varsity. His whole take on life—discipline, sports, fitness, and career-mindedness—was in the totally opposite direction from everything I was interested in. But I really dug Emile from the moment I met him. He was the big brother I needed.

As time went by, both he and Joan would become more and more important to my life. In fact, I lived with them during the first summer after they got married, in 1949. Emile had graduated, but they kept him in Annapolis as an assistant football coach. Being his kid brother-in-law was like being part of a normal family again.

As soon as fall came and I was home in Brooklyn again, I went back to hanging out in the coal bin with my buddies. By then I'd found the weirdest station of all: XERF. It didn't come on the air until nighttime. Their broadcasts started with a guy whose voice sounded like Johnny Cash, in this real calm tone, saying, "This is Paul Kallinger, your good neighbor along the way, from XERF, with 250,000 watts of power in Ciudad Acuña, Coahuila, Mexico."

He would do some pitches for products, play some wild-ass hillbilly music, and then yield the airwaves to a string, lasting all night long, of the most amazing preachers you ever heard in your life. Man, they hit you with everything a human voice was capable of. They'd bring it down low, like they were sharing the most important secret, then they'd get a Bible-thumping frenzy going, like they were laying God's Own Rule Book on the line and woe on the head of those in radioland who wouldst not pay heed! In another instant they were whooping about the joys of finding salvation, then they'd bring it down low and intimate all over again. It was like their fifteen-minute segment was a one-voice soul symphony.

Of course, each time one of these preachers got to the end of his segment, he gave out an address, and told you about something you could buy to ease the sorry passage of your soul through this troubled world of ours. "And one other thing, folks. This is a *m-e-a-n* world we're living in!" Sometimes they offered a special prayer cloth, sometimes an especially blessed picture of Jesus, or a wonderful medallion with the power to direct money or healing powers your way. Sometimes they just flat out called for donations, "to keep the vital work of this ministry alive." But they always made it sound like profit was the furthest thing from their minds.

Music was my first love, but these guys were almost as compelling. They had something real similar to a great rhythm and blues performance going on, a fervency, an urgency, an earthiness. We'd listen and we'd laugh, telling ourselves that this stuff was for suckers, but we could also feel the power tugging us in.

Around midnight, XERF would switch over to a guy called Big Rockin' Daddy, playing jump-band music, rhythm and blues with a stripped-down sound, the kind of stuff that later grew into rock 'n' roll, from artists like Ike Turner and his Kings of Rhythm, and Louis Jordan and His Tympany Five. And if any of you haven't yet heard Louis Jordan doing "Fatback and Corn Liquor" or "Five Guys Named Mo," you've still got some thrilling times ahead.

In September of 1954, when I was sixteen, Alan Freed

came on the air on WINS, New York. I'd already been listening to black stations, so the music he played was more familiar to me than it was to most white youngsters. Freed simply presented it under the name "rock 'n' roll."

In fact, my transoceanic radio had introduced me to Freed from his Moondog show out of Cleveland. First you'd hear a baying hound, then tom-toms, maracas, and a tambourine shaking a real brisk beat. "Atta boy, old hound. Hello, everybody. How y'all? This is Alan Freed, the old King of the Moondoggers. Good old Aaron Brew, formula Ten-Oh-Two, northern Ohio's largest-selling beer, makes it possible for us to be here. Howdy everybody, and welcome to the big Moondog Rock 'n' Roll Party."

When he played the records, he'd thump on a big phone book or something and just generally intensify the whole musical experience.

As soon as he came to New York, *The Alan Freed Show* just tore the town up. Everybody went nuts, especially me. That's when I told myself, "I don't care what. I'm gonna definitely be part of this." I didn't know how, I just believed there was a *somehow*.

I was still young enough that going anyplace outside of my neighborhood felt like a real major step, on a par with going to Florida or something. But I doped out the bus schedules, put on my T-shirt and pegged pants, and got myself to the first show that Alan Freed put on at the Brooklyn Paramount Theater.

The excitement of being out in the audience was overwhelming, but I had to get closer. Since it was the first show, they didn't know how crazy the fans would get, so there weren't enough security guards. I found myself a dark place alongside the curtain where I could watch the performers walking to the stage. Late in the show, Alan Freed was actually standing right in front of me, checking out the crowd.

I blurted out, "Uh, Mr. Freed, man, I love this music and I want to be here all the time and I'll do any kind of work you want me to. Just give me a job. Anything."

Freed gave me the classic answer: "Go away kid. You're bothering me."

That was a real letdown, but still I came back the next day. As I remember, it was a five-day stand, with a movie to open each show. Freed would come out in this real loud plaid jacket and blow kisses at the audience while the house band played some real down, aggressive blues vamp.

The second time, instead of bugging Freed, I asked some backstage worker if there was something I could do. This guy tolerated me because I was willing to take a little work off his shoulders.

"Go knock on the third door on the left down there, and tell those folks they've got to be ready to go on in five minutes." I double-timed down there and knocked. Bam BAM BAM. A voice said "Come in," and I stepped in to see these young black guys in matching jackets, blue satin with black velvet lapels. Some fine, fast-looking women were hanging around with them and a whiskey bottle sat on the table with the cap off.

It was like I'd stepped into paradise.

From then on, I made it to every show I could. Some of the folks around Freed were pretty slick, bebop types that probably didn't care about me any more than a bug under their shoe, but Big Al Sears, a saxophone player, started being real nice to me. I sort of became accepted — as long as I made myself useful. They called me Smitty, as in: "Hey, Smitty, go get me a cup of coffee, will ya?"

"Smitty! Get down to the delicatessen and bring back a coupla ham sandwiches."

But whenever anything really important was going down, it'd be, "Go stand outside, Smitty. We gotta talk about something."

Jackie Wilson was not much older than me, maybe twenty years old, and he was working as lead singer of Billy Ward and the Dominoes. His solo stuff—"Reet Petite," "Lonely Teardrops," "(Your Love Keeps Lifting Me) Higher and Higher"—would come out later, but you could see him as a star in the making. He had this great-looking girl working for him as his stage manager or something, and I developed a big crush on her. Then one time I got sent to remind him he was due on stage in two minutes. I knocked on the door and they both said, "Come in."

She was zipping her skirt up while he was tying his tie with a big smile on his face. I realized that she wasn't going to become *my* girlfriend anytime soon.

Another time I recall standing on the fringes when they had to get the payroll together. All these people—hangers-on, managers, valets, friends—were looking at this big wad of Alan Freed's cash like foxes checking out the hen house. You could've cut the tension with a knife.

I basically began learning show business by forcing myself on these people.

When my parents found out where I'd been sneaking off to they put a stop to it. I got grounded and forbidden from going back, which frustrated the hell out of me.

Meanwhile, my friend Richie had gotten himself a job at a gas station. That's where he learned how to hot-wire cars. On weekends, he and I, with Lenny and Klepto tagging along, would walk down the street together, pick out a car, and take it for a joyride. Sometimes it was too easy. People actually left their keys in the ignition. On General Motors cars then, if the owner just turned the ignition to "Off" instead of "Lock," all it took to start the car was your own fingers.

We never did anything bad to these cars, just enjoyed them for a few miles, then left them at a curb and walked away.

One day, as we were tooling around in someone's black '51 Ford sedan with the windows down and the radio playing loud, a police car came cruising up behind us. They busted us and took us down to the station. Our folks had to get us out. Because I was the youngest, and because Weston came in looking like a solid middle-class citizen, very polite and persuasive, I got released with no record. The catch was that I had to be put into a strict boarding school.

The Friends Academy, a Quaker school, was a serious prep school. All the kids wore very conservative threads. They all came from well-to-do families, and were gunning for Ivy League schools. I arrived in purple pegged pants with saddle stitching down the sides and pistol pockets in back, Hollywood shirts with "Mr. B." collars, and a ducktail haircut. We called them "Mr. B." collars in honor of Billy Eckstine, the great soulful singer of ballads.

The Friends Academy was actually a good school, but it felt like a prison to me. Every day it was wake up, eat breakfast, attend classes, eat supper, go to bed, wake up, and do the same goddamn thing over again. Completely regimented and dull. Occasionally, Rosamund and Gordon would pick me up in their bullet-nose Studebaker and take me home on the weekends. Marge and Weston mostly stayed away.

Every morning before classes started, you had to go into a big chapel and put your head down to meditate. You couldn't leave until time was up. If the spirit moved you to say something, you were supposed to stand up and say it to the whole congregation.

This seemed funny to me, so one morning I stood up

51

and said, "I have to go to the bathroom. I have to leave the room right now, and I wanted to tell everyone about that."

After a couple of minutes, I got up again and said, "I just shit my pants 'cause I wasn't able to go to the bathroom."

It wasn't what you'd call sharp humor, but the other kids started to giggle, in spite of themselves.

That evening I was deprived of supper. After everyone else went to bed, Mr. Jones, the wrestling coach, a real big, brawny motherfucker, took me down into the basement and ordered me to take off my clothes. Then he turned a firehose on me. If you've ever had a firehose hit you, you know it's unbelievably painful, like needles puncturing your flesh. I remember standing there, shivering and cold, with red blotches all over my belly, my arms, my ass, and my legs. Mr. Jones just quietly strung the hose back up in its rack and said, "This is what we do for extreme bad behavior."

After that I changed everything and started really behaving myself. It wasn't my world, but I made myself fit in long enough to finish out the year and not get into any more trouble. That was my sophomore year, which was the last year of formal schooling that I finished. Except for broadcasting school, which happened some years later.

In the summer of 1956 I went down to Key West, Florida. Emile and Joan were stationed there, so I got to spend a couple of months with my "other family." By then they had two little boys of their own.

Emile is a real no-nonsense kind of guy, but with a big heart. I could do whatever I wanted, as long as I helped out with the toddlers and acted right. After my term in Quaker school, Key West was a great taste of freedom. I even got my first set of wheels.

They don't make Indian motorcycles anymore, but when they did, they mostly made big-bore bruisers, in the same league with Harley hogs. But in the early 1950s Indian came out with a model that was smaller, lighter, and more like a European bike. They called it the Indian Papoose. I got a used one real cheap and spent the whole summer just tinkering, taking it apart and putting it back together. My three-year-old nephew, Randy, watched the whole process like it was a thrilling drama. When I finished, a few parts were left over and I didn't know where they were supposed to go. Even so, the Papoose ran well enough to get me around the island and have some fun. The day before leaving I sold it to another teenager there, Ralph, a real macho-type guy I'd hung around with.

When it came time for me to go into Miami and catch a train back north, Emile loaded the whole family in their wood-trimmed 1951 Ford Country Squire station wagon. I was in the back seat with the kids. As we came to the bridge out of town, all of a sudden I saw Ralph. He didn't look up to see us. He was busy lifting up the Papoose's kick-starter with his toe again and again, throwing the strongest kicks he could, trying in vain to get it started. As we were passing by he gave one last kick. It went "Ba-ba-BOOM!" and a greasy-looking plume of blue smoke came belching out of the tailpipe. I slid down to the floorboards and begged Emile, "Step on the gas, man!"

That same summer, Marge and Weston moved from Brooklyn to Short Hills, New Jersey, which is a very uppity community of the well-to-do. They put me in a trade/tech school so I could become an electrician, but I really didn't like it. I hardly paid attention at all. Now, electricity is something that doesn't allow you to goof off too many times. One day, while my mind was someplace else, I practically electrocuted myself and another guy.

Soon after that, I started my own curriculum. I rode the bus to school just like everything was normal, then walked a couple of blocks to where I could catch another bus to Newark. I was headed for WNJR, one of the stations I had always listened to in my coal bin days.

WNJR was a dusky kind of a place with a little bit of light coming in from outside. A friendly black lady who was the receptionist allowed me to sit with her in the reception area for a long time, listening to a speaker that played what was going out over the air. Somebody who looked like they worked there came through, so I walked up and said, "Hi. I'm Bob Smith. I really want to learn the radio business. Do you mind if I go back there with you and watch what you do for a while?"

It turned out that I'd asked Mr. Jim, the engineer, who was exactly the right guy to ask. He even seemed kind of flattered. Just like I did around the Alan Freed scene, I made myself useful for Mr. Jim, and all the other engineers and DJs. Most of their jocks were black, but the one known as Mr. Blues turned out to be as white as I was.

I met Mr. Blues one day when I was standing in front of the urinal. He walked in and stood right beside me. He pulled his zipper down, extracted his crank, and started to relieve himself. I was so excited to be in the company of the great Mr. Blues that I switched my pecker to my left hand and reached over with my right one for a handshake. He had to shift hands, too, and fumble with his cigarette so smoke wouldn't go in his eyes. It was an awkward moment, but sincere.

In those days, the engineer sat on one side of the jock's booth, separated by a soundproof glass. It was easy for me to hang out there with Mr. Jim while he played all this great rhythm and blues. The black jocks kind of intimidated me a little bit because they were so dynamic, but the engineers were happy to take some time out and teach me how their job worked.

There was a whole lot more to it than just playing records. They had to have a real feel for when to punch something, and when to soothe it down. They had to slide in underneath the DJ's rap, especially going in and out of commercials.

All along, my parents thought I was going to the trade school. In a way, I was. Except it was one that I had self-selected.

Day after day, I'd log about five or six hours at WNJR. Right down on the corner was a drugstore with a soda fountain that made hamburgers, sandwiches, ice cream sodas, and sundaes. I'd be in and out of there twice a day, getting everybody's snacks. The local liquor store even sold beer to me because they'd gotten to know me as Smitty, the gofer from WNJR.

One afternoon Mr. Jim called in sick. He was supposed to work with Mr. Blues from seven o'clock until eleven. They couldn't find a replacement. One of the black jocks, a guy I didn't even know real well, said, "Why don'tcha let Smitty run the board? I've seen him. He knows what to do."

Naturally, I wasn't a union member, and they were scared that there'd be a big beef if they used me. They were more worried about that than whether I'd screw the gig up.

When seven o'clock rolled around they didn't have any choice. I was supposed to be back home in Short Hills, but I was too juiced up to remember that. At the stroke of seven, Mr. Blues began doing his thing and I was performing alongside him like a champion. My segues came in right. Mr. Blues would get about three beats from the end of a live commercial and give me a wink and I'd bring in that sexy music right behind him, right on time, like an NFL lineman opening up a hole so the big star running back could blast through.

I was feeling about ten feet off the ground. Four hours went by like a couple of fingersnaps.

When I got home, my parents hit the roof. I made up a story about being at some friend's house, but they weren't buying it. Unfortunately, a couple of days later my report card arrived in the mail, showing almost solid absences.

The next thing I knew, I was enrolled in a school for problem kids, including the mentally and emotionally disabled. That was a lot tighter, but I faked being sick and once again got free to return to the radio station.

As you might expect, my control freak stepmother, Marge, and her sullen, troubled teenage stepson, Bob, were now set for a head-on collision.

It finally arrived one Saturday afternoon.

Even out in the suburbs, I still had a kind of radio studio set up. This time it was in the garage. I was fooling around with it when my turntable broke down. I knew Stewart had one in his room that he hardly ever used, so I walked in and borrowed it. Later, when he came home and discovered it was missing, there was hell to pay. Marge went into total hysterics. It was a sight to see. She gathered up all my clothes and records and threw them into the garage, shrieking the whole time. "You ungrateful little shit!" she said. "I've had all of you I can stand."

When Weston came home from a Saturday spent working at the office, she gave him both barrels. "He has to go," she demanded. "We've given him every opportunity and all he does is throw it back in our faces!"

I'd never seen Weston look so sad. There he was with his heart in a vise, caught between a child who kept fucking up and a spouse who never gave an inch. He took me aside and told me the time had come for going out on my own. He was sorry, but they'd done everything they knew how to do. Then he gave me $300.

"I hope this helps you get started," he said.

It sure did. Early the next day I was on a Newark used-car lot with my pal Richie, picking out a '49 Buick convertible, a big bomboozle that you could use to mow down trees. It was painted a dark, mossy green color, with a Fireball 8 under the hood. Richie had always wanted to get out of town. The Buick looked solid enough to get us where we wanted to go, which was Hollywood, California. I was hurt and confused by what had gone down with my parents, but I'd spent most of my life dealing with those emotions. Now I was going to get away. As a parting shot, I told them that I was going to become a famous actor.

My exodus came about the time when Fats Domino was putting out one easy-rolling, Louisiana-flavored hit record after another. One of his songs pretty much summed up what I was feeling: "I'm gonna be a wheel someday, I'm gonna be somebody. I'm gonna be a real gone cat, and then I won't want you."

Both Richie and I were good-looking young guys. There had to be some kind of Hollywood careers we could latch on to. "Man," I said, "one of us is bound to get a break. If it's me, I'll help you out, too. And if it's you, you're gonna help me out. Okay?"

We shook on it. By late afternoon, the Buick was loaded and highway bound. We were playing the big Sonomatic radio, singing along with it, when some hip DJ put on a lesser-known Chuck Berry track — "You Can't Catch Me."

It's about a guy who just got an "air-mobile" with "a powerful motor and some hideaway wings." And when the cops try to catch him for speeding on the New Jersey Turnpike, he lets out the wings and goes airborne. That became our theme song all the way out of New Jersey: "You can't catch me. Baby, you can't catch me. 'Cause if you get too close, you know I'm gone like a *coooooool* breeze . . ."

What exactly we'd do when we got to Hollywood, and how we'd buy the gas, hamburgers, and french fries it'd take to push us across the country, those were a couple of details we hadn't worked out.

The only thing we knew for sure was that my sister, Joan, and her husband, Emile, were then living just outside Washington, D.C., in Alexandria, Virginia, and they had agreed to let us sleep at their place on the first night of our journey to fame.

Chapter Four

When Richie and I invaded Alexandria in that ten-year-old Buick, two young, prowling New York types with ducktail haircuts and slick, wild-colored clothes invading a serene, sleepy family suburb full of brick split-level homes with trikes and bikes in every driveway, we were the most outside characters ever to come on the scene. We brought with us a couple of case-hardened attitudes.

In the presence of real family warmth, those attitudes melted away. When it got down to it, all we wanted to experience was being on the inside for a change.

Everybody needs a good family feeling in their life. If you haven't got it, chances are you'll go around the rest of your days looking for a way to create it. I got lucky. I got a second chance to become part of a supportive, disciplined, really sweet and caring family.

That turnaround made a huge difference in my life. I kept on being crazy and an outsider, but I also got a sense of roots and self-worth to grow from. Because the Wolfman may be wild, but he isn't a destroyer. Wolfman

Jack, the guy I've spent my life trying to become, is somebody who invites everyone else into the circle of good times.

Before you can invite people in, you have to build a sense of who you are. My second family—Joan, Emile, and all their wonderful kids—gave me a great basis. Within their scene, I started to become more of a whole person.

Richie and I arrived planning to stay one day, maybe two at the most, before pushing westward to Hollywood.

Almost instantly, though, we both realized that we didn't want to leave.

In the high desert east of Palm Springs, there's a lot of nearly identical-looking canyons, filled with cactuses, Joshua trees, and boulders bigger than houses. If you walk all the way to the head of some of those canyons, sometimes there's a spot where water seeps to the surface. The greenery thrives there, and all kinds of living creatures buzz and fly around nearby. If you've been hiking a long, long time and seen nothing for hours but hot, dry sand, big rocks, and scaly lizards, coming up on one of these places will open your mind to the meaning of the word "oasis."

Well, Richie and I had stumbled into an emotional oasis. It was a home where a happy mother and a caring father were raising three youngsters and a newborn. Everyone stood inside a circle where the helpless were protected and the strong were kind. It was a place where people weren't yelling at each other, or pulling head trips on each other, or trying to wipe away their own unhappiness by creating misery for everyone around them.

A place that felt real good to your soul to stay in.

Richie went for it like a ton of bricks. Being in a peaceful home was so new that it just lulled him. He kind of reverted to age four and spent all day horizontal on the couch watching cartoon shows.

Joan and Emile's house was a front-to-back split-level. You came in the front door to the main level of the house. The kitchen and dining room and family rooms were there. Most of the bedrooms were on the upstairs floor. Downstairs was a playroom, a spare bedroom, and a bath. Richie and I settled into that playroom. Pretty soon we completely stopped talking about our Hollywood trip. I brought my radio gear in from the car, set it up in the playroom, and resumed my habit of playing disc jockey until two or three in the morning.

After we'd been settled in for about one week, an emergency arose in Emile's family. His brother had just been assigned to the Army General Command School out in Kansas, but at exactly the same time his wife got seriously ill. She was facing a long hospitalization.

Command School was the kind of all-or-nothing opportunity that a young, ambitious officer couldn't turn down. It would make a huge difference in his entire career. But their two young children wouldn't have anyone to take care of them.

Emile and Joan immediately took those two kids in. Suddenly, the household head count had expanded to two adults, two twenty-year-old juvenile delinquents that didn't want to grow up, four healthy, barnstorming little boys, one sassy little girl, and a brand-new infant baby girl.

Something had to give. It was Richie.

Emile took me aside and set out the rules: I could stay there—as long as I got myself a job, took night classes to complete my high school diploma, helped out around the house by doing chores and ponying up a little room-

and-board payment, and generally started getting my life together. There was no room for anybody extra. Especially if all they ever did was to zone out on Daffy Duck cartoons.

Richie caught a bus back up north and I don't know what happened with his life after that, because my *own* life suddenly became a full-time involvement.

Scrubbing the pots and pans every night after dinner was my main household chore. Between night classes, and the fact that the teenage girls around Alexandria had never seen or touched a New York sharpster before, practically every night I tore out right after dinner and didn't come back home until after midnight.

Lots of times Emile had to field phone calls from pissed-off parents: "Bob was supposed to bring our daughter home by eleven-thirty and they're not here yet!" The poor guy hadn't even been married ten years and already he had all the hassles of supervising a sexually adventurous young buck.

Anyway, as soon as I got in the door, I filled the sink with soap bubbles and attacked those pots and pans. The clatter I made was how everyone knew I'd gotten home safely.

The playroom became my bachelor apartment. We soundproofed the ceiling so I could do my DJ thing until all hours without disturbing the rest of the family. There was a built-in hi-fi system in the room that I tore into and connected with my own stuff.

It was still just a hobby. But, even if I wasn't ready yet to be a Wolfman professionally, I unconsciously began to develop the character. People have asked me so many times how I came up with the idea of Wolfman Jack. I've concocted a lot of different funny answers over the years, trying to be entertaining about it, because I really didn't remember. It wasn't until I sat down to write this book that this birth-of-the-Wolfman memory came back to me.

I loved being around all the kids, and they really dug having this lively, new character on the scene, somebody who was part uncle and part big brother, who played music and stirred up excitement all the time. Every day I tried to come up with something new to win those kids over. The payoff was instantaneous, lots of love and attention, which I thrived on.

One thing the boys all loved was when, after they'd gotten into their pajamas, I'd drape a big, dark blanket over myself and say, in the deepest tones my vocal cords could manage, "The W*ooo*lfman is coming down the *halllll* . . . The W*ooo*lfman is coming to your doo*ooo*or . . . Now he's coming to GET YOU and *EAT YOU UP!*" Then I'd cup my hands in front of my mouth and go *"Awoooooo!"*

Their eyes would get as big as tea saucers. They'd either squirm under the bed, or shoot out the door and go running down the hall, yelling, "The *Wolfman's* after us! The *Wolfman's* after us!"

Finally, everybody would get too wound up and Emile would have to assert some order with a navy command: "All Stop! All Stop!"

Years later, when I was mounting an attack on the radio scene, that marauding Wolfman character who scared the kiddies for fun just synced up with all the jivemaster disc jockey role models I'd been emulating since I was a kid myself. The "Jack" part got added on because that was a hipster's style of speaking, to end your sentences with the name Jack. Like, "Dig that fine set of wheels, Jack."

It was like the answer to a question:

"Who is that weird guy over there?"

"That's Wolfman, Jack."

To help pay my room and board, I landed a job selling *Collier's Encyclopedia*s door-to-door. The whole sales force was young kids like me, all eager to get out there and score. An older guy with a dumpy-looking Plymouth coupe would take us out into the neighborhoods in the mornings and drop us off so we could work up and down the streets until suppertime. We sold those encyclopedias on an installment plan—one volume now and another one every month until you've got yourself the whole alphabet.

The company outfitted us with a big fold-out photo, about eight feet wide, of how a complete set would look in somebody's bookcase. Once I got past somebody's front door, I'd flip this life-size image out and let them drink in how substantial and intelligent they'd feel owning the whole raft of books. Then I hammered them with my sales pitch about the E-Z payments and the outstanding success their kids would enjoy in school from that day forward. I made Joan and Emile sit through my whole pitch and tell me whether I had it working good or not.

"Yes, these encyclopedias will be all your kids need when they need to look something up for school. You wanna look up elephants? Here they are in Volume Five. You wanna learn all about horses? Here they are in Volume Eight. I tell ya, I hold in my hands right now—and I'm offerin' to you—the keys to future success. Your kids can win scholarships! They can be doctors and lawyers!"

I sold enough encyclopedias off of that rap to trade in my faded Buick for a '54 Ford convertible. It was lipstick red, with wide whitewalls, a V-8 engine, dual exhausts, and a Continental spare tire riding in style up over the back bumper. There wasn't a cooler car in Alexandria.

Next, I moved up to being a Fuller Brush Man.

I don't even know if there are any Fuller Brush salesmen left in the world these days, but in the 1940s and 1950s, the whole country was overrun by guys pounding out their living door-to-door, selling everything from Bibles to shoes. The Fuller Brush Company sort of had the full range of stuff a person might want for house-cleaning jobs.

I remember how stoked I was after I got accepted to the sales force and the regional sales manager gave me a big pep talk.

"Bob," he began, "you're going to derive a whole lot more from this job than simply the money you're gonna be earning. Many, many of the most successful men in America today began their careers as Fuller Brush Men. From our training, they learned how to meet the public with confidence. This job will demand the best of you. You must meet success and failure alike with a smile and a will to go out and do even better the next day. And the next day, and the day after that. Succeed as a Fuller Brush Man, and you will succeed with every hurdle and every challenge you face the rest of your life."

Man, I was so fired up, I sincerely wished I had a roll of bills in my pocket to pay him for the privilege of being allowed to go knocking on doors all over town with a suitcase full of toilet scrubbers.

Of course, there was a big helping of bullshit in what he said. But there was some truth to it, too. And it got me going. I went after that job like a demon. All week long I'd punch doorbells and burn up shoe leather until my dogs were barking. By mid-week I'd turn my orders in. On Friday a truck would pull up at our house and drop off all the goodies my customers had ordered. Pretty soon I had so many orders that I began hiring my nephews and some of their little friends from the neighborhood to help sort all the brushes and things. Then the kids would pile in my red convertible and we'd cruise out to make deliveries, with the top down. It looked like a 1950s version of *Oliver Twist*, with Fagin taking the ragamuffins on the road.

The kids always came back home with lots of nickels and dimes jingling in their pockets and they felt like they were world-beaters.

Actually, so did I. Within a couple of months I was one of the top Fuller Brush peddlers in the Alexandria area. And I did learn some valuable lessons while I was on that job, even if they weren't the same ones that I'd heard about in my first-day pep talk.

One Saturday afternoon the company treated a handful of their top salespeople to a day at the racetrack. For some reason, early in the afternoon I decided to throw a five-dollar bill on this pathetic long shot. Everybody told me I was crazy as hell, but then that horse went out and smoked the field.

All of a sudden my hands were wrapped around the most cash I ever had in my life. I had to be a racetrack genius! So I played my hunches on all the other races, all afternoon long. By the time night had fallen and all the ponies were led away and the janitors were sweeping up the crumpled tickets, beer cups, and mustard-soaked hot dog napkins, my winnings were so far down that I owed somebody else a buck.

I came home completely disillusioned and downhearted. "What happened?" Emile asked. When I told him, he said, "Bob, you know what? You went overboard. Something good happened and you got carried away. You didn't have the experience to know how to handle it. But now you realize how much better off you'd be if you still had some of that money in your pocket."

"Boy," I said, "you're right. I've learned a lesson." And I meant it a hundred percent when I said it. But when I think of all the things I've done since those early days, going overboard seems to be my common denominator. I guess I've never gotten over how much fun you can have by going overboard once in a while.

Speaking of that tendency—one afternoon I was working a country road with my Fuller Brush sample case and I came upon some newly built houses with tall wooden steps leading to their front porches. I walked up and knocked on the door of one of these houses, all ready to go into my spiel. A lovely woman wearing a peach-colored satin robe opened up the door by only a couple of inches. She had a sweet face and a very relaxed manner.

"Hi!" I said. "I'm Bob Smith, your friendly Fuller Brush Man, and I've got a whole bunch of free gifts to give you. Can I come in and talk to you a few minutes?"

"Uh, sure. Come on in, Bob."

She opened the door and I stepped into the house's entryway. "Come into the living room," she said, walking a few feet and then turning right and passing through a doorway. I followed right along.

Once I'd walked into the living room, it took nearly a full minute before I could begin to believe my eyes. Three men and five women were lying around the living room, naked as the day they were born, but a lot more hairy. They all looked to be in their mid-thirties, slightly drunk, and game for anything. In fact, one of the guys was calmly getting his member swallowed. Another one was on his knees on the couch, right behind a woman with dark, wavy hair, and they were smiling in my direction at the same time they were doing an imitation of overly friendly cocker spaniels. My jaw dropped. My sample case of brushes hit the floor.

"Wow," I said. "Holy smoke."

The woman who had opened the door then let her peach-colored robe slip past her peaches, off her shoulders, and fall to the floor. "I'm Claire," she said warmly as I stared at the round-yet-pointy parts of her naked body, her belly button and her sable muff, "and that's my husband, Kenny." A naked man sitting on the rug waved a cheerful hello to me. A heat wave began to work its way from my shirt collar to somewhere near the top of my ears. I was too stunned to return Kenny's friendly gesture. My eyes didn't know where to land.

Then Claire gave me a nice smile and said, "Would you like to join us?"

"Well, I don't know. Wow."

Before I could say or do anything else, she and one of her girlfriends were fondling my private parts through the fabric of my pants and unfastening the belt, button, and zipper that held them up. Within a few seconds there were warm, red lips providing direct inspiration to my young soldier and I knew without reservation that I'd be lingering for a while in this strange and wonderful place.

I don't know how long that afternoon get-together had been going on before I arrived, but it stretched for another three hours after I got there. I popped my cookies the most times I ever had in my life, at least once with each of those women, with a glass of wine and a restful spell in between each. We went at it sideways, up against the fireplace mantel, down in an easy chair, up on the coffee table. Everybody was applauding. I'd never been anyplace before where balling was considered a spectator sport.

I didn't sell any brushes that afternoon, but I had an open invitation to come on back every now and then. Not that I was a big stud or anything. I just happened to get in on a remarkable situation. Any kid who was young, willing, and halfway good-looking would have made the most of it.

Which I did—at least once a week for the next couple of months. Kenny was like Peter Sellers in *Being There:* he liked to watch. It was real spicy to him to see his wife being driven to ecstasy. Sometimes there were two women there in the mood to be playful. Other times they said "not today" and didn't invite me in.

But even though any horny youngster would've suited their plans, allow me to boast anyway that I was a very sharp-looking character in those days. At least, compared to the local guys around my age. They were more or less a bunch of rednecks. I modeled myself on Elvis, but with a New York streetcorner attitude.

Since at that time I didn't have any other goals in particular, the money I was making from salesmanship went to sharkskin suits and great casual shirts, jackets, and slacks that I bought from stores in the black sections of Washington. And to generous amounts of Dixie Peach Pomade for my boogie-woogie hairstyle.

Being so different from the hometown guys gave me an edge with lots of the girls.

There was Jo, a girl from the neighborhood who used to come over sometimes and snuggle with me down in my basement room. My little nephews would hang around and bug us, knowing full well that I'd get frustrated pretty soon and give them some money to go buy candy, just to get a little time alone with Jo.

One night she took me to a local party, and some other girls there began paying a lot of attention to me.

The local guys didn't like it. They'd seen me come up in my flashy convertible, and they didn't like that much either. A couple of them stood on the sidelines while Jo and I danced, saying stuff like, "Where didja get that loud shirt, hey, off a dead nigger or somethin'?"

I decided not to hang around that scene. I slipped on my jacket, put my arm around Jo and reached for the front door knob. Just then one guy grabbed me from behind and pulled my jacket back over my shoulders to hold my arms down. Then his buddy commenced to wail on my face. The guy doing the punching had a big ring on. At first I was too dazed and surprised, and whoever was behind me had too good a grip. Then the guy throwing punches laid that ring across the point of my chin and I felt like I'd been slashed with an electrified sword. I threw my arms outward with a surprise burst of strength, breaking away from the guy holding me. In one motion I lunged forward and grabbed the guy who'd been throwing blows. Both of us went down, me landing on top of him. He banged his head on the hardwood floor real loud, and then I drew back and gave him a short, hard shot to his nose.

I was so scared, with the adrenaline rush and everything, that it felt like I had to kill him or else he would kill me. But between the rap his head took from the floor and the punch I landed, he was out cold. For a second, I thought I really had snuffed him. Blood was gushing out of his nose and dripping off my chin. Some of it was soaked into my shirt front.

When I stood up, everybody just held their breath and backed off.

I was such a mess, I didn't realize that the blood on my shirt was my own. After dropping off Jo at her parents' house around one in the morning, I dragged my scruffy-looking butt into the kitchen and began my regular chore of washing out the pots and pans. When I looked down into the dishwater, the soapsuds were flecked with blood. I picked up a towel and held it to my chin with one hand but kept trying to wash the pots and pans with the other. Being a little woozy, I didn't realize how much noise I was making. The next thing I knew, Emile was walking briskly into the chen, tying up the sash on his plaid wool robe and looking at me like I was crazy.

"Wh the hell happened to you tonight, Bob?"

"Em, I got cut here. I think I need a Band-Aid."

"My od, you need stitches."

He ide me press the towel up to my chin with both hands hen he called a doctor he knew, and loaded me into old Country Squire.

In le of ten minutes, I was up on a table in this doc 's office, getting seven stitches on my chin with no esthetic. I don't mind admitting to you that I yelled like motherfucker.

ter that, I laid off the Alexandria peckerwood party ci uit.

his incident inspired Emile to take me aside for one his fatherly talks. "You've got to decide what you want do with your life," he said.

Actually, I knew exactly what I wanted. I'd known it or a long time. For years. But every time in the past when I'd brought up the idea, back up in Brooklyn and Short Hills, it had gotten stepped on.

"I want to be a radio announcer," I said. "But Weston thinks it's like I'm a little kid who wants to be a fireman."

"Well, if you want to be in radio, are there any schools in this area can train you?"

I got busy the next day, combing the phone book and making calls. In Washington, not very far away, there was a prestigious-sounding school called the National Academy of Broadcasting. If you got through their one-year course of study, you became a legitimate radio announcer. And they had a placement service with nationwide connections.

The only hang-up was the cost: $3,000 for the year. I didn't have that kind of money, and Joan and Emile

71

couldn't give it to me, either. I felt defeated bef I even got started.

"Look, Bob," Emile said, "your father can ord to help you. Pick up the goddamn phone and call m."

"You call him," I pleaded. "He thinks the world you."

"You're the one who wants to go to school. Yo nake the call."

I got up my nerve and called my father back in ort Hills. "Papa," I said, "I've been wanting to do this my life."

"Son, the last I heard from you, you were going the an actor. How do I know you're serious about this?

After I'd given it my best shot, Emile took over 'I honestly think this is where Bob should be," he sq. "Ever since I've known him, almost ten years now, he had a strong leaning toward radio. He practices all th time. I see every day how dedicated he is."

That won my old man over. A couple of days later, check arrived, big enough to cover a year's tuition and expenses.

If any of my teachers from the Quaker academy, the trade/tech school, or the disabled kids school could've seen how I dove into my broadcast school studies, they'd have keeled over. I ate up the curriculum like it was a hot fudge sundae sitting on top of a crisp waffle. The year flew by, even the parts where we had to study stuff I didn't care much about — like classical music, for example.

I drew straight A's. I volunteered for every project. Usually I ended up becoming a group leader and even helping to teach the other students. After all, I'd learned every inch of the engineer's board from Mr. Jim of WNJR. I had already won the Mr. Blues Seal of Approval. Most of the others went home and practiced with a reel-to-reel tape recorder and a hand-held mike. I'd already been running a home studio for years, in my Alexandria bedroom, in the Short Hills garage, down in the Brooklyn coal bin.

The other kids at the National Academy of Broadcasting mainly came from wealthy homes. The lady who ran the school wanted everybody to go on to prestige careers at classical music stations. Most all the other students were grooming themselves along those lines, except a few crazy rebels who wanted to be sportscasters. One guy had the dream of hosting a make-believe ballroom dance show, where he would play society orchestra records and pretend a gala white-tie crowd was having a swanky time in the ballroom of a grand hotel.

I was positively the only one in the whole school that wanted to work for a rhythm and blues radio station. The rest of the students didn't understand my goal at all, but "How Much Is That Doggie in the Window?" was not my kind of music. Neither was Beethoven, Wagner, or Sibelius. I wanted to hear Clyde McPhatter and the Drifters do "Money Honey" and tunes like that. I actually introduced some of those kids to real good boogie-woogie music and a few of them—the girls more than the guys—really got the feeling. But it scared them. Like, if you listened to too much of that stuff, you'd turn into some kind of thrill-crazy outcast who had sex on the brain twenty-four hours a day.

Come to think of it—that's exactly what happened to me. And you folks at home can do it, too!

Anyway, at the end of the term you made an audition tape in the format of the kind of station where you wanted to work. Then the school would send them out, with your own cover letter, to stations all around the country.

I made mine in the same kind of bag as John R., Symphony Sid, and all those others who had been inspiring me since I was a little kid. I created a jive-talking character called Daddy Jules—which was a play on "the family jewels"—and put together a whole sample show of hard-cooking tunes.

Emile sat down with me at the typewriter after he got home from work and together we cranked out seventy-five letters to radio stations in every corner of the U.S. Then I went out and got seventy-five blank tape reels and started making duplicates of my audition.

The way things turned out, my demo stuff never got mailed. Immediately after the term ended, I went back to the school to pick up my diploma and some equipment that was stashed in a locker. Walking down the hall, I bumped into the president of the school. She was talking with an older guy I'd never seen before.

He turned out to be a pivotal character in my young life.

"Bob, I'd like you to meet Richard Eaton, the president of United Broadcasting Company. He owns a station here and one in Washington and another one in Newport News, Virginia."

I grabbed his hand and shook it, while he stared at me like a man trying to figure out the solution to a puzzle.

"Mr. Eaton's stations are aimed at Negro audiences," she continued. "In fact, he came to ask me if anyone in this graduating class might be interested in pursuing a career in his organization. That's why I thought of you, Bob."

Now I began staring right back at him, wondering if he could be for real. "Yes, Mr. Eaton. I'd like that very much."

I later found out that Eaton had been a newspaperman in the 1940s. Right after World War II he bought himself a small station. It was just a Class 4, which meant 250 watts maximum. High on the dial. It was what people in the radio business call a "cripple," a station with either a weak signal or crummy facilities. Or both.

But the revolutionary thing Eaton did was to make that cripple into the first radio station in America that was programmed to appeal to black listeners. They were getting just a little more prosperous in the postwar years, as the Jim Crow laws and exclusionary clauses and other segregationist bullshit gradually began to recede. Advertisers realized that it'd do them good to reach those black folks.

Eaton's venture did so well that over the next ten years or so he was able to buy another small station in Baltimore, another in Richmond, and then the one in Newport News. Which was where the job opening was.

At that time, all Eaton's stations were within driving distance of his headquarters in D.C. Later on he expanded to L.A., Miami, Cleveland, New York, and a bunch of other places.

He was a tough, tough operator. He didn't pay too much. But he was important in the evolution of radio in America. Eaton was the first guy to prove that you could take a marginal station, program it for a specific audience like an ethnic group, and build it into an empire.

It was a great twist of fate for me to get hooked up with the guy. In time, a partner and I had a lot of luck by expanding on Eaton's basic idea.

WYOU, the Newport News station, wasn't much more than a peanut whistle. The broadcast signal barely made it past the city limits. They cranked it up around sunrise and turned it off at sundown. One jock, a truly remarkable cat that I was soon to meet, was carrying the whole load by himself, seven days a week. Whoever joined him on the gig would have to do just about everything from sweeping the floor to selling advertising, plus take over half of the airtime.

Even though the station was oriented to black listeners, most of the merchants they wanted to sell airtime to were white guys. And there was a competing station nearby over in Norfolk, also catering to black listeners. It had a stronger signal, better ratings, and it ran for more hours of the day. So WYOU was a tough sell, and Eaton thought he might improve the odds if he hired a white guy to work with the black jock who was already at the station.

Not realizing what I was getting into, I was crazy enough to go for it. And Eaton was crazy enough to hire me.

Newport News, for anybody who hasn't been around that part of the country, is a tough, hardworking town across the Chesapeake Bay from Norfolk, Virginia, near the Atlantic Ocean. Major shipbuilding activity and a huge navy presence have been in that area for more than two hundred years. When the *Monitor* and the *Merrimac*, the world's first ironclad ships, fought each other during the Civil War, they went at it just offshore from Newport News.

It's the kind of place where you use a capital B when you call it Blue-Collar.

When I got to WYOU, Newport News, Virginia, my existence went up about twelve levels in intensity. Radio wasn't a hobby anymore.

Once and for all, it was my life.

Frances was her name. But as a toddler, my sister could only say "Tantan." And that was what she wanted to be called, from that day on. Loving and caring were her total life. She was the first black person I ever met, she introduced me to black gospel music, and Tantan made it clear—through her actions—that living means putting your heart and soul into your work, and all the people you love.

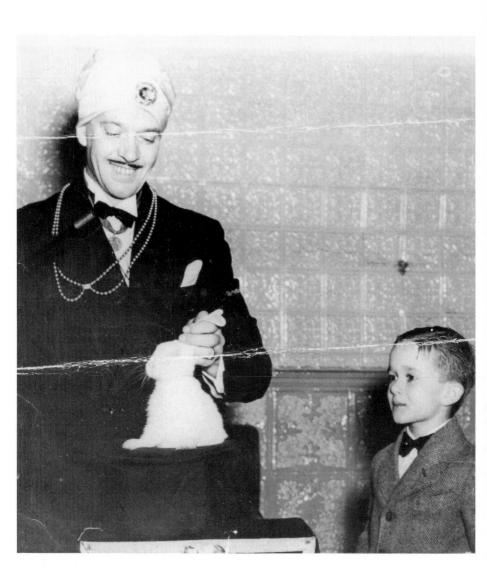

This is my dad, Weston Smith, as his alter ego, "Kandu the Magician."
Assisting him is me, under the stage name "No-Kandu." These gigs
happened wherever a handful of kids were gathered, and they gave me
a taste for applause—something that I still can't get enough of!

My grandfather, who was a college professor, and my father, who was a writer, editor, and businessman, holding up a very young version of me for inspection.

If you want to sound like me, you've got to start working the lungs and vocal cords at a very early age.

My fascination for fine wheels developed early. Later on, I'd be more interested in Cadillacs.

I have nothing but happy memories from when my original family was together. Here's me, with sister Joan and my mom, Roxie, who now spends lots of time at my home in North Carolina.

The same crew, but with my father in the picture. He was a sweet guy, blind to anybody else's faults, but very smart and talented.

Joan and I always had a special closeness. She took a lot of responsibility for my upbringing, and that experience helped her become a terrific mother to her own kids later on.

You can see it in her eyes. My stepmother was not a happy woman. She coddled my stepbrother, Stewart, but he eventually rebelled. I was always the odd one out.

It seems like I was always a split personality. Both of me are all dressed up for my junior high graduation. High school graduation never happened, but I did get it together for a G.E.D.

This was the picture that started things off, earning Joan the title "Miss Stardust." She could've gone on to a Hollywood career, but she really wanted to have a family of her own. And she met exactly the right guy to partner up with. (*Wide World Photos*)

One of her many modeling gigs was with Bill Holden, at an aviation show. This was just before he starred in the classic movie *Sunset Boulevard*. (*Wide World Photos*)

This ain't a holy trinity. Klepto, master of shoplifting, who built my first record collection for free, is on the left. I'm in the middle, and my partner in hot-wiring cars, Richie Caggiano, is on the right.

One of my first cars was a lipstick-red '54 Ford convertible with a
Continental spare in back. With wheels like that, it wasn't hard to get
girls to take a ride.

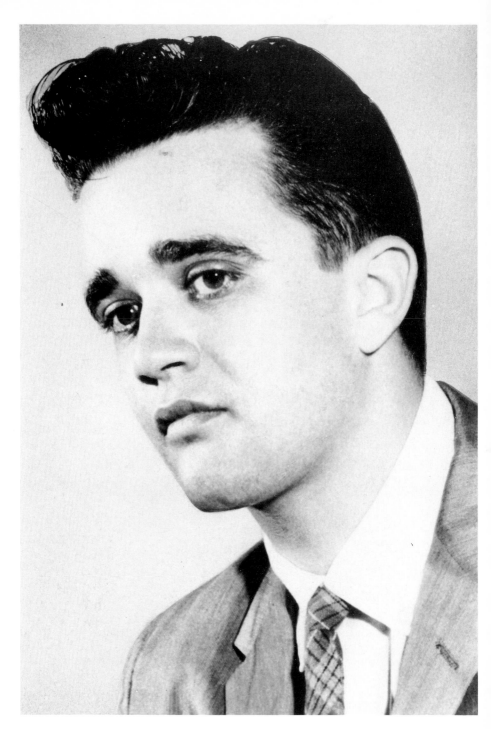

This might've been a school picture, just before I dropped out. Anyway, dig the soulful expression. This was a kid who wanted to be a movie star. It took a long time before George Lucas granted my wish, and by then I looked a little different.

Chapter Five

Trade-out is a vital fact of life in the radio business. Lots of times, businesses get their advertising spots practically for free if they trade merchandise or services for it. My first stop in the city of Newport News—thanks to a trade-out arrangement—was the old Warwick Hotel. Eaton had swapped them radio ads for a cheap rate in one of their smaller rooms.

It was a beautiful old hotel, probably built in the 1920s, but the Warwick had definitely seen better days. Since this was an industrial neighborhood in a working-class city, though, there wasn't anything nearby that looked much better.

You walked through a lobby and there was a garden. Beyond that, all the way in back of the hotel, was a wing of rooms that could be rented on a weekly basis.

WYOU was down a side street from the hotel. Instead of walking back to the lobby, you could turn left in the garden and come out an alley that led you to the street. In the middle of the block, there stood WYOU: an old, weatherbeaten wooden structure with paint peeling off the sides. It must've originally been a sailor's hall, or a whorehouse. Some kind of a dive, anyway.

The WYOU building probably should've been condemned long ago, but at least it was really big, a lot bigger than we really needed. That was going to come in handy.

I walked in and met a light-skinned black lady who was the receptionist. Just as pretty as she could be, with the nicest figure I'd seen in a long time. She told me to turn right and go up the steps to the office. There I met Tex Gathings, the only other jock at WYOU.

Tex was a black guy in his mid-forties who'd worked for Richard Eaton all his professional life and who must have weighed about 350 pounds. He was a good-looking guy, though. He had a great voice, but he didn't sound the least bit ethnic. He had the diction of a Harvard professor.

That's why Eaton had hired me. I was white, but could sound black; Tex looked black but sounded white. Part of the gig was making personal appearances at local public events and part was selling airtime to white business owners.

Between us, Tex and I had all the bases covered.

WYOU catered to the merchants in the area who sold to the black community. The format was soul, jazz, and rhythm and blues. I came on in the afternoons as Daddy Jules, the character in my demo tapes. My pay was only $60 a week, which worked out to less than a buck an hour, plus 15 percent commissions on whatever ad sales I could hustle on the side.

That was Eaton's methodology. Get 'em cheap, and keep 'em hungry.

It didn't take me long to figure out that hustling on the side was gonna be my lifeblood. As soon as I got more connected in the community, I got all kinds of action working. Some of it was even legal.

I really bonded with Tex. He became my father, in a sense, during that time. The man was such a solid pro at all aspects of radio work that coming under his wing was just like being accepted to graduate school for a master's degree. He treated me totally as a real friend. In return, I'd do everything for him, run all his errands and such, without his asking for it. We got to be real tight.

As it turned out, Tex really had gone to Harvard. So had his brother, who was a doctor. Tex drove a big, creamy-white 1960 Thunderbird and lived in a very classy apartment, where he kept a huge aquarium full of exotic fish. He could rattle off the scientific names of all of them.

Radio guys are often very lonely people who have a strong wish to express themselves. Tex was from the same mold as almost all the great radio men and women I've ever met—a very inward type, but with a taste for excitement and an appreciation for beauty. Even though he loved his work, the aspect of going out to perform in public, doing promotions and things like that, was just alien to his shy nature.

Tex and Eaton were both real good to me. They had enough confidence to put me in the important afternoon drive-time slot, from noon until sundown, and they let me concoct my own playlist and fly with it. They took a real chance with me—which was just as great a form of compensation as getting money. I might've been pretty persuasive, too. When I want something, man, I know how to get it. I'll go around the corner a few times if I have to. And I'll do everything I can for the individual I gotta please.

One big plus I brought to that station was the deep

record collection I'd been building up—with Klepto's expert help—ever since I was a kid. Since my friends and I never listened to anything except rhythm and blues, I had several boxes full of wonderful old sides. Some of it was stuff that hardly anybody else had.

My collection, and my well-schooled knowledge of what I was playing, made me very hip with the WYOU audience. They couldn't figure out whether I was white or black. I knew too much of the kind of stuff that only black folks are supposed to know.

Even though Tex's accustomed style of speech was sort of Ivy League-inflected, he gave me an invaluable straightening out on the finer points of black diction. The first time he heard me do a set, he took me aside right afterward and said, "Hey listen, man, I know you're not trying to be Amos and Andy. But if you're gonna make these people really believe, you want to do this thing right." He coached me on pronunciation until it got real, real authentic. Because few things sound more lame than a white guy getting an African-American accent wrong. There are lots of subtleties to black diction.

Tex's coaching was a milestone in my development. I wanted the black community to dig my work and really accept it. I was really trying to be one of them. I wanted to reach them. And while reaching them, I would be reaching those white people that needed it, too. I always knew that white people needed this music, because it had the power to pull them out of their doldrums.

Tex was a jazz fanatic, so he also taught me a whole lot about the soul side of jazz. His favorite part of the week was when he got to do *Jazz on a Sunday Afternoon*. That was his baby.

I used to sit in the studio with him every afternoon when he did the show and while the records played he would fill me in on what the different artists were all about. Tex got me aware of exciting people like Della Reese, Sarah Vaughan, Eddie "Lockjaw" Davis, and lots of other artists. I got to where I couldn't live without my daily fix of Jimmy McGriff and Jimmy Smith and their smoky, soulful Hammond B-3 organ workouts.

Eventually, I got into it so much that Tex let me take over his show. That was a real graduation.

One of the key times of the month at WYOU was when Richard Eaton came to town. I never got to know the man well personally, but Tex told me a lot about him.

Ever since getting his radio empire together, Eaton had lived in the top floor of the Shoreham Hotel in Washington, with a magnificent collection of eighteenth-century French antique furniture. He was married to a French woman. They had one kid of their own, and they had adopted thirteen more—all war orphans.

Eaton would come down to Newport News in a limo, driven by his chauffeur, and he'd stick his head in the door of the station for about five minutes. He had a limp and he walked with a cane, which made him look even older than he really was. But he was incredibly tough. A lot of our advertisers were very slow to pay off their bills. He'd go down into the ghetto, gimping along on his cane, collecting $10 from a barbecue joint, $150 from a shoe shop, $40 from a fortune-teller, and so on until he'd personally collected every penny that folks owed him.

He always got it, too.

Just before his driver eased him into the limo and took him back to his digs at the Shoreham, he'd come up to Tex and then to me, quietly slipping each of us a hundred-dollar bill. Then he'd look me in the eye and say, "You're doing a good job, kid. Keep it up. Take care of my man over here."

It was always "Yes, sir, Mr. Eaton. Yes sir," as if God

had walked through the door and directly touched your life.

The competing black station in the area was playing raunchier, more down-to-earth stuff. And they were really doing a great job in the ratings. So the down-home records I had brought in sort of advanced WYOU's cause. It wasn't long before we began catching up with the competition.

Nowadays, you'll never see me in a necktie or a suit. But back when I was young and ambitious, on the make in Newport News, I always wore slick clothes. I'd make deals with the store owners that serviced the black community, a little bit of advertising and a promise to pay on time, and I'd walk out wearing great skinny-lapel suits, usually linen or silk, with a selection of narrow ties and some sharp handkerchiefs for the breast pocket. Except for the color of my skin, I could've stepped onstage at any moment with Sam and Dave's Soul Revue.

Most of the time I was in debt close to three grand for my wardrobe acquisitions. And I was always meticulously groomed, my hair slicked back nice, my nails professionally manicured. Even my car—a brand-new Ford Galaxie 500, white with black interior, picked up via a trade-out and a long-term, low, E-Z payment schedule—was immaculate at all times.

I worked like a mule at WYOU, practically twenty-four hours a day. Relentlessly. And I couldn't have been happier. While I was growing up, going through a succession of schools and disappointing my folks more and more with each failure, the prevailing thought was maybe, if I'd straighten out, I could someday hold down a job as a garbageman.

That gave me an incredible motivation to be a success, to show them what I really had in me. I guess you'd say

I was a compulsive worker. And I still am to this day. It's what sometimes happens to people who get sick of being pegged for worthless. They run all their lives on "I'll show you!"

Other than Eaton's occasional generous handouts, WYOU paid diddly-squat. I was always open to learning different ways of making money.

One day I was trying to sell airtime to a black guy who owned a nightclub. He was one of those guys you sometimes meet in the ghetto, with a regal quality and yet a sly aspect at the same time. Real smooth and in control, very knowing, with great radar at work behind his eyes, constantly checking you out. After we'd cut a deal, he said to me in a real soft voice, "How'd you like to make fifty bucks extra, on the side, just for yourself?"

"Sure," I said, leaning in. "What do I have to do?"

"I've got this package that I need to have delivered over in Norfolk."

Almost a week's pay for something I could do in less than two hours! I didn't ask what was in the package. I just took it, pointed my car across the bridge, and made my run.

The delivery place was another nightclub, which as I remember was called the Starlight Room. Everything went off without a hitch, and over the next few weeks I made more runs for the same guy. Finally he told me what I was carrying: marijuana.

"You ever tried this stuff?" he asked.

"No. What do you do with it?"

He smiled, and produced a packet of rolling papers from his inside pocket. With precise but very casual movements, he rolled a joint that looked almost as tight and smooth as a factory-built Camel straight. He lit the number, sucked down the smoke, and held it in. After looking into my eyes to see if I understood that this was the way to do it, he extended the joint into my hand. I followed his lead, then passed it back. This was absolutely the first time I'd tried marijuana. I didn't really know what to expect.

A minute or two went by and I started to sense that the sun, which I hadn't paid any attention to all day, was penetrating the threads of my silk suit in a benevolent, caressing way, suggesting that I'd enjoy relaxing and maybe leaning my butt against the fender of the coral-colored Cadillac we were standing next to. I took that suggestion and eased back. I could hear Tex Gathings's show coming out of somebody's apartment window, just above street level. The music was speaking to me in a little different way than before, easing its phrases into my ears. The tension was still there in the music, but I heard the release, too.

Thus came my introduction to the herb. And shortly after that I was granted a small bonus: enough pot from each shipment for a doobie of my own.

This was in 1960, before grass was really happening. In just a few years, it would be big on every college campus in the U.S.A.

Being around the black community all the time in Newport News, I got to know all the good local musicians. There were a few guys who were really exceptional. I convinced a local club owner to book one of their bands on Friday and Saturday nights. I made a fee, and I got these guys working. Pretty soon I had a management thing going with three or four black groups. That's how I got to know Gary Anderson, who went by the stage name Gary "U.S." Bonds. He started with the Church Street Five in Newport News. I met him even before he made a record. You could tell from his freshness and his energy that he was going to make something click.

It wasn't long before a Norfolk guy named Frank Guida got him a record contract. By late 1960, Gary "U.S." Bonds had his first national release out. The sound was primitive, like someone put a band in an empty wooden hall and hung a single mike way off at the back of the room. Daddy G., on saxophone, answered the lyrics in that call-and-response style that traces right back to African tribal music. "New Orleans" kicked off a great string of hits over the next couple of years: "Quarter to Three," "School Is Out," "Dear Lady Twist."

Bruce Springsteen used to do a version of "Quarter to Three" as the closing song of his concerts. One day he actually met up with Gary and helped him to get a record deal and have a little comeback.

Being at the Warwick Hotel introduced me to another source of cash. Somebody named Leo, who I got to know on station business, had a list of ten or so ladies who needed to make some money on the side. Most of them were married and their husbands were either out of work or off on long navy tours. So they took care of their household bills by turning occasional tricks.

I knew all the staff at the Warwick, all the bellhops and everything, so I spread the word: "If somebody comes into town and they want a little action, contact me over at the radio station."

When a call came in, I would get Leo on the phone and tell him what room number at the Warwick was requesting service. An hour or so later, the lady who had taken the job would drop by at the station and pay me five bucks commission. When a big navy ship or a freighter was in at the docks, I was making twenty, thirty dollars a day from the girls entertaining over at the hotel.

Some of them showed me their appreciation in ways I had never expected. It was just like that Woody Allen

85

joke: "Sex without love is a hollow experience. But, as hollow experiences go, it's one of the best!"

An even more successful money-on-the-side thing came from taking advantage of WYOU's big, unused side studio. I got the idea of doing an afternoon dance party, a local version of *American Bandstand*, where kids would come in after school to dance and make requests and dedications while I played records and talked to them from behind the glass in the regular studio.

I dropped off leaflets at all the high schools in the area: "Enjoy the Party! Come by WYOU and Dance with Daddy Jules." Gradually, the crowd started to build. At first it was all black, then an adventurous 10 percent of white kids. Before long it was a 50/50 scene.

Tex started getting nervous that the Ku Klux Klan would come down on us in some way. Fortunately, I don't think they ever got wind of it. The white kids were just as much into having a great dance party as the black kids. There were never any fights, just people having fun and getting along great together. The place was packed every afternoon, Monday through Saturday. We set up a microphone so the kids could say, "Hi. I'm Shirley from Newport News, and I want to dedicate the next song to my boyfriend, John."

There was no admission charge. The money all came in through the slots of the Coke and candy machines that Tex and I had installed in the dance room.

Those coins added up real good. We made enough off of the machines to get me out of my little room at the Warwick and into a little more upscale setting—a trailer park on the edge of town.

The Daddy Jules Dance Party also helped us beat that other rhythm and blues station in the ratings. So all of a sudden, this little peanut whistle, semi-worthless station was churning some real heavy money. The airtime sold like there was no tomorrow. We barely needed salespeople. The clients would come down in person to sign up because they wanted to be sure they wouldn't get squeezed off the air.

As the station's business gathered momentum, a guy named Al Kelly joined as a salesman. I was supposed to introduce him to some of our clients.

On Al's first day, we went to the Fred Astaire Dance Studio together. While I listened to Al pitching the manager, in walked a beautiful young girl with long, pale blonde hair. She was a vision of innocence—like somebody out of a dream.

I walked over to her right away, as if I was one of the Fred Astaire bigwigs. "Yes, ma'am," I said with a big, friendly smile. "Can I help you?"

That was how I met Lou Elizabeth Lamb, a shy girl from the backwoods of Tidewater North Carolina, and that was when I began a full-scale assault on getting her into my life.

Lou worked for a two-bit local advertising agency that printed Elks and Kiwanis club brochures. Every morning before work she stopped at the local Woolworth's lunch counter to pick up coffee and doughnuts. One day, the manager of the Fred Astaire Dance Studio was there and he told her she ought to come in and try out for a dance instructor position.

So there she was, trying to convince me how good a dance teacher she'd be, believing all the while that I was someone who could hire her.

Finally I admitted, "I'm really not part of the dance studio, but I happen to know the manager. I'd like to introduce you." And then I took her over to this guy that she already knew and said, "This young woman is just a fantastic dancer. You definitely ought to hire her."

He looked at me like I was a creature from outer space,

then he told Lou, "We're having a dance tonight to celebrate the graduation of a group of pupils. I'd like you to
come and see how you do, mixing with the customers."

She agreed. I stepped in and asked, "Why don't you
come to the dance with me?"

No dice.

I was coming on too strong for her, she said. My Yankee
accent, my sharp clothes, and my fast-talking ways
marked me as a character to watch out for.

That didn't slow me down. When I signed off at the
radio station later that evening, I jumped in my Galaxie
500 and went over to the dance. She kept on keeping
her distance. Meanwhile, the studio manager, who was a
real dapper-type guy, started monopolizing her attention.

When I saw her leave with him, I was determined to
at least find out where she lived. I trailed them in my
car.

To my surprise, the Fred Astaire manager pulled his
car over after three or four blocks. Then I saw Lou get out
very quickly, flinging her sweater around her shoulders,
slamming the car door closed and striding away in her
high heels. He peeled a quick U-turn and smoked off in
the opposite direction.

I calmly drove up behind Lou, rolling down the window on her side and saying, "Well, excuse me, but it
looks as though you're in need of a ride."

She bent over to check me out and said, "Oh, it's you.
No thanks. I just got away from one animal. I don't need
any more problems tonight."

"It's not like that," I said. "Here . . ." I shut off the
car and extended the keys to her. "You drive. You'll be
in control."

"No funny business."

"No," I promised. "No funny business."

She started thinking it over. "It's a brand-new car," I added. In the next instant, Lou stepped around the car and opened the door while I scooted over to let her slide behind the wheel.

My heart was beating so fast I thought it was going to jump out of my throat.

All you young folks out there, I can't tell you any surefire way to know whether you're really in love. But here's a tip: if you really like talking to someone—not just getting hot flashes south of the border or going gaga and melting as you stare in each other's eyes, but I mean really having good, flowing, sweet conversation—that's one of the best signs you can ask for.

I just let her enjoy the driving. Then, as we sat in the car in front of her house, we both began talking, sharing all kinds of things about what our lives were and what we wanted them to be. Oh, every once in a while I'd try to get my fingertips on her sweater, but she'd nudge me away. Mainly, we talked to each other. We didn't stop until faint early-morning light was beginning to show in the sky. By then she'd heard all about how I grew up, and I learned that she was a little girl who would always wait until everyone in the house had gone to bed, then sneak in and watch the TV with the sound down real low, just trying to figure out what the world was all about beyond North Carolina farm country.

She was also the oldest of eight kids, and had been baby-sitting practically all her life. Her family had roots in that part of the country that went back for about three hundred years. Lou loved all that history, but another part of her didn't want anything to tie her down—traditions, marriage, kids, whatever. She wanted to break free and travel.

Well, by the time I walked her up to the house, I was

positive that I was in love with her. I asked to see her the next day, but she put me off. It turned out that she had about six boyfriends chasing her around and I was going to have to be patient about working my way into the schedule.

Lou was staying with her Aunt Ica, which is pronounced "EYE-sah" (I didn't make this up: she was from real down-South people). Later on, when I met Aunt Ica for the first time and told her what I did for a living, she got all prim and frosty on me and said, "Little black birds and little white birds should *not* fly together." That was her outlook. It was totally different from the way my mother and father had taught me. Behind her back, I started calling her "Aunt Cold-As-Ica."

At the time that Lou and I met, I was also going out with about three or four girls, having a good time. But Mr. Suave immediately got real lovesick. I couldn't get Lou out of my mind. I dropped all my other girlfriends.

Lou and I would neck a lot and hold each other close. This was one woman who could really kiss. But I just couldn't get any further, and it drove me crazy. Weeks went by and we still hadn't had any sex, and Lou was still going out with other guys.

I called up Joan and Emile, and said, "I've met the nicest girl. Her name is Lou Lamb. I think she's going to be the one. Can I bring her to your place for the weekend?"

My scheme was to show her I came from some good, normal-type people, so there wasn't any reason to be afraid of me—no matter how out of line my style of living seemed. All she really knew about me was that I spun records at a black station, hung out with a lot of shady-looking people around town, and dressed like a pimp.

Actually, I *was* a pimp. But only part-time. And she didn't know about that stuff yet.

The visit to Alexandria worked. Lou was very shy and proper, but everybody took to her real well and made her feel like part of the family. From then on, I started believing I could win her over.

Of course, even though Lou was being real coy and careful, she wasn't at all uptight like her Aunt Ica. She wasn't prejudiced about skin colors, and she also sort of liked the fact that I was a little crazy. She was always interested by the action I got into.

I took her to the Starlight Room one night to see Jimmy McGriff work out on the keyboards. She'd never been anyplace before where there were mostly black folks and just a few whites mixed in. But she did love the music. Meanwhile, as Lou sipped a cocktail and enjoyed the music, I excused myself and retrieved a two-pound package of grass from the trunk of my car, scored my deal, and returned to our table in time for McGriff's last three tunes.

Another time at that club we took in a big Ray Charles concert. This was right when white folks were just beginning to be aware of Ray, around the time of his *The Genius Sings the Blues* and *Genius + Soul = Jazz* albums. His shows were the most intense musical experiences happening anywhere in the country at that time. The best way to get a taste of what Ray was doing onstage then is to buy a copy of his *Live at Newport* album. Check out "Tell the Truth," and the announcer's frenzied intro: *"Ladeeez and gentlemen, the high priest! The high priest! Ray Charles!"*

Later on, Ray and I got to be real good friends from working *The Midnight Special*. I got to see him a lot and talk to him.

I can tell you, whatever soul voltage you feel from his music, you get a double dose of it in person. The master musicians, the ones who make a real mark, they're usually the kind of people who love other human beings. That's how I feel about Ray.

If you listen close to his music, you can pick up what some of his influences were, like Nat "King" Cole, Louis Jordan, and Charles Brown. But the way he cooked those influences up, added a whole lot of gospel, and put in all that fervency and incredible musical ability of his own, that's what makes him one of the most overwhelming musical forces this country has ever had. Calling him "The Genius" or "The High Priest of Soul" doesn't even go far enough. When the whole soul music scene exploded in the later 1960s, with Motown, Stax-Volt, Atlantic Records, and everything else, the fountainhead of inspiration was Ray Charles. And, as I'm sure they will readily admit, Ray did as much to inspire Joe Cocker and Van Morrison as Otis Redding did to inspire Michael Bolton.

The reason why Lou liked a little more excitement than the average southern white girl, and why she could get intrigued by a slick Brooklyn Yankee hustler, was that during his day her own old man had once been one of the top bootleggers around northeastern North Carolina. So had his father before him, and his grandfather, too. Lou kind of had a warm spot in her heart for maverick, bandito-type people.

In that part of the country, there's a long tradition of sidestepping the laws on pleasure-inducing substances. Maybe you've heard that old folk song: "Get you a copper kettle, get you a copper coil. Fill it with new-made corn mash, and no more will you toil."

That was how lots of North Carolina families survived

the Depression. Folks couldn't do it through the crops in the fields, they had to do it with the still on the hill.

The area Lou came from sort of surrounds the Great Dismal Swamp, and all around there's nothing but green fields, thick woods, wide rivers, and bayoulike creeks full of poisonous snakes. If you can call to mind that Creedence Clearwater song "Green River," then picture water moccasins slithering on the surface as boats go by, you've got the general idea.

In country like that, it's very easy to hide—and extremely risky to go snooping. Bootleggers were local heroes, the only home-grown success stories. That's why people down South became so crazy about stock-car racing. Bootleggers had to know all about hot camshafts, oversize pistons, and multiple carburetors so they could make a normal-looking car go like a bat out of hell whenever it was time to outrun the law. Someone who was as good at distilling white lightning as they were at souping up engines and driving back-country dirt roads at breakneck speeds could make a hundred grand or more a year off their down-home talents.

When Lou was a girl, on certain nights her mother would sit in the parlor with the wife of her old man's bootlegging partner. The ladies would keep their hands busy and their nerves in check by stitching quilts until all hours in the morning. Lou soon figured out what their quilting bees meant: something hot and heavy was happening in the moonshine business that night.

Finally, around the time Lou was fifteen years old, her father got popped by the Feds. They took away all his delivery trucks and broke up all his stills. It was either go back to straight farming after that, or risk a long prison stretch. Of course, old Thomas Lamb had stashed a few bundles of cash in secret places around the county, so the family still got by okay.

As I kept pursuing Lou, along the way I got acquainted with another guy who was hustling to make a living amongst the black community. Red Guavi owned a run-down grocery store near WYOU. I moved from my trailer house into an apartment right above Red's store, and the two of us immediately put our heads together over plans to open a nightclub.

About the only regulation that stood in our way was getting a liquor license. The easy way around that was to run a club where people brought their own liquor in. The club could sell "setups," a couple of glasses, some ice, and a bottle of 7-Up or ginger ale. Of course, then you wouldn't get in on the real heavy money of nightclub owning—which is selling the liquor. But we had a plan for that.

Red found an old Quonset hut for lease in the industrial zone. It used to be a machine shop, but now it just looked like a giant, upside-down washtub.

And that's what we called it: "the Tub." Even with some tables on the floor, there was room for at least four hundred people to dance. We hired a way-out local artist real cheap to decorate the inside walls with murals of Jazzbo beatnik-type characters in shades and berets, bent backward blowing horns and hunched over conga drums, wailing away, with lines of musical notes curling off and flying through the air in all directions.

Tex and Eaton let me push the Tub on WYOU, free of charge. All that was left was to book some of the great local musicians I knew and just let it rip.

The very first night, the bass player in our combo failed to show up. His instrument was there, brought along by the drummer, so I—not having a clue as to how to play the damn thing, but at least knowing how it should look—jumped up on the stage and faked my way through three whole sets.

We got around our lack of a liquor license. A friend of Red's, a little Greek guy, covered that angle.

Virginia has state-owned liquor stores called ABC stores, which stands for Alcoholic Beverage Control. They close up by late afternoon, so if anybody gets in the mood for a bottle after sundown, they're out of luck.

Red's pal would make a run to an ABC store in a different nearby town every day, picking up $100 to $200 worth of liquor. Then he'd go back behind the Tub, climb up the hill, and stash all the bottles behind tree stumps and under bushes. When people came in that didn't have their own booze, if we knew they were somebody we could trust, someone would sneak out and fetch a bottle that we'd sell to them at triple our own cost.

Grass was available, too, at a nice markup.

The entertainment was always black. Our crowd was mixed races, but mostly black, so the police really never paid much attention and they never caught on to how we were getting around the law. All the other clubs in town at that time were either strictly black or strictly white, so it's amazing that we didn't get more attention from either the cops or the Klan.

Newport News was going through some heavy stuff about race relations at that time. Black people would come into the downtown Woolworth's and sit at the lunch counter, and all the white folks would get up and leave with big scowls on their faces. That was the way it was. The atmosphere around town was so tense that you expected fighting to break out any day.

Over at the Tub, though, people were just having a good time, getting excited by the music and dancing, just sweating their heads off. We had a guy playing piano now and then who was a combination of Errol Garner, Les McCann, and Jimmy McGriff. I was his manager at the time, and he had a really bad heroin problem, so keeping him straight was a whole 'nother job. When he was all right—which was most of the time—he was unbelievable. The only thing that held him back from becoming a big name was the fact that he was self-destructive. But he had been around Newport News a long time, so he was a real good draw for the club.

Other times we had Gary "U.S." Bonds and the Church Street Five with Daddy G, so the place was fantastic no matter when you came. Either it would be rocking real good or else in a steamy jazz mood.

As it got late in the evening, some of the best local musicians would show up. Everybody would get in there and jam.

Men paid three bucks a head to get in the Tub, which included a small setup. Women got in free. Lou would be at the door, collecting money. Red was in charge of the setups, and I took care of the band. Everybody had a real good time. There was a good, loose feeling to the scene at the Tub. And WYOU kept doing better than ever.

When everything is going real good, though, sometimes that's when you have to watch out.

One day Richard Eaton took a close look at the WYOU balance sheet. He flashed on the fact that this insignificant station he had picked up long ago for practically no money at all was suddenly doing so well in the numbers that its value had gone way, way up. The time was ripe to sell it. The numbers could slip back anytime. It'd never have that kind of value again.

Max Resnick, another radio man from D.C., laid a lot of money on Eaton for WYOU. Unfortunately, that marked the end of the good times Tex Gathings and I had been having.

Right off the bat, Resnick dumped the winning formula we had going. He decided to make WYOU into a "beautiful music" station. He completely blew off the black audience and identity that we'd built, even down to changing the station's name to WTID.

Resnick's dream was to make this little peanut whistle sound like WCBS in New York. Right away he let Tex Gathings go, which was really a painful thing for me.

I almost got the ax, too. Resnick didn't like my voice. I wasn't polished-sounding enough. To keep a job, I had to stop being "Daddy Jules, gettin' down with the kids here this evenin' " and begin calling myself "Roger Gordon." I had to drop the rhythm and blues and play Frank Sinatra, Mantovani, and the loaded-with-strings, late-era Nat "King" Cole pop stuff—the "quality" part of the pop music business at that time.

Some of it was fairly hip stuff, but it wasn't where my heart was. To this day, I feel a lot worse about cracking open a mike and announcing, "Good morning. This is Roger Gordon bringing you *Music in Good Taste*," than I do about the fact that I was transporting weed and brokering mattress action on the side.

Resnick placed an ad for salespeople in *Broadcasting* magazine. As a result, into my life came one of the most unusual, crazy, brilliant, and influential people that I ever met.

The really amazing show business stories aren't always

about the famous people. The mastermind, behind-the-scenes, brainiac types like Mo Burton are generally the most remarkable folks of all.

Mo was a dyed-in-the-wool New York Jewish liberal, with the accent to match. He came from a family that had emigrated from Russia and worked its way into prosperity. He had completed all the studies to become a rabbi. But that wasn't the right trip for him, so they sent Mo to New York University, down in Greenwich Village, to become a lawyer. That's where he began hanging out with beatniks, painters, poets, and authors at the Cedar Bar and the White Horse Tavern, and all the other places where a small, influential band of folks were spending the 1950s dressed head to toe in black, drinking espressos, smoking French cigarettes, and talking about French movies.

Mo was just as brilliant as anyone else in that crowd, but he was also one of those guys that was around campus twice as long as it actually takes to graduate. He didn't want to let go of the action, the ladies and the social scene. One day he was putzing around the library, leafing through a copy of *Broadcasting*, when he got a bug to jump into the real world by trying out the radio business.

With no experience at all, but a real fast tongue and a willingness to work cheap, he got on the phone and convinced Resnick to give him the advertising sales job.

Shortly afterward, Mo arrived in Newport News on the Greyhound, looking sharp. He was about Danny DeVito's size and shape, wearing a groovy pair of slacks that he'd bought on Fifth Avenue in New York, with a green shirt and a black tie, and Italian loafers over lightweight nylon socks that had a subtle red diamond pattern on the ankles.

Mo walked to the curb in front of the bus station, opened the back door of a cab and said, "Take me to the Warwick Hotel."

"Yes, sir," the cab driver said, flipping on the meter. Then he checked his rearview mirror, made a U-turn and stopped right at the curb directly across the street.

"That'll be seventy-five cents, sir."

Welcome to Newport News, sailor.

Mo checked into the Warwick, got situated, then walked into the studio while I was on the air being Roger Gordon in the afternoon. I had a red silk shirt on, with the top three buttons open. "Summertime" by Mantovani was on the turntable.

"I've heard," Mo said for openers, "that you're the guy to talk to if someone wants a piece of ass."

I took a look at him and said, "Hey, how ya doin'? Listen . . . Lemme make a call on your behalf here."

He returned to his trade-out room in the back of the Warwick Hotel, got his brains blown out, and came back to meet me for dinner when my shift was over.

We were friends from that day forward.

I slipped an iridescent deep blue silk jacket over my red shirt and we got into my Galaxie. "I'm taking you to a nice little steak joint," I told him. As we drove along, I could tell that he was looking at me and thinking, "I know for a fact this station doesn't pay worth shit. How the hell is this guy living this way?"

When I was driving him back to the Warwick, I noticed that Mo started playing with the car's radio. He ran the little cross-hair slowly from one end of the dial, concentrating on the job like a professor examining a rare manuscript. Different stuff would come on and he'd listen for maybe half a second, dismiss it, and keep exploring the band for something more interesting.

We started talking about New York and all the radio

stations and personalities we each liked listening to. It turned out that Mo was a radio junkie just like me. Except while I concentrated on black stations, he liked absolutely everything that was marginalized, nonmainstream, ethnic, or far out.

I said, "Do you want to go listen to some records? I don't mean that *Music in Good Taste* shit. I've got my own records upstairs at the station."

That was it for Mo. I took out a stack of prime 1950s black music and, without any kind of drink, smoke, or pills, we both got loaded from pure shots of music. Just having a great time.

As soon as Mo got around the community a little bit, he figured out how much better people liked the station before it changed. He told Resnick, "You're crazy, man, to take this station—as hot as it was—and try to make it a 'good music' station. It ain't gonna work. You ain't makin' no money." Finally, Resnick agreed to ease off some of the sappy stuff and bring our playlist more into the Count Basie realm, into Les McCann, Joe Williams, and even a little Jimmy Smith and Jimmy McGriff. I had to keep on being Roger Gordon, but at least I could come out of a record during my drive-time shift saying things like, "I know that makes you feel good. I know I just touched a button somewhere in someone's soul. I know they just dig the way he do his thing."

We had a guy on during the middle of the day who had a deep old "big-balls" kind of voice, but he had no soul. He was just like a machine: "WTID. We're happy to have you with us. Mantovani's 'Unchained Melody' was the last selection we played. Before that you heard a thing by Kay Starr called 'The Wheel of Fortune.' "

The funny thing was that we still had many of the old

advertisers, and their commercials sounded odd with the new format. After Mantovani was through, this stiff, pompous, white-bread voice would have to say, "And now, I'd like to tell you about Sister Margaret and her magical ways. Yes, she is prepared to give you the Lord's lucky number. And with that you'll have a complete lucky time. If you need a magic potion for a strange love affair, or if you'd like to fall in love and you're lonely, Sister Margaret can fix you up in that department also. She knows the way. She'll read what's happening. She'll tell you how you're doing. That's Sister Margaret."

And in the morning, Max Resnick himself went on the air. Here's a guy who's very conservative, a very kosher-type Jew. He liked to do the news. But he had this nasal, sort of flute-y, fruity voice. He'd say, "And now you folks out here in Newport News are going to really enjoy this music we have playing for you. Look at that sunshine shining out that window. Isn't it something? I know I feel good because the sun's shining. I'm such a meshugunah that I forgot to read you this about Louis Lipp's Grocery on the corner of Church and 14th, which is offering such a fine bargain today . . ."

Resnick quickly brought in a bunch of high-powered, high-priced radio executives and salespeople from D.C. But Newport News was a little more of a down-home environment. Their big-city style didn't impress the local merchants. When it came to selling ads, they were all sucking wind.

Mo and I were like the outcasts, sitting in the back at the meetings while everybody else ran through their flip charts and showed off their professional polish. But we were the only ones actually pulling in business, because we were out there in the street, hustling our way around a community that we understood. Especially Mo. He liked to call Resnick's big-shot salesmen "The Joint Chiefs of Staff" because they were so high up that they didn't take orders from anybody.

As the highest-billing salesman on the station, Mo Burton soon came to wield a lot of power.

He taught me a lot about selling, so I was able to make a few commissions and add to what I made for being on the air.

Resnick saw the light, reluctantly, and sent his cannons back to D.C. He let us get at least partway back to rhythm and blues. I started doing *Jazz on a Sunday Afternoon* again, featuring Mose Allison, Dave Brubeck, Cannonball Adderly, and folks like that. We started to get our adult black listeners back again. Overnight, Mo became the general sales manager, then actually a partner with Resnick.

I was still pursuing Lou, but I still couldn't pry her away from her other dates. She was adamant. Nobody was going to monopolize her time or draw her into a serious commitment.

By this time, Mo had bought himself a beautiful, brand-new jade green Chrysler Imperial. He couldn't drive it very well because all he knew about was riding subways and taxi cabs all his life, so he'd never got any car-handling skills together. I would drive us around while he fiddled with the radio dials with all the intensity of a NASA technician guiding a moon shot. We'd tune in John R. from WLAC down in Nashville, and XERF, and all that other crazy stuff. We'd listen to everything happening on the dial, and give forth opinions of what was good about it, what was bad, what was the psychology of it, did it turn us on, and what they should do to make that station a real killer.

In between talking radio, I'd tell him how hung up I was on Lou. I was a lovesick puppy.

One of those cruising and talking nights, Mo told me that his parents owned a bar and grill in an especially rough part of Newark, New Jersey. When he was a schoolboy, Mo's old man made him sit on a barstool and watch the bartenders make change, to be sure nobody would skim from the cash register. Maybe that set a pattern, because Mo became a brilliant manager of money. As a result of which, he eventually became the owner of several stations—all of them bought cheap, built up through brilliant programming and hard work, and then sold for major money. Kind of like Richard Eaton, but even more so.

Today he's worth something in excess of $20 million. I rank him as one of the best deal-makers that ever walked. Believe me when I say that I got taught the fine points of the radio business by a genius.

Maybe you've noticed that some athletes who are great players are terrible later on as coaches. Lots of people are incredible in their field, but their perfectionism gets in the way of working with lesser lights. Mo was like that: dynamite with the business stuff, but unable to handle dealing with people. His mind just raced too fast. He'd get impatient with anybody who couldn't keep up. If anybody didn't see things his way, he went into a tantrum.

He needed a front man, and that's where I started to fit in.

Before long, Mo got real tired of dealing with Resnick and his limitations. He put together a super-sweet deal— practically no money, and many years to pay that little bit off—on a puny, failing little daytime station down in Shreveport, Louisiana. He asked me to come along and help him run it.

About this time, Lou had finally relented to all my months of pleading and agreed to marry me. Well, first she yielded to my incessant pawing and finally allowed me to peel the garments off her fine, young form. Which led to impending motherhood, a state she hadn't envisioned for herself. I brought a lot of agony down on her, and she spent a great deal of time driving my car around trying to think things out. I would be on the air, dedicating songs to her, trying to reel her in. One of our signals was if I played "Call Me," by Chris Montez. I know, it's not a hip song. But when I played it, Lou *would* call me and we'd work our problems out.

The most important course in my whole life was set the day she put aside all the plans she had for herself and agreed to be my bride. Without Lou in my corner, I would've been a goner long ago. She is beyond doubt the most remarkable person I've ever known. And our two wonderful kids would've never made it on the scene. Lou and I have weathered a lot of storms over the years — many of 'em storms that we stirred up all by ourselves. But I can't imagine anyone else who could be so perfect for me.

Marrying me, Lou stepped into a whole bunch of problems — most of them financial. When WYOU changed hands, free advertising for the Tub got cut off. As a result, the business went down. I just let Red and his Greek pal take it over. And I had to stop with the hookers and the marijuana, because Lou didn't want a husband who lived behind bars. All my hustles on the side had to go. When they went, so did my fine new car, which got repossessed.

I found a funky 1949 Plymouth business coupe in the want ads for fifty bucks. Instead of a back seat, it had a flat space that went all the way back into the trunk, like a traveling salesman might use to carry merchandise and samples. Since there wasn't any rear seat, the car's top only went halfway back. It looked like a tank turret. Stick a gun on the roof and it would've looked like the pygmies were starting an army. The brackets that were supposed to hold the front seat upright were busted, so we had to keep a two-by-four wedged into place to keep it from flopping down flat.

On the day of our wedding, Lou was driving down Jefferson Avenue on her way to the wedding chapel, fifteen minutes late and pressing for speed, all dressed up in her wedding outfit and with, as they say, a bun in the oven. She went over a bump in the road and the board popped out of position. The seat back dropped away. The only way she could keep from falling back and crashing the car was to clutch the steering wheel for dear life. She arrived at her own wedding that way, with white knuckles on both hands, wondering what the hell kind of life she was getting herself into.

Well, that was the start of our married life. We never went on a honeymoon. There was no time for it. Had to work. And we've never gone on any kind of pleasure trip since then. Our whole life has been a honeymoon. We've just kept moving along, doing the work, and being together.

Lou and I celebrated our thirty-fourth wedding anniversary a little while ago. Our two great kids live nearby and we see them almost every day. So I'm going to go out on a limb and say that things eventually turned out real well for us.

Anyway, that fifty-dollar Plymouth kept getting shakier by the minute. And Resnick barely tolerated me. It looked like the best thing was to throw our fates in with Mo and his Shreveport station. It was time to pick up stakes and move on down the road.

On Christmas Eve of 1961, Lou and I packed everything

we owned into a slightly better car, one that we'd bank-rolled with an advance from Mo Burton, and drove down to spend Christmas Eve with her family in North Carolina. By noon on Christmas Day we were reaching the outskirts of Durham, headed south by southwest, to see what Shreveport was all about.

"Well, darling," I told Lou, "at least you're realizing your dream of seeing the world."

Chapter Six

Our car was packed with everything we owned, and several things we didn't, such as my not-quite-paid-for silk suits. And my young bride was packed, too, with the baby girl taking form inside her.

All three of us drove through the night, passing through Atlanta, then Birmingham, on our way to Shreveport. When the sun went down I locked the car's radio on XERF, the high-powered Mexican border station that had captured my fancy since back when I lived in Brooklyn. The crazy preachers, wild music, and off-the-wall advertisements seemed just as amazing as they had when I was a kid.

XERF was the most powerful commercial radio station in the world, a big blaster doing business out of Del Rio, Texas, pumping a quarter-million watts from a transmitter somewhere deep in the Coahuila desert, beaming out old-time, prayer-cloth-selling preachers, fervent gospel singers, hillbilly mountain music, all kinds of stuff that was just a little too weird, a little too dangerous for American stations. XERF sold gain-weight plans, lose-weight plans, baby chicks, pep pills, sex-drive-boosting pills, songbooks, records, hair dye, anything that could be stuffed into a box or corked up in a bottle and sent off in the mail for "cash, check, or money order."

On cold nights, when their signal took a big skywave skip off the ionosphere, XERF reached nearly every nook and cranny of the United States, plus parts of Canada, Japan, Germany, Australia, Russia, New Zealand, Sweden, England, and most of the asteroid belts around Jupiter, for all we know. The signal may have been staticky as hell in some areas, but it had the horsepower to get around.

To somebody normal, it probably sounded like bedlam. To me, it was the biggest stage in the world. Preachers ran every night until midnight, carrying on about saving your soul, selling holy-magic this and that. There was Reverend A.A. "Let God Be Your Dentist" Allen and his Miracle Restoration Services. There was Dr. C.W. Burpo and the Bible Institute of the Air. There was the king of them all, Reverend Frederick Eikerentrotter, best known as Reverend Ike, preaching "get out of the ghet-*to* and get into the get-*mo!*"

After midnight they mostly ran gospel records and Spanish-language stuff that didn't sound so exciting.

I was beginning to wonder if there was some way I might become part of that freewheeling station.

The station Mo had bought, however, was in a totally different bag. KCIJ, my new place of business, was going to involve nothing but country music, country gospel, and white preachers. I wanted desperately to get back to the rhythm and blues thing.

"Ya gotta be patient," Mo counseled. "After this station is successful, there'll be other chances down the road."

Shreveport's a big town alongside a river, like New

Orleans, but way up near the eastern edge of Texas and only a little bit south of Arkansas. In Confederate times, Shreveport was the capital of Louisiana.

Mo was worried how local folks would take to a Brooklyn hipster and a New York Jew stepping into their business community, but we were treated fairly okay. I guess the fact that we were associated with a country music station made us seem like regular folks.

KCIJ had formerly belonged to Bob Neal, the guy who had managed Elvis Presley up until about 1955, when Colonel Tom Parker came along and took away the gig. That's why Elvis got some of his first major exposure over Shreveport radio in 1954, on a KWKH show called *The Louisiana Hayride*. The Grand Ole Opry wouldn't have any part of wild, young Elvis, so Neal booked him on this big 50,000 watt Shreveport station. He knew that it would be dynamite to get Elvis out on that big signal.

James Burton, Shreveport's hottest local guitar player, also graduated from *The Louisiana Hayride* and went on to play lead in Ricky Nelson's band, and then later on for Elvis. You may not know Burton by name, but you've heard his "chicken-pickin'" country-rock guitar licks a million times, either played by him, or by the hundreds of players who imitate his style.

KCIJ, Bob Neal's own station, was a 250 watt peanut whistle at the 1050 spot on the AM dial. It only ran during daylight hours. It was the epitome of low-budget. Neal would come on the air as Uncle Bob, plunking on a ukulele and reading the funny papers. He'd bought the station at a time when he was managing Johnny Cash, but then he and Cash parted ways, and suddenly he was short of cash all the way around.

The crazy thing was, in spite of his background in country music, Neal was only running a little bit of country in the morning. The rest of the time, he was trying to make KCIJ sound like a high-toned CBS affiliate. And losing his shorts in the process.

When Mo had initially gone to check the station out, the answer to KCIJ's problems came to him in a second. Full-time hillbilly would turn this station around. And that was exactly what we went and did.

Just because you make a smart deal and a good programming decision, though, that doesn't guarantee you a success. You've also got to work like a maniac. KCIJ was one of the hardest-working gigs I ever had. I was the station manager, program director, early-morning disc jockey, and slightly more than one half of the advertising department.

Every day began with me getting out of bed before sunrise—a feat that I have seldom attempted since.

The farmers in those parts liked a certain brand of overalls called "Big Smith," and the fact that Lou was a great down-home southern-style cook had begun to show around my newly expanded beltline. So I became "Big Smith with the Records." I signed on at sunrise, put on the coffee, cracked open the mike, clanged an old cowbell that was hung from a big old nail in the wall.

"Friends, we're gonna give you a song now by Lester Flatt and Earl Scruggs, called 'I'm Using My Bible for a Road Map.' But first I want to remind you that Kathy's Meat Market has a sale on bacon now for just thirty-nine cents a pound, and she's got those pig ears for twenty-nine cents a pound, and you gotta stop by there today!"

That would kick off a long stretch of Ferlin Husky, Cowboy Copas, Red Sovine, Hank Thompson, Hank Williams, Stonewall Jackson, and other local favorites.

It wasn't my first love in music, but I played my Big Smith role to the hilt. That hillbilly stuff was making a home for Lou and the bundle she was incubating, so I was plenty grateful.

Because of KCIJ's low power, we couldn't charge much for commercials. The name of the game was "Work in as many ads per hour as humanly possible." I'd let a tune run through maybe two verses, long enough to let its flavor come across, then I'd rattle that cowbell and pitch a local barbecue joint or car dealership. "Yes, sir, folks. That was Ersel Hickey singing 'Bluebirds over the Mountain.' And if you want to be as happy as a bluebird, you'll wanna know about the *unbelievable* values this week at Hobson's Grocery. Yes, old Mr. Hobson will always greet you with a big smile on his face. If you smile back, why he just might give you extra groceries."

If you were funny and entertaining when you broke in to the records, people didn't seem to mind. After all, they'd already heard those songs at least a thousand times apiece. It actually took a fair amount of skill and energy, cutting in and out like that and ad-libbing to keep everything moving along.

Around ten o'clock I'd hand the mike over to Reverend Billy Franks, who played country gospel records and did some preaching. Another preacher would take over at noon. Finally, another hillbilly DJ took over and ran the station until sign-off at sundown.

Meanwhile, between 10 A.M. and dinnertime I was out on the streets, hitting up local businesses for advertising. We were dirt cheap. "A dollar a holler" was our motto. I'd duck into these hardware stores, groceries, and burger joints asking, "How many spots do you want?" The orders would all get written down on the back of a brown paper bag. Then I'd come back to the station and log them in.

Sunup the next day, I'd be ringing the cowbell again and singing the praises of all our terrific new sponsors.

Mo and I, within a couple short months, turned around this money-losing little cripple and began operating it on a profitable basis. In fact, from the time we took over the station never had a money-losing day. And it was a particularly good time to climb out of debt. Joy Smith, our beautiful baby girl, came into our lives in July of 1961.

I was out somewhere selling ads. Lou's water broke a little sooner than we'd expected and she went to the hospital in an ambulance. By the time the news reached me and I got to the hospital, Joy had already emerged and Lou was just beginning to come out of the anesthetic. She took a funny look at me and said, "Oh my God, you've turned black."

"Lou, honey, it's me. We've got a brand-new little baby girl."

"No, you're black."

Somehow, from the drugs they'd given her, she came out for a minute seeing the colors of everything reversed, like a photo negative. "I love you black," she said. "Come over here and kiss me."

Having our first child was a great feeling. Here was suddenly a living, breathing extension of the love we had for each other. And another reason to keep trying to succeed.

By fall, the station was influential enough that I was able to work a trade-out deal with the local Oldsmobile dealer for a brand-new 1962 Starfire convertible. It was salmon pink, with a four-barrel carburetor and dual exhausts. But that wasn't radical enough. I took it over to a local upholstery shop, and in exchange for advertising time, had my new cruiser enhanced with tuck-and-roll zebra skin seats.

No sense in looking just like everybody else.

Besides, if I had to be a hick on the air every morning, at least I could have some cools later, on my own time. Owning an Oldsmobile was a big thing to me. I had always been crazy about them. The Rocket 88 was the elite hotrodder's car of the early 1950s. It had one of the hottest V-8s of its time, but it was lightweight enough to really fly, and yet kind of luxurious, too.

The first rock 'n' roll record of all time, in fact, was a tough little boogie shuffle called "Rocket 88." That record made it to No. 1 on the R&B charts all the way back in 1951. It was credited to Jackie Brenston, who did the singing, but the song was really by Ike Turner and his Kings of Rhythm. If you saw the movie *What's Love Got to Do with It*, it's the song that Ike sings in that sweaty nightclub scene near the start, which for me was the best part of the whole movie.

You women have heard of jalopies
You heard the noise they make
Well, let me introduce my new Rocket 88
Man, it's great, just won't wait,
Everybody loves my new Rocket 88
We will ride in style, cruising all along . . .

That was how my new convertible made me feel. It had a huge, VistaVision dashboard, a big oval speedometer, plus a chrome-plated map of the world stamped in the middle of the deep-dish steering wheel. With the custom zebra skin upholstery, my new Starfire looked half Sabre Jet, half El Mocambo Cocktail Lounge. There was nothing sweeter on the road.

Meanwhile, Mo and I made a great team. He preferred being in his office, making calls and cutting deals, so I became KCIJ's front man, as well as Mo's protégé in learning the business end of radio.

Unfortunately, there was an ongoing source of friction in our relationship. That was my ambition to perform.

Mo was interested in Bob Smith, the up-and-coming radio businessman. That was fine—as far as it went. I liked being successful that way. But I also had a longing to be hip-deep in my favorite music, rhythm and blues, and projecting it out to the public.

One thing that really impressed Mo was when I developed contacts with the wild preachers on XERF. I got some of them, like Reverend A.A. Allen, to run on our station. It was real cheap for them and a great revenue source for us.

Through that, I quickly learned how the preachers' gig worked. They taped their programs and paid stations a fee to run them. For XERF, with its big signal, it cost maybe $1,500 a week for a fifteen-minute program, five days a week, Monday through Friday. All that mail-order stuff brought home big cash. The key was to concoct a show that got people stirred up and made them feel connected. Once they identified with the show, they'd want to go on and buy the merchandise.

As much as I loved Mo, I also spent a lot of time daydreaming about getting an enterprise of my own going. Somehow, that daydream always included XERF.

One night I sat straight up in bed. Lou woke up, rubbed her eyes, and looked at me. "What's wrong, honey?" she said.

"Wrong? There's nothing wrong, baby. I just figured out what I want to do with my life, that's all."

"What're you talking about?"

"It all just came to me: KCIJ is doing good, and that means I'm gonna be stuck doing country forever. But what about XERF? I could get on that station doing a wild character, do the blues, just mesmerize the folks.''

By the time I pulled my next daybreak shift as Big Smith with the Records, I had a few more details worked out. I'd do exactly like the preachers do, make my money on mail order. Except there wouldn't be any preaching. Instead, I'd stir people up with the power of the music, and a crazy DJ character who had the same blend of coolness and hipness as all the great ones that had zapped my imagination when I was a strange little kid transfixed by what was coming through the radio.

It still took lots of hours of woodshed time to invent the Wolfman. And the way I was working for Mo, I didn't have many hours to spare. Whenever possible I turned on a tape recorder and worked on making my voice even deeper and richer than it had been for the Daddy Jules gig in Newport News. I cooked up an animalistic personality, drawing on all the hundreds of 1950s horror movies that I'd watched in my time. That's still my favorite kind of flick to this day: giant radioactive spiders that trap humans in webs as thick as cable, next-door neighbors who turn out to be Martians with pulsating brains on the outside of their skulls, beasties that get woken up by atomic testing, anything with zombies, vampires, or werewolves. Great entertainment.

And back in my mind I must've remembered the fun I used to have with my little nephews, scaring the daylights out of them by doing a growly wolf voice.

Mo didn't know anything about these woodshed sessions. I knew it would just bring up a fight between us. Also, he was preoccupied with looking for angles to build up the business. Everything about the format was doing great, but KCIJ's potential was limited by that puny 250 watt transmitter. Our prime audience was way out in the country, but the signal couldn't get out and blanket the sticks like we needed it to. More reach would easily make more money.

Mo and I still liked driving around at off hours, me piloting his green Imperial and him piloting the radio knobs. From what we heard over the air, and from checking the local ratings, it was obvious that a local rock 'n' roll station named K-REB was losing money. It was on a beautiful place: 950, right in the middle of the AM dial, 5,000 watts. It covered maybe two hundred miles in all directions.

A guy named Lawrence Brandon had bought K-REB about a year before. He was a blueblood type, and a war hero, but also a real soulful guy who eventually became a very close friend of mine. At exactly the same time Brandon launched his venture, a heavy hitter named Gordon McClendon, owner of the No. 1 Top 40 stations in Dallas, Houston, and San Antonio, was laying plans to make Shreveport the fourth outpost of his empire.

McClendon had all kinds of resources—money to pay the better jocks and to hold attention-getting contests. Brandon was completely blindsided, never knew what hit him.

Mo got together with Brandon. "You've got the facility," he said, "and I've got the format. Let's combine our stations!"

"What are you going to do with KCIJ?"

"I'll move it out of town, if the FCC will let me. A guy over in Marshall, Texas, wants to take it over. His signal is close to mine on the band and he wants to boost his power, but the FCC won't allow it as long as KCIJ remains on the air."

Mo was proposing something that had never happened before, but it turned out that the FCC just loved it. Shreveport had nine radio stations. Ever since the oil companies had left for Houston, only four were still doing good business. By reducing the number, we made it easier for the others to survive. And we allowed some guy in Texas to expand his business. In fact, today the government gives station owners a big tax credit if they eliminate a weak station that's preventing stronger ones from growing.

So Brandon became a partner in an everybody-wins kind of deal. It worked like this: the two stations got telescoped into one, with a big signal, a successful format, and Brandon and Mo as co-owners. The increased power meant we got a better price for our airtime, so money started rolling in better than ever.

I wasn't a partner, but they treated me almost like I was. Everybody was pulling down pretty good coin.

Meanwhile, I took a chance and played my Wolfman Jack demo tape for Mo. All it did was get him mad. Mo has so much horsepower in his brain that sometimes he can't fit the words together fast enough to go with the ideas. When I tried to show him how excited I was about Wolfman Jack, his mouth went into freewheeling, just spewing craziness and profanity. "Motherfucker, you're working for me. You ain't doing that other shit."

When Mo got fired up, his tongue could cut the legs out from under a charging rhino. He reamed me out, fired me, banished me off the property, then hired me back in practically the same breath.

That was just one of five, six, maybe seven different times over the years that Mo fired me. None of them were pretty moments, let me tell you. He didn't want me excited about anything that might shift my focus away from running his station.

But later on when I laid the Wolfman tape on Lawrence

Brandon, I got the opposite reaction. He flipped for the Wolfman.

Brandon was new to me. He was sort of my opposite number, always dressed in that old-money style: a well-pressed button-down shirt, a proper coat and tie, and a pair of looks-like-he-goes-to-Princeton pants. He was in his mid-forties and he had a wife, a couple of teenage daughters, and a stately pad. But he connected with the spirit and the potential of *The Wolfman Jack Show*. "I'd like to help you get this on the air," he said.

During all this scheming, deal-making, and rising prosperity, Lou gave birth to our son in September 1963.

Tod Weston Smith rounded out the family at four, a very agreeable number. He was such a good-looking little baby, I made the nurse hold him up to the window so I could count all his fingers and toes and everything. Being a complete egomaniac, I found that having a son was a very wonderful thing. He was just like I wanted him to be: rebellious, just like his old man.

My life was real together and going fine. Lou and I were very much in love, raising a family. All that stuff she had felt about not wanting to be tied down, well, as soon as she looked into the eyes of her very own kids, that went out the window.

The only problem was this Wolfman Jack character I'd invented. He kept invading my thoughts more and more of the time. He was a happy-go-lucky cat, real hip, who just wanted to make people feel real good, feel nice and sexy and alive. To do that, he needed to get his big shot on the airwaves.

I loved my two brand-new babies, heart and soul, but the Wolfman was wanting to get born, too.

Chapter Seven

It was December 1963.

Mo had left to spend holiday time with his people in New York. Brandon and I were sitting around KCIJ on a Wednesday afternoon, running things. By now we had more than half of all the preachers from XERF on our station in Shreveport. We knew by then that a guy named Arturo Gonzáles ran XERF, because that was who the preachers all did business with.

I came up with a totally irresponsible plan. "Let's grab the Wolfman Jack demo tape," I said, "and drive down to Mexico to see what XERF looks like. We'll get in touch with Arturo Gonzáles and see if he'll cut some kind of deal with us to put Wolfman Jack on the air after midnight. We'll take some money with us, have a good time down in Mexico and maybe do the wamboozie with the girls down there." To my surprise, Brandon was excited enough to go along with the idea.

When I told Lou I was ready to make a run at XERF, she said, "Go after it, darling." Just like she's done throughout my career, she got behind me one hundred percent.

Thursday morning we put the Oldsmobile's top down, stuck the tape into a briefcase, and about $2,000 in our pockets. We took our shirts off to improve our tans, and started cutting a big diagonal across Texas, down to where the Pecos River runs into the Rio Grande, a six-hundred-mile run with nothing but sagebrush and cactuses and all kinds of rabbits running around the road. We were headed right for La Frontera, the old frontier, where guys like Judge Roy Bean, Bigfoot Wallace, Jim Bowie, Sam Houston, and Pancho Villa all used to hang out.

It was dusk when we hit the Rio Grande. We crossed right on over the border to the Mexican side. There was Ciudad Acuña, one of the dirtiest little border towns in the world, the kind of community where anybody who still had all his own teeth was considered a pantywaist. It looked like Dodge City must've looked a hundred years before—high wooden sidewalks, no pavement, a street full of deep muddy ruts down the middle, thick dust on all sides. There was barbed wire and broken glass cemented into the tops of buildings and fences, kind of a low-tech frontier security system that got you wondering about the local crime rate.

We headed straight for Boys Town, a section of Ciudad Acuña that had about two dozen cantinas and fifteen or so brothels lined up on both sides of the street. That part of town was just buzzing, in a red-glowing, liquored-up sort of way. A lot of military boys were knocking around in their soldier and sailor suits. Local guys were swerving around in their cowboy boots, with pearl-handled pistols older than their granddaddies stuck in their belts. Mariachi bands were playing in the joints, or else out in the street. Drunks were slouched against the sides of the buildings, and everybody else was upstairs getting laid.

Boys Town was famous in every military base, high school locker room, and frat house in the whole state of Texas. Except for XERF, the town's economy was pretty much mattress-based.

Brandon and I started asking bartenders and other various folks how to get out to XERF. "You can't actually get there," people said. "There's no road." But after a while this old Mexican guy walked over and told us he had a cab. There were fifty or sixty random whiskers and a half-dozen knife scars on his face. He looked like a basset hound coming off a two-day Benzedrine trip. His pants looked like slept-in Korean War surplus. "Hey, for thirty dollars," he said, "I take you to the station."

We looked at him, then at each other. Even as roughed-up as he looked, he actually seemed like an all-right guy, and we didn't cross the whole state of Texas to quit a few miles short, so I said, "Okay, let's go."

We locked up my car and parked it near the border crossing. We greased the guards a little bit to keep an eye on it. Then we jumped into the back seat of his cab, which was an old '49 Chevy fastback. Spare parts were sitting on the floor, an old clutch disc and some bent push rods, half wrapped in shop rags and Mexican newspapers.

Once we were out beyond the town there was no kind of road at all, just sand under the tires making this crispy noise, and pitch-black views out of every window. Our guy just kept driving on, the headlights bouncing all around the sand dunes, around the rocks, over some train tracks, past miles of scrub. Maybe half an hour went by.

"Hey, man," I said, "how do you know where you're goin'?"

"I know the way. We'll get you there."

121

I whispered to Brandon, "He's probably gonna take us out in the middle of the desert somewhere, kill us, and take all our money."

Suddenly there was a big red light blinking in the distance, just throbbing very high up in the sky.

In a couple more minutes we could see that it was a radio tower, XERF, the Promised Land. There wasn't much light on the scene, but we could make out two big buildings close by the tower. Stucco walls and red-tile roofs. A dozen or so banged-up cars and trucks were parked around the station. All of their headlights were glowing.

"That's kind of strange," I thought.

Our driver pulled his Chevy up in front, shut off the motor, clicked off his lights, and told us he'd wait right there. We looked in the first building. There was a diesel generator in it that looked like a locomotive waiting for someone to bolt its wheels back on.

We walked over to the other building, which was the studio. There was a set of double doors. I opened one of them and heard the Reverend Bishop Sheldon preaching from a reel-to-reel tape machine. He had the whole hour between 11 P.M. and midnight.

Just before going in the door I looked back at the old Chevy that had brought us to XERF. Its headlights were glowing just like the others.

Later on we learned what that was all about. So much energy rolled off that transmitter tower, it vibrated the filaments in headlights until they lit up. You could hold a fluorescent tube up to the tower and it would do the same thing. Any bird that flew too close while the power was on would seize up with a birdie heart attack and fall to the ground, dead as a stone. People working at the studio would get a kind of drug-free high for the first few hours. Then they'd start to get loopy and need to take a heavy nap. XERF had an atmosphere like no other radio station in the world.

Off to our right side we saw a tremendous transmitter. It took up about three quarters of the building—250,000 watts of power requires a lot of room. Right next to it was a 50,000 watt transmitter that they kept as a standby.

The first studio was like a little lounge area. That seemed like the place where everybody was. The next studio was where the DJ would sit, then the next was the engineer's studio, where they had the turntables and tape machines.

Brandon and I walked into the lounge and found ourselves right in the middle of eighteen or twenty guys holding a big, important meeting. They didn't see us at first, so we just watched.

Even without knowing Spanish, we knew that something had these guys pissed off and scared. One of them spotted us. A good-looking young fellow. Mario Alfaro was his name. He was the only one who spoke much English.

"Hi," he said. "I'm Mario. What can we do for you?"

The others kept looking at us real suspiciously, so Mario led us out into the hallway.

"I'm Bob Smith," I told him, "and I just came in from Shreveport with my partner here, Larry Brandon. We want to talk to the owner of the station. We have this idea to put Wolfman Jack on the air, this disc jockey character who's like an animal. We want to put him on the air playin' rhythm and blues, and we want to do some mail-order business."

Alfaro filled us in. The owner wasn't around, we couldn't talk to him. A whole lot of heavy and complicated stuff was going down with the station, which was exactly what the meeting was all about. The station had fallen behind in paying wages and taxes, so the Mexican government had sent in a receiver—they call it an *interventor* down there—to take over the business and make sure the government got its back taxes paid. Only this *interventor* turned out to be a crooked, nasty son of a bitch. Went by the name of Montez. Wore a slimy iridescent green suit and a skinny black tie, with a permanent stain around his shirt collar where the pomade that melted off his hair ran down the back of his neck.

Under Montez, the guys who ran the station still weren't getting paid regularly. When they complained, thugs and pistoleros would rough them up. They didn't have any money or guns to fight back with, but they weren't willing to take any more abuse, either.

Some of them were voting to kill him.

Before I can tell you about what went down between nasty Montez and Mario and his boys, I've got to let you know how this whole one-of-a-kind XERF situation came together in the first place. I mean, you might wonder how the most powerful commercial radio station in the world happened to be out there in the middle of a Mexican desert, and how XERF became the site of my world premiere live performance as Wolfman Jack.

Back in the early 1920s, commercial radio broadcasting was a new phenomenon across America. Almost overnight it became the hottest thing going. In the year between 1921 and 1922 alone, the United States went from having just eight commercial radio stations to nearly six hundred.

People were actually spending more on radios than any other kind of furniture or appliance, hundreds of millions of dollars annually. They bought big wooden table models and jukebox-sized, hunchback-looking floor models. Some of them had speakers, some just had airplane-style headsets. People would crowd two heads under one set of headphones, if they had to.

The whole family would get all clustered around the radio at night. They'd tune in anything that was on the air. Radio was the big-time excitement of the day. It could sell you soap, it could preach you the airwave gospel.

Radio really was a miracle, especially for lonely people out in the sticks.

One of the earliest stations in America was KFKB, which stood for "Kansas Folks Know Best." It broadcast from Milford, Kansas, a little south of the Nebraska border.

KFKB was owned by Dr. John Romulus Brinkley, a wildcatter out of that great, super-persuasive American tradition of snake oil salesmen. Brinkley did three old-time religion broadcasts on KFKB every day, telling people to put two dollars in an envelope and write him about their medical problems. He'd read the letters on the air and then tell folks they'd get well with his special tonics, one dollar per bottle.

He backed up his wisdom with a 1914 diploma from the Eclectic Medical University of Kansas City. But, as you might guess, good ol' Eclectic was the kind of place that would certify just about anyone as a doctor, as long as they laid the right "tuition" on the president. Brinkley, at age nineteen, had earned his E.M.U. diploma in one month.

Once he got KFKB going, his biggest moneymaker was to preach that there would be more Christian babies in the world, and lots fewer cranky, out-of-sorts Christian mamas, if the men in the family just had more get-up-and-go under their Bible belts. More divine energy for spreading the faith, if you understand what I'm saying.

In 1919 he hired a PR guy to help get the word out. "A man is only as old as his glands," Brinkley would say. "Come at once to the Brinkley Hospital before it is everlastingly too late."

Well, thousands of guys named Clem and Wilbur and Clarence drove up to the Brinkley Farm outside Milford, where big flocks of goats were penned up. Each customer would pick out a healthy-looking goat, then check into the Brinkley Hospital. The doctor would supposedly make a potion out of the goat's nutmeats, then slit open the patient's scrotum and insert the sauce.

Folks around Milford used to have a favorite joke: "What's the fastest thing on four legs?"

"A billygoat who just caught sight of Dr. Brinkley."

It wasn't just farmers that dug Brinkley's pitch. Rich Americans and Europeans of that time were already getting monkey gland injections in Switzerland, so the whole thing seemed scientific and upscale.

Harry Chandler, the owner of the *Los Angeles Times*, invited Brinkley out to L.A. in the early 1920s and even got him a special temporary permit to practice medicine in California. This took some heavy influence, because the American Medical Association hated Brinkley and his carnival jive with a passion. Chandler himself may have even gotten his own pills supercharged, but nobody knows for sure. At any rate, Brinkley did forty thousand bucks' worth of surgery for the high and mighty of L.A. society.

Chandler also owned a shiny, new radio station, which is where Brinkley got the idea to get started with KFKB.

Radio broadcasting in the 1920s was an anything-goes kind of situation. Some stations were so straitlaced, they wouldn't even play music that had saxophones in it. Others would air practically anything. The government finally decided to step in and create an agency to regulate radio.

The Federal Radio Commission, the forerunner of the FCC, came along in 1927. Brinkley was their first big target. KFKB got voted the most popular radio station in America in 1929, but by 1930 their license was yanked.

Brinkley and his fans got real mad. He ran as a write-in candidate for governor of Kansas and almost won. He actually had the most votes, but election officials threw out thousands of ballots because people had written "Doctor Brinkley" instead of the official ballot form of "J.R. Brinkley." Across the state line in Oklahoma, where he wasn't even running, Brinkley came in first in several counties.

Being the owner of a station, of course, he had used radio as the cornerstone of his campaign. And he hopped all around the state in his private plane.

Those tactics impressed guys like Huey Long in Louisiana, the Kingfisher, and W. Lee "Pass the Biscuits, Pappy" O'Daniel in Texas, who each later became governor of their own state by running a Brinkley-style, radio-driven campaign.

To keep his radio scene going in spite of the Feds, Brinkley headed for Del Rio, Texas. According to what the old-timers around La Frontera told me, he took his wife across the Rio Grande and adopted two little boys from an orphanage in Ciudad Acuña.

Those boys were both less than ten years old at the time, but within a couple of days, they had themselves a license from the Mexican government to start up a brand-new radio station. It was a little unusual to award a major commercial license to a pair of youngsters who still had puberty to look forward to, but technically it was all legal.

The original call letters were XERA. Brinkley put up a 50,000 watt transmitter. Later on the government let him kick it to a half-million watts. If you lived in Del Rio or

Ciudad Acuña, you didn't even need a radio to tune in XERA. Signals hummed right off telephone wires, barbed wire fences, and metal fillings in your teeth.

The reason they had so much power was because of a treaty between the U.S., Canada, and Mexico to regulate how many radio stations were out there, and how many watts they could use to send out their broadcasts. Since the States had lots of people, we got the right to have a large number of stations. But the power had to be kept low, so one station's signal wouldn't conflict with another one in a nearby locale; 50,000 watts was the top limit. Because Canada and Mexico had smaller populations spread out over great big geographical regions, they were allowed to license a small number of stations with super power. At night, these muscled-up signals could take a big bounce off the ionosphere, a layer of the atmosphere, and end up practically anywhere on Earth.

Patent medicine companies loved advertising on XERA because it reached the outlying areas where people didn't have doctors around and were ready to believe in home-remedy type cures. There was so much advertising, within five years Brinkley had two more Mexican stations, XEG and XENT. In 1938 he moved the Carter Family, America's "First Family of Country Music" and Johnny Cash's future in-laws, down to Del Rio. For a couple of years, they sang live on the radio, performing "Wildwood Flower," "Keep on the Sunny Side," "Lulu Walls," and all their other mountain music tunes for sponsors like Kolorbak Hair Dye and Peruna Tonic.

The goat gland business continued to be Brinkley's biggest gold mine. He operated now out of the top of the Del Rio Hotel, charging as much as a thousand dollars per scrotum overhaul. He wore big diamond rings on each hand, diamond pins on his lapels, diamonds on his cufflinks. He lived in a great big mansion, he had private airplanes, a fleet of cars, a couple of yachts, and some Texas oil wells.

The local goats didn't have much to be happy about, but thousands of new customers had fresh stitches in their nut sacks and a love song in their hearts.

Of course, sooner or later the whole thing had to go down the tubes. First the AMA sued Brinkley and won. Then he lost a number of courtroom wrangles with some angry ex-patients. By the early 1940s he was filing for bankruptcy. The Mexican government shut XERA down and Brinkley kicked the bucket not long after.

Time went on and some of the people who'd been associated with XERA wanted to get it rolling again. One of them, Arturo Gonzáles, was very ambitious. He had even holed himself up with books and became a self-taught international lawyer. He learned everything by mail order, passed the bar exams and all that stuff.

With the help of some American financial backers, he got the station going again, this time under the letters XERF.

Gonzáles grew into quite a figure. He always wore very well tailored Western clothes and a perfect Stetson and rode around in a brown Cadillac limousine. His cousin was the chief of police, his brother was the mayor, and Gonzáles became the undisputed Godfather of Del Rio, Texas. He had the biggest El Rancho Grande, a two-thousand-acre spread, with a huge, palatial hacienda, and lots of people on his payroll.

Around 1956, Gonzáles made a deal with RCA to bring in a monster, quarter-million-watt transmitter, identical to what they had sold the U.S. government for aiming Voice of America broadcasts at Russia.

The price of this transmitter was equal to the wattage

it delivered: a quarter-million dollars. The driver tubes *alone* were worth a fortune. A driver tube is sort of like the amplifier in your home stereo system. At a normal station, they might be about three feet tall. XERF's were water-cooled, made with platinum, and stood almost seven feet.

Once he had that 250,000 watt reach, at 1570 on the AM dial, his main source of income came from selling fifteen-minute and half-hour chunks of XERF time to those crazy preachers from all over the United States. Their tapes were lined up from about seven o'clock in the evening until twelve midnight, one after another. They pulled in bread like you can't believe. When the sun got low in the sky, it was Paul Kallinger, "Your Good Neighbor Along the Way," playing an hour's worth of country music. Then *The World Tomorrow* started the religious programming off. When the sun was completely down, along would come C.W. Burpo, then J. Charles Jessup, Reverend A.A. Allen, J. Harold Smith. They usually finished up the evening with Reverend Bishop Sheldon, who had a big church up in Philadelphia.

Gonzáles noticed, gradually, that every time he raised the rates on the preachers, they complained a little but they always had the bread to go along. Nobody ever dropped out. It didn't take him long to realize the preachers were making beaucoup cash. So the next step was figuring a way to get himself a deeper cut.

Well, the way it was told to me, he got together with each of the preachers and proposed a one-time deal: "Reverend, if you give me one million dollars, cash, I'll give you a lifetime contract. In other words, you will hold exclusive title to your current time slot on XERF. You will never make another payment. That time will be yours for the rest of your life."

It sounded great. They could recoup the million within

a few months: it would be pure gravy from then on out. For a lifetime!

In the contracts he wrote up with the preachers, Gonzáles put a small clause down at the bottom, saying that everything became null and void if XERF ever got taken over by the Mexican government.

Just a technicality, right? The station runs great. Who's worried about them taking it over? In Mexico they give out licenses for about twenty years, and they renew them right away almost without question. They don't do much checking up.

All the preachers signed on the dotted line.

Gonzáles wound up with several million bucks in his hands. He built his magnificent El Rancho Grande and still had plenty left over. There's all kinds of crazy stories about what he did with the rest of the cash. Some people say he bought property all over the world. Some say he buried the cash in a secret location on his ranch.

Anyway, soon thereafter the station fell behind on its taxes and wages.

Gonzáles ran the radio station like everything was normal. A couple of years went by without incident. But when the unpaid taxes eventually got up around half a million dollars, the government folks down in Mexico City started paying attention.

Mexico is a very socialistic country. They need those taxes to provide medical and dental care and lots of other services. They sent the station some letters, which were ignored. Then they definitely got mad. "Listen," they said, "you have forced us to put the station in the hands of an *interventor*. He will run XERF until enough profits have been generated to pay off this tax debt."

That's when that evil guy, Montez, came into the picture. He was the officially named *interventor*.

But here comes the kicker: Plenty of cash had been

spread around in Mexico City, guaranteeing Montez the *interventor* job. The very first thing Montez did was to hire Gonzáles as XERF's U.S. representative, in charge of handling business with the preachers. Gonzáles humbly took his Stetson in hand and told all the preachers how sorry he was about their million-dollar contracts suddenly becoming worthless. But if they wanted to stay on the air, they had to start sending money again. There was nothing he could do about it, those government people had him over a barrel. And by the way, the price was now double what it used to be.

XERF was the preachers' lifeblood, probably 95 percent of their incomes. They had no choice. Every one of the preachers sued Gonzáles, of course, but with all his international law training he didn't have much trouble keeping them at arm's length.

Montez was now making over a hundred and fifty thousand a month from the preachers. Out of that, one or two grand would go to the tax people, just enough to keep the regulators off their backs.

The scam could have worked for eight or ten years. Raise the prices a little bit now and then. Pay off the taxes very slowly. Then let Gonzáles step back in for a fresh start.

As things moved along, Montez apparently got too greedy for long-term thinking. He started nicking a few bucks here and there, trying to stretch out his end of the deal. He slacked off paying the workers. He didn't care if programs got played, or if the station got behind on fuel bills for the generator, or if the insurance payments were allowed to slide. Montez just basically let things swing in the breeze while he kept more and more money for himself. Gonzáles wasn't in a position to do much about it.

And that was the moment in history that Brandon and

I stumbled upon. We had landed in the middle of the luckiest moment of our lives.

All the workers were owed back wages. Their old cars were all funky, beat up, and falling apart. Some guys had babies on the way. Some of them had family members needing medical care. Everybody was at their limit. And when they protested, Montez sent his men down to beat the shit out of them.

This was a massive opportunity. "Listen," I told Alfaro, "why don't you guys appoint your own receiver if this guy's such a crook, y'know? Send somebody to Mexico City and get it all straightened out. That way they won't be screwin' you."

"We have no money," he said, "and we would need a U.S. representative to deal with the preachers."

"Here I am," I said. "Here I am, man. They sent me down here from heaven. All you gotta do is let me be the representative. I'll call the preachers. I'll get them to send the money to us instead of Montez. You guys run the station, and we'll have a deal. It'll all be legal and everything."

Brandon and I went with Alfaro to each guy and started talking Mextex, promising to straighten out their problems, trying to make them start believing in us. Then we sat down to talk some serious business.

These guys had a union. That could pull a lot of weight with the government. In spite of all the corruption and bribery stuff, Mexico is very much for the workers. A union-backed guy would have a good chance of replacing Montez, especially since the back taxes were still looming large.

Pulling off this *interventor* switch would take some organizing, which Alfaro and his buddies could do. They put forth Fernando Ramos, the head of their union.

Fernando was on the elderly side, and in Mexico you've

usually got to have some years under your belt before you get any status. He was the perfect choice. It would also take thousands in ready cash to get the job done. Brandon could get the money by sticking his hand in the KCIJ till—hopefully putting it all back before Mo could find out, because we'd get our lungs ripped out if he ever knew.

On top of that, pulling off this big maneuver was going to take some stupid impetuousness, blind luck, and shameless double-crossing.

That's where I came in.

Chapter Eight

If there's any talent I've got, it's for really getting across how excited and enthusiastic I am. That's something you just can't fake. Well, Mario was not only the sole English speaker among XERF's workers, he was also somebody the other guys respected a lot and somebody who could really communicate enthusiasm in his own right.

Mario, Larry, and I and all the rest of the guys hashed out details and promises all night long, with no time for sleep. Some wanted to trust us, some were very doubtful. They already knew that Montez was a heavy. Throwing in with us might expose them to even more of a big risk. But it also gave them a chance to get their dignity back. The only chance they had, in fact. By the time the sun came up on Friday, Larry and I had a solid deal with the union.

Brandon went to the bank in Del Rio and wrote a countercheck for fifteen grand on KCIJ's Shreveport account. Praying, all the time, that this scheme would come through in time to put all that money back.

Next, Alfaro put us together with two bright young

lawyers in Ciudad Acuña. They understood the problem. After some discreet phone calls, they said they wanted to spread a few thousand bucks around in Mexico City, with guys higher up than the ones who had been greased before. Enough grease in the right parts of the machinery could swing legal control of the station over to the workers' union.

Of course if it didn't work, we could all end up in a very deep, funked-up condition for a long, long time. Getting caught was a definite consideration. Montez was not going to like two brash out-of-towners stepping on the toes of his custom-made snakeskin boots, trying to pry the deed to his gold mine out of his hands. It didn't matter that this was 1963, the dawn of the electronic age and all that. Ciudad Acuña was nothing but a frontier town. Complicated hassles down there often got worked out with simple, direct bullets.

Mo, on the other hand, was not the kind of guy who, upon learning that a partner had misappropriated his hard-earned funds, would laugh the whole thing off. We could end up as guests of the state of Louisiana, up at Angola, learning traditional chain gang songs from the original artists.

I always wanted to have soul, but I never wanted to go that far to get it.

Still, the union guys and the lawyers sounded like they knew what was happening. I was dying to get on the station anyway. If I could just get on for one night, I didn't care if I went down in flames and took good-hearted, almost-innocent Larry Brandon with me.

So be it.

The lawyers took about six thousand bucks, Fernando Ramos put on his freshest shirt—peach, with gray stripes and a black collar—and all three of our emissaries boarded a flight to Mexico City. Brandon and I took charge of the local scene.

One advantage of growing up in Brooklyn is that you learn to hustle real good, and to line up your protection early. It's either that or get kicked around all the time.

By mid-morning Larry and I were over a couple plates of huevos rancheros and two strong mugs of Café Bustelo, figuring out how we might guard the station once folks got wise to our maneuvers and tried to grab it back. There was no telling how long it would take the lawyers to do their thing in Mexico City, but we still had nearly five grand in our pockets.

We rounded up two of our new compadres, Mario and another guy, then rented a truck and took off in the direction of San Antonio. The plan was to ring the station with barbed wire and sandbags, make it look like we meant business, and back up the impressive decorations with enough firepower that nobody would want to bother us.

San Antonio was due east, more than two hours' drive. As soon as we reached its outskirts, we grabbed a phone book and found out where all the feed and seed stores were. Our first move was to purchase hundreds of burlap bags. There was plenty of sand in the Coahuila desert to fill them. Then we made a circuit of all the local army-navy stores and bought massive amounts of guns and ammunition.

Nobody ever asked us what we were doing. In Texas at that time, you could buy all that kind of stuff you wanted.

In one store we found a hairy-looking 60-millimeter machine gun left over from World War Two, sitting on a big tripod with its muzzle sticking way out. I pictured Montez and his boys out there on the dunes, checking out the station with their spyglasses and spotting this ugly mother on the roof.

"Larry," I said, "this'll scare the shit right out of 'em."

The storekeeper couldn't legally sell a machine gun in working condition, so there was no firing pin. But by a strange coincidence, he happened to have a friend down the road who had the right firing pin and two thousand rounds of ammo for immediate sale. No questions asked, of course.

Besides our 60-millimeter beauty, we wound up with a couple dozen .30-.30 rifles, which the guys called "treinta-treintas," and enough Smith and Wesson revolvers to give each guy in the crew a pair, plus enough holsters, bandoleros, and barbed wire fencing to stage a range war.

Around noon on Saturday we met up with the rest of the station workers behind an abandoned motel on the outskirts of Del Rio. Each guy took some of the firearms and crawled under their car. Somebody who had brought a spool of wire from the station cut off two-foot lengths and handed them to the guys so they could wire the rifles and pistols up around frame members and axles. The machine gun had to go in pieces. One guy took the tripod, one guy took the barrel, another guy took the rest.

Brandon and I crossed the border with nothing but burlap bags in the truck. The Mexican border patrol checked us out with a fine-tooth comb. All the local guys, who had ammo under their seats and guns below the floorboards, cruised through with a smile and a wave.

As soon as we reached the station, everybody started filling sandbags. People in Mexico have a different style of working. At first it looks like they're going slow, but they hit a moderate pace and then they go for hours without slacking up. Little by little, our guys got the entire station circled with a sandbag barricade. Then they strung barbed wire over the top, plus a wire with naked light bulbs every two or three feet.

Last of all they put that machine gun up on the roof behind its own ring of sandbags, a true "piece de resistance."

With that accomplished, each guy got his own rifle and pair of six-guns. They dug it completely. They started walking patrols with their bandoleros crisscrossed on their chests and their treinta-treintas slung over their shoulders, sometimes with the barrel pointing up, sometimes with the barrel pointing down, whatever looked and felt cool to them at the time.

Me and Brandon savored the moment, a pair of Robin Hoods with their band of Merry Mexicans.

We drove back across the border and checked into the Del Rio Hotel. After a couple of heavily needed baths, we turned our attention to the preachers. It was money time.

Because I'd hustled their business for KCIJ in Shreveport, I had phone numbers for all of them. I grabbed a phone and started working my list again, this time for a whole new cause.

"Hello, this is Reverend J. Charles Jessup of Gulfport, Mississippi, isn't it?"

"It is. And who am I speaking to, sir?"

"Reverend Jessup, you remember me. This is Bob Smith."

"Well, how are you, Reverend Smith? Praise the Lord."

"Praise the Lord, Reverend Jessup. How're you doing? I wanted to tell you that we got a new thing going and I'm in control now of radio station XERF here down in Del Rio, Texas. You know, where you're on the air from eight to eight-fifteen every night, Reverend Jessup? Oh, yeah. You love that XERF, don'tcha, man. It gets around. Well, about this time slot you've been enjoying . . . Listen Reverend, we just took over the station. We're the new American representatives. And I figure that your program is worth about four thousand dollars a month. You must be paying at least that much. I don't have the contracts in front of me at this moment, but I can tell you that we're going through a terrible repossession time here. We have to break new ground on the rates. We're going up to eight thousand a month. In order to stay on the air, you're gonna have to send us, in the next couple of days, at least four months in advance. Of course, that will be thirty-two thousand dollars, all in cash. We're not set up in our offices here just yet, so you'll have to send it here to the Western Union office in Del Rio, Texas."

"Excuse me, son? I didn't get all of that. Would you tell me that again?"

"Reverend Jessup, if you don't get the cash money to Western Union for four months in advance, right away, y'understand, I'm gonna have to take you off the air and put somebody else in your place."

"Now hold on there! I've paid Arturo Gonzáles two months in advance already. How much money do you people want from me down there? You keep squeezing me dry!"

"No, no. Mr. Gonzáles doesn't run the station anymore. I'm Bob Smith, and I'm running the show down here now. I have to get the money by Monday, serious business here, Reverend, or we're gonna take you off the air."

"Well, son, I think you're really putting me on. I'll have to talk with Mr. Gonzáles. Good day to you!" Click.

I called them all. Each one turned me down just like that. The next thing they probably did was to call Gonzá-

This is the one school where I posted flying colors, the good old National Academy of Broadcasting. Everybody else was into classical music, or else society orchestra stuff. I was a hard-core rhythm and blues guy—once again the odd man out (back row, far right).

Miss Lou Lamb Smith, of very, very rural North Carolina, took my hand in marriage this day and the excitement has never stopped. No honeymoon, we couldn't afford it, and the family car was a $50 wreck. Yeah, but we had L-U-V, baby. And a kid on the way, too.

My first radio job. Picture taken by my proud sister, whose young family had adopted me—the screwy kid brother—and helped me find direction. Two disc jockeys covered the whole day at this little Newport News station. I was a hipster type called Daddy Jules. My broadcast partner, a Harvard-educated black man, did a lot to help me get on track.

The hits just kept on coming! This is at home in Shreveport, where I was Big Smith with the Records, with the two beautiful babies Lou had brought into the world—Joy and Tod.

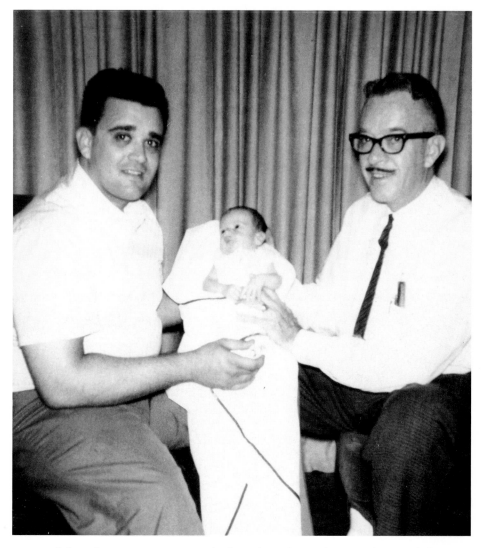

We didn't always communicate the best, but I know for sure that my father dug being a grandpop.

Two years can make a big difference. (top) Here I am with Lou at Don the Beachcomber in Las Vegas, in 1966. At this point, I was only Wolfman Jack on the air, and just plain Bob Smith, radio businessman, the rest of the time. (bottom) By 1968, my wolfishness was beginning to assert itself more and more. This is in Las Vegas, too, at the International.

This was our first Christmas in California. With the December weather, rattlesnakes didn't come in the house nearly so often. That was a nice present.

(top) Through all the years of our marriage, Lou and I have always had romantic feelings for each other. The caring runs deep, and that's kept us together.

(facing page) In this early '70s shot, I'm just as good at faking the trombone as I was at faking the bass in my nightclub-running days, when the real musicians didn't show up.

Wolfman Jack: Leading Exponent of Avant-Garde R & B

Wolfman Jack
Alias XERB's Bob Smith

HOLLYWOOD—Just who is Wolfman Jack? He's a dj who has been heard over the entire Northern Continent by transmitters as powerful as 250,000 watts. He is also Bob Smith, General Manager of the 50,000-watt XERB, where his alter ego character Wolfman Jack is heard and loved nightly.

The station contends that it is a "soul" station, yet it programs Blood, Sweat and Tears. The reason is simple: the station is five years ahead of its time. XERB spends ample time surveying record shops in black communities to arrive at a playlist which fully accommodates the tastes of the supposed black music listener and record buyer. Bob Smith declares, "The Tommy Roes and the Archies, that's what they're buying as well as the expected blues items, and therefore that's what we're playing."

This liberal position for a "soul" station coincides with underground or some FM programming where the playlists have increased considerably to provide extended selection.

Smith further stated that his station's surveys show that Blood, Sweat and Tears and Creedence Clearwater are ranked tops in requests and record purchases. "It's the old axiom of supply and demand, and a station's first obligation should be to supply its listeners with what they want to hear regardless of tradition," Smith added.

In addition to being involved

The Wolfman Jack Show recently bowed in Las Vegas and proved to be a giant draw.

They are currently negotiating for future Vegas engagements and a possible TV show which Wolfman would host. It was also announced that the premise for the television series would be more than the run-of-the-mill variety show but one which contains much commentary. A show that would make innovations, for that's what Bob Smith, alias Wolfman Jack, is all about. with this almost revolutionary soul radio station, Smith puts on the Wolfman Jack roadshows featuring concert acts.

—Ron Baron

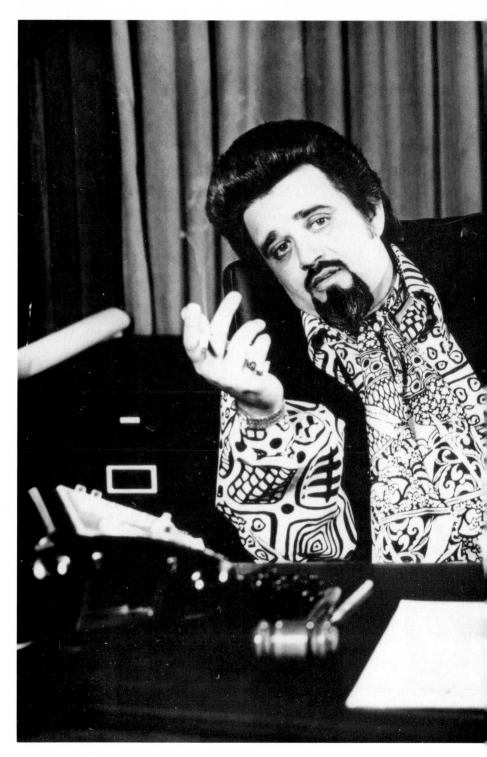

This responsible-looking guy was the businessman who ran XERB from a
Sunset Boulevard office. This is one of my typical conservative outfits: note

how the pattern on my scarf nearly matches the pattern on my shirt. The goatee and pompadour tie the whole look together, sorta *GQ* style.

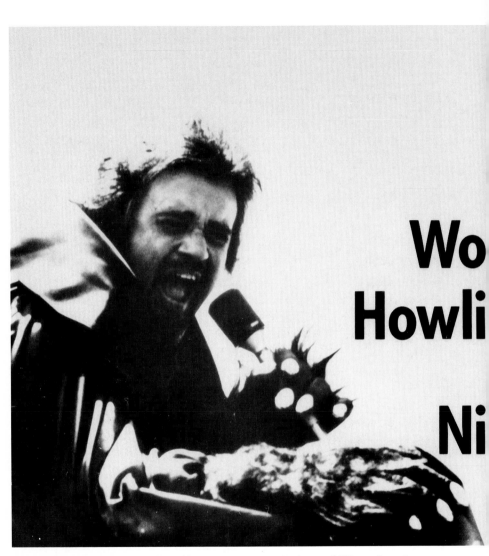

This was one of the first big entertainment-industry billboards to be put up along Sunset Strip. I was suddenly off Mexican radio and joining a small

**Wolfman &
Alice Cooper.**

Hollywood Bowl

July 23rd.

an Jack

prowling rock & roll.

s. KDAY 1580 AM

but influential L.A. station where we pioneered free-form type programming
on the AM band.

Me with Jerry Wexler, who wrote an excellent book of his own recently.
We're both crazy about the voodoo/New Orleans sound of Dr. John.
Producer of many classic soul and R&B sides, Wexler was one of many

cool, heavy people who dropped in at the studio. Steve Stills and John Lennon were among the others. *(Jeff Dunas)*

At nights, and especially under a full moon, this guy booted Bob Smith out of the driver's seat. Notice the ad for Wolfe Chevrolet.

les. I guarantee you, he didn't know what was going on. Who the hell is this guy calling the preachers, telling them he's taken over? Who would do that?

He probably figured it was either some idiot, or else some new scam by Montez.

Next I found a little record shop there in Del Rio and I rifled through their bins looking for good sides. It wasn't any record collector's paradise, but I did manage to find four LPs that were all right: one each by James Brown, B.B. King, Lowell Fulsom, and Elmore James.

By now Brandon had conceded that his Ivy League look didn't go over in Mexico. He threw his jacket and tie into the back seat of the car and undid the buttons on his collar points. I handed him the records and we drove out to XERF just in time to watch the crew fire up the generator for that night's broadcast.

That's when I got to know Archie, the engineer in charge of the generator, and when I got a real sense of what this station meant to all the guys who worked at it.

This crew was responsible for the most powerful radio signal in the world, and they really respected that.

Archie looked like a Mexican version of Pee-wee Herman, a real short, skinny guy. But when you touched his muscles, he felt like he was made out of metal. The generator he had charge of was a monster with pistons on it as big around as dinner plates. Archie would get up inside and adjust stuff, then tell his assistant to throw the switch. Just as the engine began to go "Cha-dowm-dowm, chung chung chung chung chungchungchung," he would jump out from behind all the moving cranks and flywheels and gears. If he had been about half an inch wider or half a second slower, he would've gotten his ears chopped off every night.

141

Archie's generator was off in its own building, but when you sat in the soundproofed studio in the other building, it vibrated the seat of your chair. You could hear it growling very faintly in the background.

The engineer for the transmitter was a guy by the name of Pedro. He had a sharply trimmed 1940s-style mustache and wore a mesh stingy-brim hat with a silver and black striped band. The transmitter was his baby. Pedro kept it sparkling clean. You could just about eat off the tops of the driver tubes.

He was a classic tubehead kind of a guy, always had his shirt pockets stuffed with little wires, circuit testers, and electronic whatever-the-hells. He kept a soldering gun stuck in his pants pocket and a tiny screwdriver behind his ear, too. Nearly every time you saw Pedro, he was busily doing little private, mysterious things with the tubes. He'd put this one over here and take that one over there and tweak it just a little bit, polish it with a special cloth, then run little tests on all the nearby circuits.

In Mexico they don't have the money to be always going out and buying new machinery. Anybody that can keep old equipment running like new is a very honored and valuable guy. Somebody that we would just call "mechanic" they call "maestro."

Out at XERF, the maestros were married to their machines, and they were some of the proudest men in that part of the country.

When the transmitter went on at six o'clock, the crew did their nightly ritual. They brought out a big pot and started charcoal burning in it and they just sat in the sand around the glowing coals like a tribe of Indians, just listening at full crank to whatever was on the air. The whole air was humming, the transmitter, the tower. The generator was rumbling the walls and the ground. The little red light was blinking up on top of the tower, about three hundred feet up, and birds were flying around, trying to cram in a few last beakfuls of insects before the sun went down. Every couple of minutes another bird winged in too close to the tower and flamed out.

They ran some Spanish-language thing up to seven o'clock, then Paul Kallinger, "your good neighbor along the way," who I used to listen to up in Brooklyn. Then came the preachers' time slots.

In towns and cities all across America, all those preachers were kicking back, expecting to hear their prerecorded tapes roll. Instead, I opened XERF's mike at seven o'clock and came on with "Aaaoooooooooo! All *right*, baby. Have mercy! Good golly, Miss Molly! This is the Wolfman Jack Show, baby. We gonna par-ty tonite! We down here in Del Rio Texas, the land of the dun-keys."

In the background I was playing a great blues instrumental called "Jivin' Around," by Ernie Freeman, off my demo tape. He was the same guy who hit the Top 10 back in 1957 with a song called "Raunchy." So with Freeman's band cooking behind my rap, I continued, "I gotta tell you, baby, the old Wolfman gonna make you feeeeel good. Gonna get down! Gonna make you feel it tonite!"

I was nervous as hell, but I was a lot more pumped up than I was scared. I hadn't slept in a couple of days. I know I did some weird stuff that night, probably the strangest I ever did in my life. There weren't any commercials to cut to, so I had to rap my head off. It was just me and the tunes: "Here's Elmore James and his *funky*-funky slide guitar. Makes me want to get naked every time I hear it, baby. I'm runnin' around naked in the studio right now, beatin' my chest. And I wantcha ta reach over to that radio, darlin', right now, and grab my knobs. Aaa*ooooooo!*"

Mario Alfaro was running the board, Brandon kept looking out across the desert, half expecting some posse to roll in and blow us all away. I was in a state of totally adrenalized, twenty-five-year-old, feelin'-like-pure-God-head glory. The Wolfman had busted out into the world. I knew, down to my toes, that from then on I would do whatever it was gonna take to keep the Wolfman running wild, for all time.

Millions of people were out there, listening to my craziness. It was like I could feel their vibrations coming back to me through the air. Not many people have ever been on that trip. Not many people ever get to feel what I felt that night. The energy off that transmitter alone almost levitated me off the ground, made me feel like I was high on grass and everything else. The sensation of a whole world of listeners out there, beyond the desert, digging something wilder than they'd ever heard before, gave my head a spin that has kept it reeling to this very day.

I ran the mike from seven at night to four in the morning, at which time a Spanish program took over until sign-off at seven in the morning. All night long grabbing tacos and Mexican beer and shots of tequila while the records played, just floating. What a time!

Sunday morning, knowing we had freaked out thousands of people nationwide, Brandon and I returned to the Del Rio Hotel and got a long, deep sleep.

Three o'clock on Monday afternoon found us parked in front of a streetside pay phone located one door down from the Del Rio branch of Western Union.

I commenced to work the list again.

"Reverend Allen? Hey, this is Bob Smith down here in

Del Rio, Texas. You didn't hear yourself on the radio last night, didja Reverend?"

"No, I didn't! Who was that crazy animal playing that devil music?"

"That was Wolfman Jack. We brought him in from Mexico City. He used to be in porno flicks down there and he just loves doin' radio. He's the only thing I can afford right now. That's what I'm gonna do if I don't get the money here this instant. You'll be off the air for another night, Reverend. And by next week someone else is gonna replace you in that time slot. Have you got a piece of paper? Here's the number for Western Union . . ."

"But, sir . . ."

"Hold it a minute, Reverend Allen. Write this number down or you're not going to be on the air tonight."

"Yessir, Reverend Smith. It is 'Reverend,' isn't it?"

"No, man, just Bob Smith."

"Well, Mr. Smith, what is that number?"

"Here it comes. . . . And go down to your local Western Union office and give them thirty-two thousand in cash. It'll probably cost you another thousand to send it, but what's a thousand dollars between friends, right? Send it down so I get the cash immediately, 'cause I need the money, brother. And if I get it, you'll be back on the air tonight."

In less than half an hour the first currency was coming through. Meanwhile, I had called two more preachers. Bing! Another thirty-two grand, then another.

I was working that pay phone for all it was worth—in fact, more than it was worth—when a black Ford cop car pulled up behind my Oldsmobile. The guy got out, left his red light on, and came walking our way. Brandon was busy packing bundles of money into the car's trunk.

I was standing there with a grip on the pay phone, sweating like a mule, not wearing any shirt, just sneakers, Levi's, and a pair of shades.

The cop walked up to me just as I had gotten Reverend Jessup ready to come on board.

"Excuse me, son."

"Excuse me, Officer, I'm on the telephone. Yes, Reverend, if you can send that right away. Here, I'll give you the number . . . I'll be right with you, Officer . . . Send that right here to the Western Union office, in cash . . . Love that cash, Officer, y'know what I mean? . . . Okay, Reverend, thank you very much. Goodbye. Yes, Officer, can I help you?"

"Somebody says you're moving a whole lot of money into your trunk, son."

"Well, you see, we're running the radio station now, Sheriff. You know, XERF? And I'm collecting from the preachers. We're gonna immediately put it in the bank over there, so don't worry about anything. As a matter of fact, if you could stay around and protect us—just shut your light off so we don't attract a crowd."

He looked a little bewildered for a second. There wasn't any apparent reason to run me in, but he still couldn't figure out what the hell my program was.

"Here, Officer," I said, tucking two sharply folded C-notes into his shirt pocket. The guy smiled and tapped it down into place, then stepped back into his squad car and drove away.

That set the style for me. From that day on, I carried bunches of large bills with me. Whenever I talked to somebody, I'd tuck a hundred or two in their pocket first. We got to know each other real good, real fast.

Meanwhile, the preachers were tapping Western Union so hard that the Del Rio bank had to bring over more cash. By 5:30, when the office shut down for the day, the Oldsmobile was packing over $350,000. A little risky, but we didn't have any intention of throwing it into the local bank. For all we knew, Gonzáles could get some cousin who was a judge to freeze the account.

Mo had returned to Shreveport over the weekend. I called and tried to tell him what had gone down, and what a huge opportunity we had in our hands. But right when I got to the part about drawing off KCIJ funds, he completely lost his mind.

"You what? You stole money? I'm sending two leg breakers down there to drag you thieving bastards back. You're fired, you son of a bitch!"

"Yeah? Well, that's fine, Mo. Because this is the deal of a lifetime, and I was gonna cut you in. So fuck you very much!"

I hung up and said to Brandon, "You're gonna have to talk to him later, man. He wants to kill me."

I was rattled. Mo had fired me before, but this time it got me where I lived. Behind all the exhaustion, and all the chances we'd been taking, I started to worry about my family.

What if I just let them down? What was I going to do, how was I going to keep my two little babies fed and clothed, with a decent place to sleep? Just crazy thinking like that. But in the meantime, all those bucks were piled behind the back seat, waiting for us to tap in to their mystic powers.

Brandon rented a dark blue Cadillac sedan. We transferred most of the money into his trunk and he headed back to Shreveport to see if he could do anything to improve Mo's emotional state. I turned back and drove the rest of the money out to XERF. By now the border guards were getting used to me, so they waved me through.

When I arrived, all the guys working at the station and

all the guys sitting around the fire came up to the car. I
led them around to the back and stroked the taillights,
wiping off the desert dust. Then I took out my keys and
popped open the trunk. They went absolutely bananas.
The greenbacks were practically gleaming. All of a sudden the insane gringos who had dropped in on their
scene, the guys they weren't sure about hooking up with,
were the greatest combination to hit town since Viva
and Zapata.

Even today, a few bucks is a good day's wages for most
folks in Mexico. A salmon pink Olds Starfire convertible
stuffed with American currency out in the desert was
enough to create a religious transformation.

Then I started taking care of some of the promises I'd
made. "Esse, you can't keep that beat-up old car running
any longer. Take this and get yourself something better,
man."

"Hey, Ernesto, they tell me your new baby's gonna
arrive any day now. Here's a thousand dollars, man. Buy
yourself a new playpen and some pretty clothes. And
somethin' nice for your wife, too."

I gave everybody a grand. I said, "You're gonna like
this arrangement a whole lot better than the old one."

Then we threw a big party.

Pedro, besides being a great engineer, was also a monster talent when it came to barbecuing goats. He set some
guys to digging a big pit in the sand and he started roasting
four or five choice cabritos. Somebody went to Boys
Town and came back with a car full of fine-looking hookers in tight party dresses with ruffles and flounces, which
created even more of a festive atmosphere around the
old station. Some Federales happening by on horseback
joined the party. We had a great time on into the night.
The preachers' tapes were rolling. The big XERF was

cooking. I got on the mike at midnight. "It's time! Baby gonna find out your Wolfman gonna blow your mind. He ain't gonna blow your nose, he gonna blow your *miiind!* B.B. King himself gonna sing to ya all about that Sweet Little Angel of his. He just looooves the way she spread her wings! You hang in there, now. It's all happening on *The Wolfman Jack Show*, on XERF from Del Rio, Texas!"

The next day we called all the preachers. Everybody was happy again. As long as they kept making money off that station, they didn't care who the hell they were paying. To them, a few thousand more was nothing but a burp.

Larry Brandon deposited the money we'd made, gave Mo his stack back with considerable interest, and we all became friends again.

With Mo calmed down, there was still one corner of the situation to be dealt with. I had a feeling that we'd be hearing from them real soon.

Chapter Nine

The cash was coming in, but Fernando Ramos and the lawyers still hadn't nailed down the government approval in Mexico City. Until that happened, until we were officially declared to be legit, I was a bandit.

Fortunately, the guys soon came flying back with all the right papers and signatures in hand. By the Tuesday following the debut of *The Wolfman Jack Show*, we were respectable citizens again.

In the meantime, we had not heard a word from either Montez or Arturo Gonzáles yet. So we just kept cooking along. On trips to Ciudad Acuña I traveled with four bodyguards. All of us wore crossed bandoleros over our chests, an accessory that can turn any old outfit into a very exciting fashion statement.

I kept up my habit of stuffing C-notes into the pockets of people I met. It's an expensive way to start a friendship, but it sure turns you into the life of the party real fast. Since I was an upstart in foreign territory, I wanted to have as many friends as possible. It had also really helped when we divvied up some of the loot with the radio station's workers. Everybody in town was either related to one of those guys, or else lived next door to their cousin. I decided to become known as a generous young man. Like my Uncle Tony might've done.

There wasn't any phone out at the station. In all the hustle, I hadn't talked to my wife in a long time. Finally, after nearly a week, I got through to Shreveport.

"I have to come down and see all this for myself," Lou said.

"I dunno, baby. We've got legal control and all, but it could still be dangerous for you here."

She insisted, strong-willed woman that she is. And me, selfish bastard that I am, began thinking how long it had been since the two of us had gotten up close and personal in bed together. We have always had a passionate thing between us.

Lou drove down alone, all the way from Shreveport. She arrived just about an hour before I was supposed to drive out to the station for my midnight show. Her fine young body got my mind spinning. I couldn't wait to get her up in the hotel and start making love. The Del Rio Hotel was built of wood, with five floors that all opened onto a central balcony. Lou thought that was great. It reminded her of a movie set. "I feel just like a dance-hall girl," she said, "going upstairs with a cowboy."

Two flights of stairs later we were alone, stripped down, having a great time and telling the world about it, while XERF played low in the background. I'd almost forgotten how great it could feel. But all of a sudden, in the midst of one of the pretaped religious shows, we heard the sound of bullets ricocheting off walls. Somebody out at XERF opened the mike. I recognized Mario Alfaro's voice, shouting, "Pistoleros! Ayúdanos! Pistoleros!"

Lou said, "What the hell are they doin'?"

I didn't say anything. I reached over, grabbed the radio dial, and turned it all the way up: *Pyyingggg!* "Pistoleros! Ayúdanos!"

"They're shooting up the radio station," I said. "They're trying to kill my boys!"

"Oh my God!"

I grabbed for my boots. "Stay right here," I said. "I gotta do something about this. Where's my money?" I pulled on my clothes, grabbed about thirty hundred-dollar bills out of the dresser, and said, "I'll see you later, baby."

Lou didn't try to hold me back, she knew I had to protect this opportunity. Part of me kind of wished she would've tried, though. I was a lot more scared than I wanted her to know.

I drove straight for Mario Alfaro's house, which was on a dirt street around the corner from the main stem. We had a major stash of guns and ammo there. Mario's wife was frantic. News travels fast on a quarter-million watts. Everybody in Ciudad Acuña knew that there was a shootout going on. I scooped up all the artillery and went out into the streets, laying cash on anybody who would help me. It took a couple of hours to get enough people together. Most of the townspeople didn't want to risk their necks.

Finally, four or five of Mario's cousins and several of Archie's friends joined in and we were all ready to go. Between us we had half a dozen pickups, four junked-out old cars, a garbage truck, and a couple of motorcycles. This was the brigade that was going to rescue XERF.

I led everyone out across the dunes in the dark, through the passes, out to the transmitter. The top was down on the Olds Starfire. A taped Wolfman show was playing, but the guys kept switching on the mike to let us know that bullets were still flying.

As we got close to the station, we all started honking our horns, whooping, firing shots into the night sky. I was clutching the Olds's steering wheel in one hand and trying to lift myself out of the seat so I could shoot over the top of the wraparound windshield. In our headlights, we saw about twenty men on horses riding outside the circle of sandbags and barbed wire, like Indians circling a wagon train in a Western movie, shooting in at our guys—who were crouched in doorways and behind window frames shooting out.

The big machine gun was silent. That guy in San Antonio had sold us the wrong firing pin, so the most fearsome piece in our arsenal had only gotten off four rounds before it jammed up and became useless.

Seeing our ramshackle mobile attack force, the riders reined in their horses and started wheeling around, splitting up in confusion. The men inside the station had been under barrage for two or three hours by now, trying to keep the pistoleros at bay without using up all their ammo. Now they picked up fresh courage. They swung the station door open a crack wider and started popping more and more rounds at the bandits. Four guys darted out and scurried to positions behind the sandbags. The pistoleros checked out the changing situation and all of a sudden split in all directions as fast as their ponies could go, twisting around in their saddles and shooting back at us as they made off into the desert.

We stopped all the cars and trucks and let the pistoleros ride off. Everybody in the posse and in the station just cooled out for a few beats. Nobody riding with me had been hit, but a couple of workers in the station had taken creases. Meanwhile, two of the bandits were lying out beyond our barricades, still as rocks, with their faces in the sand. Both were dead. One had a crater in the back

153

of his head big enough to hold a golf ball. The other one was gut-shot.

We packed our wounded guys into the back of an old green van that belonged to the station, and somebody drove them to the hospital in town. Around daybreak the Federales finally arrived, almost as if they'd been waiting for a winner to emerge before coming on the scene.

From the back of a jeep they took out a folding table and two chairs. They set themselves up a little field desk and the commandante began to conduct a hearing.

Mario Alfaro saved my life that morning. We had all kinds of illegal, smuggled-in firearms, including that nasty-looking but worthless machine gun. The Federales didn't speak any English, so Mario had to take over. All I could do was smile and slip the last remaining C-notes to the commandante when Mario gave me the sign.

After examining the two dead pistoleros, the Federales agreed that the one with a hole in the back of his head was accidentally shot by his compadres. It wasn't clear who had tagged the other guy, but the conclusion arose that no charges needed to be filed.

Smiles all around.

"Our business is done here, Señor Wolfman, and much good health to you."

The word that spread around Ciudad Acuña over the next few days was that Montez was behind the shootout. Gonzáles was lawyer enough to know that since we now held the papers to the station he had to deal with us straight up. First he tried intimidating us with demands to inspect our books, and with threats of lawsuits, but that phase didn't last long.

Pretty soon his communications got real friendly. Nothing was ever said about the shootout. He only referred to it in a sideways kind of way, saying he regretted the problems we had been experiencing with Señor Montez and his "unprofessional behavior."

Gonzáles still held some good cards in this poker game. He knew that we had to keep our promises and pay off the station's tax debt on a steady basis. Once we did that, he'd be running XERF again. In the meantime, getting rid of greedy old Montez was probably a bonus.

So everybody was now reasonably happy. Except for Montez, who was still pissed off enough to want me dead. For his pride if nothing else.

A week went by. I came back to the hotel one night, and the desk clerk did this funny thing. I stepped up to the counter and slipped him five bucks, asking for messages.

"Nothing for you tonight, Señor Wolfman," he said. But as he spoke the words, he pointed the first finger of his right hand toward the outside corner of his right eye. Then he lightly touched the skin and pulled it down a fraction of an inch, so a bigger area of the white of his eye became visible.

I thought he had some kind of weird tic. I hadn't been down below the border long enough to know that he was flashing me a message in sign language. Any Mexican could tell you what it meant—*"LOOK OUT!"*

I went up to my room, kicked off my boots, clicked on the TV and lay back on top of my bed. Then the phone rang. It was the desk clerk, talking in a whisper: "Señor Wolfman, watch out! Montez! I couldn't tell you before. He's been waiting down here for you. He's going up the stairs now."

I grabbed a revolver, latched the skinny little chain across the door, turned out all the lights and crawled under my bed. Footsteps came slowly up the hall. They stopped. A second passed, then the door crunched. The chain ripped out of the woodwork. Light from the hallway showed me a heavy black boot attached to a flash of iridescent green pants leg.

Next I saw muzzle flares from two guns and heard the bullets thumping. Wood splintered and glass shattered as shots sprayed across the bed, the chairs, the mirrors, the lamps.

I kept my head low, looking up just enough to sense where he stood, and counted how many shots he took. During the shooting, he stepped a little ways inside and the door swung shut behind him, completely cutting off the light. Neither one of us could see a thing. When he'd squeezed off twelve rounds, I fired two in his general direction. All of a sudden I heard him yell "Cabrón!" and some other Mexican swear words that I hadn't learned yet.

The door opened again, and slammed shut real quickly. The next thing I heard was quick but uneven steps going down the hallway. And then total quiet. Nobody ever came out of their rooms to see what had happened.

I never saw Montez again. He sort of vanished from the region, at least as far as any of the cantina bartenders and bordello owners knew when I asked them. But that didn't mean he had given up.

Three days after that pistol jamboree in the hotel I was driving the old panel truck out to the radio station, a little before midnight. Eight guys were riding along, in the seats and in the cargo space, headed out to relieve the first shift.

Halfway across the desert, just after we went over the railroad tracks, we came through a space between two hills. All of a sudden, quick bursts of rifle fire on both sides. Something burned, right at the tip of my nose, like a hot matchhead had been pressed there. I tromped on the gas pedal. A bullet *pinged* against the van, real close. We were bouncing over rocks, fishtailing in the desert sand, almost out of control, but I didn't back off the accelerator until we'd gotten inside the ring of sandbags.

I've still got a little crease on the end of my nose from that first bullet. The second one dug into the back side of the van's door frame, six inches behind where my head had been. We counted two more hits on the back doors.

Nobody knows what eventually happened to Montez, but those were his last shots. Between my spreading money left and right, and the influence Gonzáles had all the way down to the bedrock, Montez didn't have many friends left in Ciudad Acuña.

It had been a hairy ride, but now I felt safe enough to find a place for the family and actually take up residence in Del Rio.

We moved into a big house that actually was where Gonzáles had lived before he stung the preachers for those millions and established his big Rancho Grande. And we tried to blend in a little with the community. We were invited to become partners in a thriving local bordello, but before I could start daydreaming about what my ownership privileges might be, Lou nixed the idea.

As it turned out, we didn't stay very long in Del Rio. Maybe just eight months. It wasn't the most comfortable or cosmopolitan place after all. One day an elderly Mexican peasant walked up to our front door, rang the bell, and silently handed Lou a fresh-killed goat wrapped in Mexican newspapers. We took that for an unfriendly sign from somebody. But while we were there, we were sitting right on top of the most powerful clear channel in the world. I had the nonstop mouth I was born with, the rap styles a generation of crazed hipster jocks had fed into my head, and the world's finest rhythm and blues music within easy reach in my record bins. Everything right in place to realize XERF's full potential—cash, check, or money order.

XERF was moving a ton of mail-order stuff off the Wolfman show. Pretty soon I had to hire a couple of women just to open the envelopes. Checks went into one pile, money orders into another, cash in the middle of the table.

There was the Wolfman Jack Official Roach Clip. "What you do, friends, you get ready with this clip, which features the likeness of the ol' Wolfman himself, and you catch those speedy little buggers by the hind legs as they run across the floor."

There were Florex tablets, which were guaranteed to give you a whole lot more romantic dash. On a trial basis, we had a thousand bottles of them packaged, with a hundred pills per bottle.

"Yeah, Wolfman Jack with you, baby. You won't believe what your Wolfman got for you now. Oh, my gracious. It's sittin' right here in front of me. It's called Florex. F-L-O-R-E-X. It's a little pill here. There's a hundred of them here in the bottle. If you give a little pill to that one that you love so much . . . Y'know, maybe the marriage is getting a little stale in the naughty department. Well, one of these pills in mama's orange juice . . . She's gonna want to take it, y'understand.

"I've got a letter here from Thomas Edney and he says, 'Wolfman, I received your bottle of Florex and I got so excited that night I proceeded to take at least two or three pills. I gave my mama two or three pills. And I've got to tell you, it has never been as good as it is now in my whole life.' "

At first those pills sold gradually. Then I hired a lovely young black woman who had a sultry voice to match her looks. She recorded the exact same pitch, adding a few words directly to the ladies about how much romance these marvelous pills would bring back into their lives. "Your husband will be bringing you flowers every day, just because you ordered this bottle of Florex."

After that woman's voice went on the air, we were selling those pills almost as fast as the factory in Mexico City could make them.

Of course, Florex wasn't anything but a little sugar coating wrapped around plain old aspirin tablets. But that didn't keep people from ordering them over and over again, and sending me page after smoking page of firsthand testimony to their spicy powers. We bought 'em for $1.50 a bottle and sold them for $3.95, so there wasn't really any huge profit in them. Mostly, it was fun to think about people feeling their oats and making it with each other instead of fighting or complaining all the time. It was kind of a Dr. Brinkley trip, except I didn't have to slice the nuts off any poor billygoats to do it.

Eventually the Feds told me: "Stop advertising these pills. They're worthless." Right about that time we had ordered fifteen thousand more bottles. I thought we were going to get stuck. But that sexy woman's voice had made such a lasting impression, and people were having such a good time being convinced that Florex made their blood run as hot and horny as a teenager's, we sold out all of those last fifteen thousand bottles without even having to advertise.

The Wolfman Jack Show had all kinds of record packages, too. These were my favorite item. I really went to pains finding great records that were obscure. Even if you're a real oldies freak and listen to your local oldies stations all the time, you may not know that there's so much more. Lots of these oldies stations emphasize the candy-ass side of early rock 'n' roll. But it was that more playful, naughty, dangerous, stimulating music that originally caused kids to stay up past midnight and play that radio so low that their parents couldn't hear. That's what it's all about!

I tried to uncover a little bit of that spicy history in every record package, with great but lesser-known tunes that would get people excited all over again, like for instance "Buick '59" by the Medallions, "Blue Light Boogie" by Louis Jordan, "Mama He Treats Your Daughter Mean," by Ruth Brown, and "The Things That I Used to Do," by Guitar Slim. It goes so deep.

Of all the mail-order stuff we used to pitch, maybe the craziest was the baby chicks. My rap went like this:

"Friends and neighbors . . . If you're not raising your own little chicken farm in your backyard, then you're just not takin' advantage of a real opportunity! I mean, this could grow into somethin' BIG!

"All you need to start is one hundred tiny little baby chicks. And the Wolfman's gonna send 'em out to you. Straight to you' doorstep from Red Top Chicks. Just think about it. They give you food in the winter, feathers *all* the time, and fill your whole life with hours and hours of fun and companionship. You can *talk* to them, take 'em for *walks* in the park, and give them all cute little *names!* I mean, chickens have feeling too, y'know.

"All it takes to get your chicken farm started is a measly three dollars and ninety-five cents. Cash, check, or money order.

"But that's not ALL I'm puttin' in the offer. Send in your order today and I'll send you ABSOLUTELY FREE a life-sized, autographed picture of me that *glows in the dark!* Just close your eyes and imagine the funtime inspirations your whole family can have sittin' around in a dark room together, watching me glow for you!"

And I truly was glowing in those days on XERF, because I was a young buck doing my thing right where I always wanted to be, hitting the airwaves with gale-force blues, rhythm and blues, and the most soulful rock 'n' roll, all sent your way through the treetop-tall platinum-coated driver tubes of the most powerful commercial station on the planet.

XERF was my own personal "Rocket 88." I was riding in style, baby, cruising nationwide.

Chapter Ten

As you might imagine, the action going on at XERF attracted a lot of attention. Record company people wanted us to play their stuff, newspaper and magazine reporters wanted the inside story on this Wolfman Jack character. But it was real hard for folks to personally get in touch with us out in the desert. There was no address except a P.O. box in Del Rio, Texas, and no marked or paved roads to XERF.

One day this dusty-looking guy wearing a suit and necktie actually showed up at the transmitter, looking a little fazed from the trek, claiming to be a reporter from *Time*. He was real disappointed. The only person who met him was a smooth-faced young man with a Brooklyn accent. "Wolfman Jack?" I said. "Oh, you won't find him here. He lives down in Mexico City. I think he stars in porno films or something. We just get the tapes he sends us in the mail, and we play 'em on that machine over there."

Record companies, especially the ones that featured black artists, started noticing that we were playing their records—even if they weren't part of the mainstream Top 40. And we were helping them reach a whole lot more people. I got a real nice letter from Ahmet Ertegun, the head of Atlantic Records, home of Ray Charles, Solomon Burke, Wilson Pickett, Don Covay, Joe Tex, Percy Sledge, and Clarence Carter. He thanked me real profusely for getting that Atlantic soul sound out to a wider audience.

Some of the other record companies showed their gratitude with payola checks. Even though the whole country had gotten angry over the disc jockey payola scandals back in 1959, and my old hero Alan Freed had gone from the top of the heap to the bottom of the barrel because of his involvement, there were still lots of people offering disc jockeys cash, free travel, or lots of other illicit bonuses for airtime. But by the time the record companies began sending me their stuff, I was already making fantastic money. I wasn't some cash-starved small-town jock anymore. And I didn't want anybody to get the idea that there were any strings attached to my playlist. I picked records for my show based on whether they got me excited. Period. I wrote "VOID" on those payola checks and "return to sender" on the envelopes they'd come in.

One afternoon, the same grizzled-looking driver who originally brought Larry Brandon and me out to XERF showed up with James Brown riding in his cab. James and his band had a day off from a swing through Texas and he decided he just had to check XERF out in person. I'd never met anybody else in my whole life as energetic as him.

At the time he arrived, a radio crew guy named Ernesto was just climbing down from our three-hundred-foot-tall transmitter tower. It was his job to climb up there and replace the red lights on the top whenever one of them burned out, so no stray airplanes would run into the tower. I was joking around with James and I said, "D'you think you'd like to have a job like that?"

"Hell," he said, "that ain't nothing." Then, dressed in his tight, custom-tailored, collarless charcoal gray suit and a wicked-looking pair of red patent leather shoes, he grabbed ahold of the tower ladder and went climbing straight up to the top. When he got there, he hooked one leg around a ladder rung and leaned out to wave to us all with both hands. I thought I'd have a heart attack, but all the guys on the crew thought it was the greatest thing they'd ever seen.

Even though it was a lot of fun to operate out of that no-man's-land, common sense sort of took over and Lou—by then known to all as the Wolfwoman—brought me and the kids back to Louisiana. And then, as you learned in Chapter One, came my original live Wolfman Jack stage performance and a couple of cross-burning scenes with the Ku Klux Klan.

They say it's better to die like a lion than to live like a dog. And I have to agree with that, basically. But after dodging a few bullets and after hosting an impromptu Klan get-together on my front lawn, I decided that it would be a little bit smarter if this new Wolfman character would restrict himself to appearing only inside nice, safe radio studios.

The Wolfman Jack Show continued on XERF for a long time, through taped broadcasts. But three or four years went by before the Wolfman showed his face in public again.

I swung back toward living my life as Bob Smith, the hard-driving radio businessman. Back in Mo Burton's good graces once again, I got reinvolved with the day-to-day running of KCIJ. His confidence in me returned completely. Late in 1964, he bought himself—once again for practically no money down—another obscure little peanut whistle on the verge of bankruptcy. This one he decided to let me run all by myself.

It was KUXL, a 1,000 watt daytimer at 1540 on the AM dial, way up in the north woods of Minneapolis, Minnesota. The signal was just powerful enough to cover Minneapolis and St. Paul. It was a great chance to see if I could make another station produce like the other ones had.

Thanks to Prince and Morris Day and some of those other contemporary musicians who emerged from Minneapolis, people realize now that it's a real hip city. But all we knew about the place in the early 1960s was that when you looked at it on the map, you saw Canada on one side and Iowa on the other. At least, we thought, it didn't look to be Klan territory.

Lo and behold, we came to find out that Minneapolis was a great place to live.

Maybe it has something to do with being near the headwaters of the Mississippi River, maybe it's the open-mindedness of all the Scandinavian folks who settled there. Anyway, the first thing that impressed us about Minneapolis was seeing a whole lot of black and white people together—as friends, as sweethearts, as neighbors—actually walking hand in hand down the boulevard. It was one of the nicest places for good racial mixing that we'd ever seen.

Of course, after the XERF experience, I was extremely into the preacher thing. I knew them all. They would do damn near anything I'd asked them to because I still controlled the business on XERF and another superpower Mexican station, XEG, out of Monterrey, Mexico. XEG used to broadcast with 100,000 watts from about a hundred miles below the southern end of Texas, so it covered the central part of the United States.

We filled the morning time on KUXL with all these great preachers. They paid $150 for fifteen minutes, which wasn't much more than loose pocket change to them. From noon until sign-off, a guy who called himself Preacher Paul played choice rhythm and blues.

Wolfman Jack wasn't even on KUXL. As far as the folks in Minneapolis knew, I was just Bob Smith, a guy who ran a little radio station.

Wolfwoman and I moved into the most beautiful house we'd ever had. It was just outside of town in Lake Minnetonka, real close to the lake, with big views of rolling hills. She was the most gorgeous she ever was in her whole life, and we were both very happy to have our kids growing up in such a great setting.

I kept taping the Wolfman show, running it on XERF on my regular time, from midnight to 4 A.M. Sometimes I even did the first program of the evening, an hour of heavy, shit-kicking, honky-tonk country music like Hank Snow's "I've Been Everywhere," "Detroit City" by Bobby Bare, and Little Jimmy Dickens's "Truckload of Starvin' Kangaroos."

By now the Mexican government had collected all its back taxes. Nobody was shooting at anyone. Me and old Arturo Gonzáles had become the best of friends. XERF was back in his hands, free and clear, and he raised the rates on the preachers' airtime all over again. Everything worked out fine. The only people that got screwed were the preachers, and they had some real deep pockets anyway.

Of course, they kept suing Gonzáles for a refund of the cost of their "lifetime contracts." And to this day I think they're still trying to get some of that money back. Good luck, fellas.

Running KUXL in Minneapolis was fun, a challenge. The trick to making a radio station profitable is taking the less-desirable airtime and turning it into something special for a certain group, so they'd be loyal listeners. Anyone can sell the morning and evening drive times. That's always in demand. Most radio stations set those rates so high that they practically support the whole operation. Then they more or less end up giving away the off-hours.

If you create special niche programs, stuff that draws a loyal audience at non-prime times of the day, you create pure profit.

For example, I got some young Jewish guy there in Minneapolis to come up with a half-hour program specifically for his people. Then I sent him out among the Jewish community merchants to sell airtime. He was an instant hit.

All the new programming at KUXL started making good money almost immediately. Lou and I loved Minneapolis a whole bunch. I missed performing, though. Tape-recording my shows for XERF didn't give me that great sensation of connecting with an audience, the kind of feeling you get when you know people are hearing you at the same instant you speak.

Something happens to me when I perform. It's an awareness, a kind of back-and-forth electricity transference between me and the audience. It hypes me up like you can't believe. It's one of my happiest times, and I can't get that feeling any other way except being live on the air.

In order to get to where my heart was, into performing, I had to plunge my head even deeper into the radio business. I had to get a business trip of my own into orbit. Even though I appreciated Mo Burton for teaching me so much, I wanted to call my own shots. I knew I'd never make it big while I was working for somebody else.

That's why one day I went to Chicago to see Mr. Harold Schwartz. He was the official American representative for four of the Mexican border blaster stations: XEG in Monterrey, XELO in Laredo, XERF in Ciudad Acuña, and XERB in Tijuana. He was the king of border radio. He'd definitely made the most money. Schwartz was the original guy who got the preachers started on XERF in the 40s, sort of as a continuation of the Dr. Romulus Brinkley era.

He teamed up with a fellow named Teo Bacera, who owned XEG and XERB. Together, they covered the whole U.S.A., except for the East Coast. They sometimes ran *The Wolfman Jack Show*, so they knew all about me and I knew them pretty well, and we got along just fine.

Schwartz is retired now. He's got a town in Florida that he built. Most people for a retirement project, they might build a birdhouse or an electric train set. Schwartz is the kind of guy that started his own *city*.

XERB, the Tijuana station that he represented, only put out a 50,000 watt signal. That made it the weakest of all the border blasters. Because XERB only hit the West Coast, I wasn't familiar with the station from long ago, like I had been with XERF.

I walked into this elegant building in the Windy City and I walked up to Mr. Schwartz's office. The reception area looked like the front of a Beverly Hills law firm. Nice reception lady, tasteful artwork in ornate gold frames, and absolutely no french-fry grease spots whatsoever on the carpet. Schwartz met me with a big smile on his face.

He reached across his desktop, which was about as wide as an aircraft carrier deck, and gave me a friendly greeting. Meanwhile, a stock market ticker tape over on one side was clacking away the latest Wall Street reports.

I convinced Schwartz to let me start running Wolfman Jack on XERF, XEG, and XERB. All three at one time. It was easy to win him over because he knew the recent history of Wolfman on XERF. I used to do a mail order spot there for Keystone Cosmetics:

"Are you really happy? You got plenty of money in your jeans? You got your health and everything? Well, chances are you're pretty happy. I can't do nothing about your health. But I can give you all some ideas about putting some money in your pocket. A little more money than you ever expected before. I don't care who you are, man or woman, you could earn big extra cash selling popular Keystone cosmetics and grooming aids. You'll be proud, because the company is nationally known, respected, and highly advertised.

"Well, friends, the products sell themselves. Now, lookahere. If you are not satisfied with your income, if you'd like a little more money in your pocket, why don't you check this thing out right now? All you've got to do is write a card or letter, with your name and address and zip code to Agent, A-G-E-N-T, XERF, Del Rio, Texas. And we're gonna send you back a complete brochure. That's Agent, A-G-E-N-T, XERF, Del Rio, Texas."

The Keystone people gave us a dollar for every response. And whenever we did that spot, about two thousand postcards would show up at XERF within the next few days.

Schwartz had always kept tabs on that kind of stuff. He knew the kind of numbers we were doing.

Also, my XERF shows advertised record packages. The

box number was XERF, Box 1050, Shreveport, Louisiana, and Box 1050 was loaded with orders practically every day. These things also impressed Harold Schwartz.

I had become involved with a guy by the name of George Garrette, proprietor of Uncle George's Record Shop in Minneapolis. We joined forces on producing and pressing oldies albums—*The Lucky 40*, *The Big 30*, *Wolfman's Blues Special*, all kinds of different packages. We were the first ones to come on really strong with oldies packages. As soon as the deal with Schwartz was set, I began plugging Uncle George's Record Shop on all the Mexican stations. Each order was making us maybe a couple of dollars and everybody was doing great business—Uncle George, us, and the stations.

After about four months of running record package ads, I began to notice something wild about the mail responses from XERB. They kept climbing and climbing. Pretty soon they got to be around six hundred pieces of mail daily—as much as the other stations combined. The 50,000 watt "weak sister" was outdoing powerhouses that ran at up to five times more watts.

I had to learn what the hell was going on.

I found out that lots of local stations around America had applied for licenses close to the 1570 frequency of XERF. That meant they would blank the Mexican stations out in their local marketplace. Since fewer people could hear the pitches, fewer people were sending in their cash, check, or money order.

But XERB, which reached Los Angeles, San Francisco, and a lot of other big markets, was still flowing free.

There had to be a way to make some great money out of what I'd learned, but I wasn't sure just how. I thought and puzzled about it nonstop for a couple of weeks. Suddenly one night, I sat up in bed and shouted, "I GOT IT!"

This scared the hell out of poor Lou.

"What've you got?" she asked.

"Baby, I got the key to our future."

I went back to Mr. Schwartz and said, "Let me take over operations at XERB. Let me set up offices in L.A., program the station, and take full charge. I can make that station produce more income than what you're getting now."

And he agreed to it. Of course, Schwartz structured the deal in a way where he couldn't lose. He kept control of the station's money. He gave me an allowance of three grand a month to set up an L.A. operation and hire some jocks. When the station made extra money, over the top of what it used to make, I would get paid a percentage. That was the big incentive—a piece of the pie. Plus a whole new set of big-league challenges. Anybody who starts a career in radio or television, the main thing they want to do is work their way up from the little local markets to the majors. L.A. and New York are the biggest prizes.

I wasn't independent yet, but—if I could make XERB take off the way all the other stations in my past had taken off—I was gonna be on my way.

By this time my sister and brother-in-law, Joan and Emile Achee, were living just outside Los Angeles. He'd left the navy to become an executive for an aerospace company. Their kids, the same pipsqueaks who had helped me for nickels and dimes on my old Fuller Brush gig, had grown up to be strong, athletic, great-looking kids in their early teens.

I called up the family and said I was coming out to California to look things over for a business venture.

Late one night in 1965 I showed up at their ranch-style suburban home. I was in my Cadillac, with Arthur Hennings, a radio technician from KUXL, by my side.

Arthur, who was black, called himself Fat Daddy Washington on the air and played rhythm and blues. He and I asked Joan and Emile where most of the black people of Los Angeles lived. I guess they thought I was looking for a place to drop my friend off. Then, when I asked how far it was to Bakersfield, they really started scratching their heads. I didn't take the time to explain. Me and Arthur got a spare house key, then took off into the night.

We didn't come back until around three or four in the morning. When Emile saw me at breakfast he said, "What the hell were you two doing last night?"

"We're out doing a survey," I said. The whole purpose of our trip was to test XERB's reception around Los Angeles and parts nearby, using a little transistor radio. The business plan I'd cooked up was insanely simple: I wanted to program XERB as if it were a local L.A. station. That would give me two advertising bases—the preachers and local Los Angeles merchants. If my transistor radio could pick up the signal in Bakersfield, and inside barber shops, shoe stores, and beauty parlors in all the black neighborhoods of Los Angeles, then I was confident that plan would work.

My idea for XERB was to run preachers from seven in the morning until twelve noon. Then from noon until seven of the following morning, we'd play black gospel and rhythm and blues.

Anyway, me and Arthur must've startled a few folks when we came walking into their stores with both of our heads pressed up against a single tiny radio. But pretty soon we'd figured out that XERB's signal covered the area pretty good.

Then we went over to KGFJ, the dominant local black radio station, which was located in the heart of Compton. We marched up to their sales manager with business cards in hand and said, "We represent Uncle George's Record Store of Minneapolis, Minnesota. We're thinking about buying some airtime from you folks to sell our R&B record packages."

It was halfway true, and we looked legit. So those nice folks gave us a stack of carefully researched information, the full demographic rundown on the black community of Southern California—where they lived, their purchasing power, and what kind of music they liked best. A whole market survey, for free.

I drove back to the north country, packed up my family, all the tape recorders, microphones, and other broadcast equipment I owned. Threw it all into a U-Haul trailer, and towed it right back to L.A. with my Cadillac. Lou followed me with her car.

Of course, leaving Minnesota meant cutting my ties with Mo Burton. I gave him a month's notice, but he still didn't like it. For one thing, his dreams of a radio empire depended on having good, bright people to run all his little stations. But I was too stoked on my own dreams and ambitions to take good care of his.

Mo knew that a big part of my motivation was a desire to do more performing, as Wolfman. He was so burned up, he had to keep saying his words over and over just to get to the end of a sentence: "So whaddya wanna do? D'you wanna, d'you wanna, d'you wanna sing and and and and dance for nickels in in in in *saloons?* Is that what you wanna do?"

I had to put all that behind me. The number one thing, besides finding a cool place to live in L.A., was setting XERB up with a Sunset Boulevard business address and making the station rock. It had to be Sunset Boulevard. About the time Richie Caggiano and I had set out for Hollywood, some seven years earlier, one of my favorite

TV shows was 77 *Sunset Strip*—"The street that wears the fancy label, that's glorified in song and fable . . ."

Sunset was where I had to be. Near all those jumping nightclubs like Pandora's Box, the Whisky-A-Go-Go, the Red Velvet, the Trip, the London Fog, and the Galaxy.

Sunset Boulevard was the epicenter of all my Hollywood fantasies. It was Hippieland, lined with palm trees, and opportunities for fame and money that were so limitless and crazy, you couldn't even imagine what they might turn out to be. It was the capital of What's Happening Now.

In January of 1966 I signed a lease for the bottom floor of a pink stucco building on Sunset. Then I placed an order at a local shop for a big, beautiful red neon XERB sign to adorn the front window.

The Body Shop, where lovely young women took off their clothes in a professional setting, was practically next door. Nightclubs, heavy on the music, were within blocks.

With the help of my teenage nephews, I put my equipment and file cabinets in place. Then I wheeled a chair up to my desk, sat down with a smile, and said out loud to the walls, "This is perfect."

Chapter Eleven

Imagine that you're about seventeen or eighteen years old, living your excitable teen years in a Southern California beach town, on a farm in the San Joaquin Valley, or maybe in one of those well-to-do suburbs around San Francisco. It's 1966. Late on a Saturday night in the summertime. You and some friends have been driving around, trying to stir up your sense of freedom. The car radio is on. You're pulling in the usual stations, sampling the Top 40—which has a few good tunes here and there—"Wild Thing" by the Troggs, "Wouldn't It Be Nice" by the Beach Boys, "Yellow Submarine" by the Beatles.

Suddenly one of your buddies twists the dial up to 1090. A voice comes on like you never heard before. It's growly but happy. Then there's the sound of muffled thunder, way off in the distance. As it fades, you begin hearing a sparse, slow-tempo, clear-toned blues piano instrumental. It's something lovely, lonely, and thoughtful—"Sweet Sixteen Bars" by Ray Charles. Woven through it you hear the strange voice, as kindly and soothing as your favorite uncle on cough syrup, saying, "Yes, yes, yes, yes."

From someplace far away comes the howl of a lonesome wolf.

"It's time for the blues," the kindly voice goes on, "and your Wolfman would like to have all my children just gather around now and experience the *feeling* of the blues. Yes, yes. He was not like other men, in that he had a dream to *be* other men and not himself. But as it turned out the other man *was* himself and he, too, was *unlike* other men.

"Today that other man is me, Wolfman Jack. And the Wolfman is *more* than me, more than I ever was. And that's why I bring that *me* to you. So *be* with me, baby, for the next few moments, anyway. They are ours, and ours alone. So rare are these moments. The ones that are absolutely just for *you* and *me*."

Suddenly an avalanche of saxophone rumbles into your head. Raw blues guitar riffs begin to cruise through your ears like a red '54 Caddy convertible invading Main Street. And now that radio voice is all fast and fired up with coal and gravel. "Yeah! Oh, I tell ya, this one gonna blow the caps right off your knees! This is Wolfman Jack, skinny-dippin' in the oil of joy down here on XERB, the tower of flower power. Fifty thousand watts of soul power. We gonna rock your soul with a steady roll and pay our dues with the BLUES! I got 'em *all* for ya . . . We have Johnny Otis, Wilson Pickett, Hank Ballard, Ritchie Valens, Clyde McPhatter, Joe Turner, Carl Perkins, the Penguins, the Platters, and the Clovers!

"Baby, I got so much rhythm and blues up my sleeve today, I had ta staple my elbow to my armpit! Aawoooooo."

That was me riffing on those California airwaves,

spreading the message into Arizona, New Mexico, Utah, Nevada, Idaho, Montana, Washington, Oregon, Alaska, and, on a clear night, across Canada to Moose Jaw and beyond.

Being in charge of XERB was the time of my life, and also my turn to take a pass at empire building. Of course, it all came crashing down around my ears before the whole picture got colored in. But it was a sweet ride, by anybody's standards.

For about five years, I had it all—boss of the station *and* doing my thing on the air, live. I assembled a "Dream Team" of great regular and guest jocks, people like Art Laboe, Magnificent Montague, Fat Daddy Washington, Robert W. Morgan, Johnny "Willie and the Hand Jive" Otis.

Sometimes I even had "The Hardest Working Man in Show Business," James Brown himself, working the microphone.

Ray Charles would call up on *his* birthday to wish me a happy time.

Within a couple of years, I also began running West Coast rhythm and blues revues nearly every weekend, all up and down the state of California, in armories, road-houses, and nightclubs of every size and description.

Historically, the West Coast was the birthplace of a whole lot of cool sounds. Lots of music lovers don't know that. First off, several great folks came from out of town to be recorded in L.A., like Little Richard and Larry Williams, who cut all their great sides for the Specialty label. Besides that, some of the best R&B music ever heard was born and raised in L.A. The Penguins cut "Earth Angel" in a garage behind a little house over on the east side. Jerry Leiber and Mike Stoller, two Jewish kids who fell deep in love with black and Chicano culture, wrote more classics in L.A. than you can shake a stick at: "Hound Dog," "Kansas City," "Searchin'," "Yakety Yak," "Young Blood," "Spanish Harlem," "Love Potion No. 9," "On Broadway," "Jailhouse Rock," "Charlie Brown," "Ruby Baby," and "Treat Me Nice," just to name a few. There was also the Olympics, plus Johnny Otis and all the great artists in his soul revues, like Eddie "Cleanhead" Vinson and Etta James. And Ritchie Valens gave us all those Latin-rock hits, like "Donna," "La Bamba," and "Come On, Let's Go."

However, outside of Los Angeles, the West Coast didn't have the kind of vibrant rhythm and blues scene like folks had enjoyed up and down the East Coast. A big part of the fun about XERB was that I was doing missionary work, getting more black music on West Coast airwaves. The natives loved it to pieces.

Of course, by that magical night in your imaginary California teenage years of 1966, the phrase "rock 'n' roll" had already been around for a long, long time. And I used that phrase with pride. But Muddy Waters nailed it right down when he sang "The blues had a baby, and they named it rock 'n' roll."

My strongest feelings have always been for the tunes that came real directly out of the blues and rhythm and blues traditions. It didn't matter what color the person was who brought the music to life. But if it was a white artist, they had to have a soulful side in order to get airtime on XERB.

So after I played, say, "Zip-A-Dee-Doo-Dah," by Bob B. Soxx and the Blue Jeans, and the singers faded out on the line "Wonderful feelin', wonderful day," I might say something like—"We got a wonderful feeling for you right now, baby. Here's Jerry Lee Lewis!"

Then, after Jerry Lee was through with one of his crazy

pianistic roller-coaster rides like "Great Balls of Fire," I'd step in and say, "Let's keep those emotions goin' with Jimmy McCracklin. We gonna do 'The Walk.' Let me see you walk. Just put your hands on your hips, and let your backbone slip. Now you doin' it, baby." Then Jimmy McCracklin would give everybody a dance lesson, which was also sort of a sex lesson, if you wanted it to be, if you were willing to let the beat and the boogie-woogie bass suggest fascinating and juicy things to your impressionable teenage mind.

When you do the Walk you're right in style,
You just twist your hips and roll your eyes . . .

"Yes," I'd say when the song ended, "time flies when you're having fun. Or, if you're a frog, time is fun when you're having flies! Hey! You know when you got the Wolfman, you always got the Wolfman Jack Blues Association. Happening right here and now. Yes, we gonna go down home where it all began, and let you in on the real thing, baby. Oh, my. The blues gonna make you cry, baby. The blues gonna make you jump and shout. When you're down at the bottom of the pit, the blues is gonna pull you out. Gonna purify your soul. Yes, indeed. With the blues, action is satisfaction. Yessir, if you are narrow-minded, the blues gonna broaden your horizons. If you're pale at heart, the blues is gonna put color in your cheeks. And this next number gonna take place right now and do it *all* for you. This is Freddie King and 'It Ain't Nobody's Business What I Do.'

"Take your time, Freddie."

That would be a typical handful of XERB minutes, something that gave me great joy to put out there on the California airwaves, but which also took a whole bunch of behind-the-scenes effort to crank up and keep going.

Harold Schwartz had given me a tight budget to run the station. Always the optimist, I believed that I'd find the ways to stretch it out and still present a great, hip radio format. But in reality it took every available dime to make that idea happen. For example, I spent a lot of bread by hiring away some of the top talent from KGFJ, which had been the preeminent soul station in L.A. until we came along.

Magnificent Montague, one of the greatest black jocks in the business at that time, was part of that KGFJ talent infusion. He was from the New York scene, and he was a walking encyclopedia of who played what riffs in what key on what record, down through immortal halls of New York funkdom.

I also took away Brother Duke Henderson, who played black gospel music for an hour every night, offering his listeners "The Mighty—I said yes the MIGHTY—Clouds of Joy!"

Brother Henderson was one of the greatest pitchmen ever. He would sell fifty Bibles every night—at $75 a pop—off his XERB broadcasts. Then, after the show, you could see him driving his car down Sunset Boulevard with one hand. The hand not visible on the steering wheel would be caressing the lustrous hair of some young thing, usually a professional, who would be busy swallowing Brother Henderson's pride, so to speak.

Even while he made his nightly journeys between the extremes of sin and salvation, Brother Henderson remained a very likable guy. The contradictions didn't bother him. And he truthfully was a very religious man. He believed in God, but he also believed in doing business and having fun.

Brother Henderson promoted the best gospel concerts all over Southern California. He'd pack the Shrine Auditorium, a huge venue near the center of the city, with the Mighty Clouds of Joy, the Edwin Hawkins Singers, Reverend James Cleveland, the Five Blind Boys from Alabama, the Soul Stirrers, the Swan Silvertones, all the reigning acts of the gospel circuit. A few years later, when Brother Henderson passed on, his funeral drew thousands and thousands of people.

There was a fortune-teller named Sister Sara who ran maybe ten two-minute spots every day on XERB. If you wanted to know your lucky number, you were supposed to contact Sister Sara. Every once in a while she'd drop by the station with a bunch of her Gypsy friends tagging along. The regular jocks would be hanging out in the studio, drinking beer and smoking funny cigarettes, just generally carrying on. Sister Sara and her people would appear in the doorway in their scarves and spangles, and everyone would hide their doobies behind their backs and rise up to say, "Bless you, sister."

I also brought Preacher Paul in from Minneapolis. All in all, I had some of the greatest disc jockeys who had ever done this kind of music. This is why XERB was so special to me. In the great years from 1966 to 1971, it was a better soul station than anything else that had ever been on the air—in New York, Chicago, or any place else in the world.

Reverend Ike ran two programs on XERB, one in the morning and one between seven and eight at night. Each fifteen-minute segment cost about $250. Every year he would come in and pay *in advance* for a whole year's worth of his programs. I'd come into the offices around noon on Sunday to greet him. Ike would pull up in his Rolls-Royce with his hair all slicked back, wearing an

$800 suit and carrying a brown paper sack filled with hundred-dollar bills—1,500 of them. He'd lay the stack on my desk and count it all out. Then we'd sit and talk a while. He'd always squeeze a sizable discount out of me, out of consideration for paying up front.

As soon as he left, I ran to the bank.

When Reverend Ike got his business covered he would disappear to go have some intense fun for a couple of days, leaving his Rolls-Royce parked at my house. "If anybody calls you," he'd instruct me, "just tell 'em that I'm all right and I'm staying with you." He just wanted to get away from everybody, including the people who worked for him, and let his hair down. All the way down to the basement.

A while ago, I asked someone to call Reverend Ike, to see if he would be willing to be interviewed, as a help to getting my life story together. He answered in soft, mellow tones, "Ah, yes. The Wolfman and I go way, way back." Then his voice got even deeper and softer as he said, "And tell me, son, just what is *in* this for ol' Reverend Ike?"

For almost a year, Lou and I lived in a rented house not far from the Beverly Hills Hotel. It was a stretch to afford a Beverly Hills address, but one of the first rules of being in show business is that you always want to be looking good. When people believe you're doing well, they'll go out of their way to be part of your scene. Which can increase your prosperity real good. And if you get to where you're really doing well, they'll line up to give you things for free. It's crazy, I know, but it's how the world works.

Anyway, it turned out that the house we picked out had been vacant for almost two years. In all the time that no people were living in it, rattlesnakes had come down from the hills and decided it was a very nice, peaceful pad just for them.

The first day we lived there, I came home from the station and saw two rattlers in the corridor, enjoying the cool slate floor. Lou had discovered them right after she came out of the shower. She was standing up on the couch, naked, with a broom raised over her head, screaming like a banshee. She couldn't move from where she was. Our kids, Joy and Tod, who were five and three then, were asleep in their rooms.

I was used to snakes because my dad sometimes had them in his magic act. But these were the first poisonous babies I'd ever faced. I grabbed a big shovel out of the garage and whacked them straight into rattlesnake heaven. The slate floor took a few dings and our shovel was always a little crooked after that.

We had a lot more rattlesnake visits at that house, although they were harmless compared to the two-legged snakes who eventually came along and took away my XERB situation. But that event was still down the road, unforeseen.

The first year or so with XERB was pretty lean times. My deal with Schwartz was that I'd get richer when the station did better, but that extra cash took a long time to materialize. We sold Lou's Cadillac. Mine, which had towed a U-Haul trailer across the country a couple of times, was beginning to show some signs of strain.

Early in 1967, somebody very welcome but very unexpected came walking back into my life and helped turn our money situation around.

Mo Burton hadn't talked to me since I left his station in Minneapolis. He was in L.A. to buy himself another radio station. By now he had the strategy down pat. He'd buy into the biggest market possible, via the least

expensive facility available, then use clever programming, hungry, ambitious talent, and relentless salesmanship to make the value of his investment climb through
the roof. He was just like one of those real estate fixer-
upper guys who buys the most beat-up house in the
nicest neighborhood in town, then turns it into a jewel.

The station Mo had been pursuing—but never got—
was called KPCC. It was a weak FM signal that belonged
to a Presbyterian church out in Pasadena. They broadcast
their programs from the church basement.

During the months he was in town, trying to buy KPCC,
Mo struck a trade-out deal with the Continental Hotel on
Sunset Strip, just a few blocks away from XERB. He had
the whole top floor. Just then, the tourist business was
down along the Sunset Strip. People were real scared of
the hippies who were suddenly all over the place. Most
visitors to the Strip area were kids staying in crash pads.
Mo convinced the Continental's manager that some ads
on his out-of-town stations would bring in customers
who weren't aware of the fact that hippies were now
running wild in the streets of Hollywood.

Ironically, over the next few years the Continental
shifted gears and became one of the favorite hotels of
touring rock 'n' roll bands. Management taped up a picture for employees behind the registration desk. It
showed a long-haired hippie/musician type and said
"Treat This Man With Respect—He May Have Just Sold
A Million Records."

By that time it was known unofficially as "The Continental Riot House." Led Zeppelin once came to town
and took over six floors, almost half of the hotel, and
had motorcycles running in the hallways and sex-a-thon
parties in most of the rooms.

Anyway, Mo saw my neon XERB sign in the window

and walked over one afternoon to say hello. He and I never really could stay mad at each other. We had too much in common.

Mo told me he had a deal with the Pasadena Presbyterians, a verbal agreement, but at the last minute they backed out of it and sold KPCC to somebody else.

Believe it or not, radio is generally a very honorable business. Usually, radio people stand by their agreements. Mo was bitterly disappointed. "I never had any problem dealing with rednecks and hillbillies," he said. "But these Pasadena church people are something else."

Like old times, Mo and I went out on the town together, me driving while he explored every station on the radio dial and we both analyzed what they were all doing wrong. As I mentioned, my car was looking a little down at the heels. When I arrived at work the very next day, I discovered Mo standing next to a brand-new Cadillac. "This is the right image for you," he said, handing me the keys. "I never want to see you driving old cars."

Naturally, it wasn't long before he and I were back in business together. This time I held the reins, with Mo taking a background, advisory role. He renegotiated the deal with Schwartz so we started receiving the advertising money directly, paying a monthly fee for the right to run the station. Since the ratings were climbing, and we were doing great business, we charged higher rates to the advertisers.

All of a sudden there was real wealth.

We shared it, and we began plowing lots of it into wonderful, expansive plans.

Before long, Lou and I got ourselves out of our rattle-snake-infested rental house and bought something of our own, high up in the Hills of Beverly, on a street called Ferrari Drive.

We also decided to get the station away from the Sunset Strip. After a year, I'd had enough of that kind of glamour. In fact, it was wearing real thin.

Pandora's Box, a nightclub two blocks east of our offices, sat on a skinny, triangle-shaped strip of real estate near the intersection of Crescent Heights and Sunset, the gateway to Laurel Canyon. It had been a beatnik hangout in the 1950s. Preston Epps, a bongo player discovered by Art Laboe, used to be the main attraction. He had a hit record called "Bongo Rock" in 1959. In 1962, Jimmy O'Neill, the disc jockey who later on became the host of the TV show *Shindig*, renovated Pandora's Box as a teenage nightclub. The Beach Boys played there for a full month, before they were real famous, and O'Neill also put together an incredible house band that included future stars like Leon Russell and David Gates.

Even back then, the city wanted to tear down Pandora's Box. It created a traffic flow problem for all the people trying to get home to their expensive pads in the Hollywood Hills. Mostly, though, the pressure was on to demolish the club because the hippies were a lot crazier than the beatniks who used to hang out there a few years earlier. They smoked dope in public, flashed bare boobies at people driving down Sunset, balled each other right on the sidewalk. They also attracted a lot of greasy, sex-hungry biker dudes into the scene. Plus, the *L.A. Free Press*, the local underground newspaper, had their offices underneath the club. So Pandora's Box kind of had the establishment pissed off in several different directions.

By 1966, the city of L.A. was ready to clear the club out of there for good. Cops began leaning on the kids who hung around, citing them for curfew violations. Cop versus hippie face-offs began happening almost every night. In fact, that's what inspired Stephen Stills to write

"For What It's Worth." The "battle lines being drawn" were the police lines. Finally, they ripped down the club and cemented over the skinny triangle to make a traffic meridian. That's what you'll see on the spot today.

Lou, for one, was glad to see Pandora's Box go. She was still a very proper Southern Belle, and every time she walked from our offices to the bank, she had to pass in front of the club. There she was, striding along in her nylons and high heels, dressed like she just stepped out of a Beverly Hills shop window, while the Hell's Angels and Iron Horsemen were standing around, smoking pot, and saying, "Hey, baby, how about climbin' on my hog and takin' a magic ride?"

Mo didn't like the hippies either. Because he came of age among New York beatnik intelligentsia, he placed a big premium on being cool and knowledgeable, secretive about your outsider status, doing a real sophisticated end run on society's rules. The Sunset Strip scene was too blatant for his taste.

And for mine, too. People were overdosing in front of our offices practically every day. You'd walk up the steps and stumble over somebody who was drooling all over his own love beads, too stoned to recall what pills he'd gotten goofed up on.

I can stand a lot of strange stuff, but when people get all sloppy dirty, like they've got no self-respect, I want to be somewhere else. Call me middle-class, but Ciudad Acuña seemed totally sanitary compared to Sunset Boulevard in 1966. It was nothing but unwashed naked people on top of other unwashed naked people.

One day Mo came in and said, "I've found a building we can buy real cheap. We'll have five times as much space as we've got here."

This was the start of our empire-making days.

Unfortunately, because I got so excited and went so deep into debt to make all my dreams come true at once, it was an empire that sort of flourished beautifully and then melted away like ice cream spilled on a hot sidewalk.

It was a lot like the racetrack experience I had as a kid, winning lots of bucks in a hurry, and then gambling it all down to nothing.

While it lasted, though, it was the best situation we ever had.

Our building was an old Fred Astaire dance studio on Sixth Street near Western Avenue, around what they now call Koreatown. It was almost a whole block long. Because money was flowing like wine, we had it totally remodeled. It was gorgeous. The hallway was all mahogany-paneled, with thick, red carpet that almost sucked the shoes right off your feet. My office was as big as one of those deluxe Las Vegas dressing rooms. Mo's was twice as big. We built a recording studio that took up the whole top story, the first thirty two-tracker ever assembled, and the most technically advanced studio in L.A. at that time.

We spent a million on equipment alone, all of it in cold cash.

Along with a hot radio station, we had a publishing company and a video production house all under one roof. The video part never got finished, but if the scene had just held together a little longer, my dream was to shoot trippy videos of all the L.A. bands that were happening then, like the Buffalo Springfield, the Byrds, the Mamas & the Papas, Sky Saxon and the Seeds, Frank Zappa and the Mothers of Invention, and so on. I can't help thinking how crazy the MTV generation would go for a library of video footage like that today.

We would do the whole XERB air shift for twenty-four hours, just like we were broadcasting live from the studio, but we were actually putting everything on tape, even the phone calls that came in from listeners. Late at night, someone would jump into my Cadillac and run those tapes down to the Greyhound bus station. They'd ride the midnight bus to San Diego. Early next morning, someone else would carry the tapes across the border and on down to the transmitter at Rosarito Beach, Baja California, a little ways south of Tijuana. That way, we were always working one day ahead of actual broadcast time.

In spite of being in a beautiful, up-to-the-minute studio in the heart of Los Angeles, we still had to do business just like I'd done it back in the days of XERF, south of the border. The first time our driver brought tapes into Mexico, a local official at the border took him to one side.

"How do we know what is on these tapes?"

"They're just radio shows. You can tune in tomorrow and hear them all on XERB."

"Perhaps that is so, señor. But these tapes might be dangerous propaganda. Therefore—who knows?—perhaps I should confiscate them and analyze them for a few days."

Of course, it was all about *la mordida*, the "little bite." The border guards wanted a cut. That was how you had to do business in Mexico those days.

It wasn't long before we knew who all the right guys were. They'd get their money every week, just as if they were on the payroll. As soon as we got hip to that, whenever the border guards saw our man's truck coming, they automatically waved it through.

Back in L.A., I cut an album with some of the best session people on the scene: the Blossoms, with Darlene Love, on backing vocals. Larry Carlton on guitar, Leon Russell on piano, Kenny Rogers singing, and some other fantastic heavyweights. Todd Rundgren, who later did a song about me, "Wolfman Jack," on his *Something/ Anything?* album, wrote liner notes. So did Leon Russell. "Only in Mexico," he wrote, "could a small defenseless baby left on the steps of a radio station by a family of traveling sword swallowers become the standard of eloquence in soul communication."

Kenny Rogers wrote a couple of songs for that album, including one titled "I Ain't Never Seen a White Man," about how everybody's the same underneath our skins. Another cut on that album was called "There's an Old Man in Our Town." When my dad, Weston, passed away, I played that song at his funeral. There literally wasn't a dry eye in the house. I even let down, although he and I never were able to reestablish the kind of warmth that we deserved to have. We tried. We were both up for it. But the old emotional currents kept holding us apart.

Among the people helping spread XERB's "soul communication," Magnificent Montague was one of the wildest and most fiery. Literally. One year earlier, the FCC had censured him for yelling "Burn, baby, burn," over the air during the Watts riots. Now, that was a slogan of praise he'd been using a long time, describing the emotional experience of a hot record, and by it he meant something like "Excel at what you're doing!" But sometimes subtleties get lost in a war zone, which is what Los Angeles had been. And keeps on being.

We ran him from three to seven in the afternoon.

The Magnificent One is a bundle of contradictions. He comes on like a street-tough character. Every other word out of his mouth is "motherfucker." But he also owns one of the world's greatest private collections of important African-American art, documents, films, letters—anything you can imagine that traces the black experience in America. He came from a real cultivated New York City background, and learned the more "vernacular" style of black diction from preachers that he shared airtime with on a Texas station when he was starting out.

Montague was there, in the room, the Christmas Eve in 1954 when Johnny Ace shot himself backstage while playing Russian roulette after a show—just before "Pledging My Love," his first national hit, landed on the charts. Later on, Montague loaned black history documents to Malcolm X in the early 1960s, which fueled his street-corner speeches.

Every day, just before doing his show, Magnificent would walk himself down to the corner at Sixth Street to a delicatessen where he had his lunch. Mo often went with him. They both loved to argue so much, they were made for each other.

There was a pet shop along the way, where the owners kept a parrot on a perch out near the sidewalk to attract customers. Every day, Magnificent would step up to that parrot and say, "Motherfucker . . . motherfucker . . . motherfucker . . ."

After several days of this, the parrot finally started saying it back. Every time some innocent person walking down the street tried to get friendly with it and say, "Hello little birdie," the bird would shoot back, "Motherfucker . . . motherfucker . . ."

Magnificent and Mo both came out of the same New York scene, and they both had real loud mouths. They'd sit in that delicatessen and put on a show for everyone. Montague would carry on like a preacher, waving his arms and speechifying like the next spin of the globe depended upon it. Mo would have to stand up to be heard, using his whole vocabulary of facial expressions and Yiddish terms. To experience both of them carrying on together, in full Afro-Hebrew roar, was a real trip.

My plan for XERB had always been to program it as if

it were an L.A. station, with an advertising base of local merchants. Of course, we ran the same wild preachers that had always been the mainstay of border radio—A.A. Allen, Reverend Ike, all those guys. Brother James Carr of Palmdale, California, preached that Jesus did not like the modern calendar because Christmas and Easter are heathen practices. "Please send me your love gifts," he would say, "so I may be able to continue bringing you this very important word from God." Brother Joe Harold Smith invited listeners to read the Bible with him, cover to cover—after buying their copies at $15 a pop. Mother Graham preached that "no affliction can withstand the power of God or the appeal of a cash offering."

Those folks were the biggest source of income. Then we went down to the transmitter and rigged the towers with directional reflectors, so the signal would bounce even further up the West Coast, in a lobe shape, instead of spreading out in a circle and wasting the signal on the Pacific Ocean and the interior parts of Mexico. It was the equivalent of juicing the transmitter up to 150,000 watts.

That transmitter modification allowed us to raise the preachers' broadcast fees a notch or two. As always, they complained for a minute, then kept right on paying whatever we asked. XERB was making them mountains of cash.

Other parts of the operation were profitable, too. Advertisers went nuts to reach the black audience through us. With trade-out, I furnished our house with some of the most out-of-sight stuff you could get in an L.A. ghetto-area furniture store at that time.

One of the coolest commercials we ever ran was Joe Tex, backed by his great soul band, promoting an aspirin company. It went like this: First some bluesy piano chords, then Joe Tex's voice saying, "What you mean you gotta headache? Why, man, everybody's got a headache. That ain't nothin'." Then the brass section kicked in, followed by some fast-pounding drums. "We got splittin' headaches, throbbing headaches, tax headaches, and sick headaches. We got headaches from not eating, headaches from overeating and -drinking.

"Man, if you ain't got a headache, you don't know what's goin' on in the world. Everybody's got a headache, like I said, and Joe Tex got the answer. BC Powder. Take a BC Powder and come back strong." Then the whole band landed on a high note as Joe signed off with "Oh! Y'all straighten up, hear?"

Ike and Tina Turner were good friends at that time. I don't know how much of that scandal stuff in her book, *I, Tina*, is true, but I did become aware, one afternoon, of Ike's fondness for extramarital sex treats. I heard he was rehearsing in a studio just a couple of blocks away from mine. So I walked in on him and he's facing toward the door, very absorbed in his piano playing, not looking up. But as I crossed around the side of the piano, I saw a female figure underneath it. I suddenly recognized that it was a woman who worked for me and she was hungrily doing some freelance work on Ike's happy soldier. Apparently she didn't notice me until a minute later when Ike, his tensions freshly relieved, looked up from the keyboard and said, "Heyyyy Wolfman! Whasappenin, man?"

Wolfman Jack was still going through life unseen by the general public. Ever since that run-in with the Klan in Shreveport, I kept him that way. There was no beard on my chin. I was still primarily Bob Smith, a radio businessman who secretly got off on doing a show as a wild and crazy character. People called me Bob, not Wolf.

Whenever fans showed up at XERB wanting to meet Wolfman Jack, Bob Smith smokescreened them with a cock-and-bull story. But it was inevitable that the Wolfman would step into the public eye again.

Of course, when promoters start promising you nice, big bundles of cash to make appearances, you tend to talk yourself out of your fears real quick.

Lou had already created the basic Wolfman Jack look. We hired a Hollywood makeup guy to carry it a little further. The guy was very busy with all his TV work, so he had to come over at three in the morning to make me up for my first California gig as Wolfman Jack, an appearance with Little Richard down in Santa Ana.

Lou was already asleep in bed when we went to work on the transformation.

First he darkened my skin by a couple of tones, then he fixed me up with a big wolf nose and glued a beard on my chin. Next came a pair of fangs on top of my eyeteeth. My wig was a big hairy masterpiece.

When he got done, I curled up in bed next to my wife. The first thing she saw in the morning was me in my beastly regalia. It was a sight she wasn't prepared for. My ears rang from her screams for a real long time.

That afternoon, as I headed out for my gig in full makeup, I pulled up to a light along Sunset Boulevard. The woman in the next car glanced in my direction, did a double take and shrieked. I knew then that the time was right for the Wolfman to meet the public again.

After that, I began to organize my own road shows and present them almost every single weekend. We'd book the local National Guard Armory, or a good-sized road house, in towns of all sizes between San Diego and the far end of the San Francisco Bay area, plus all up and down the San Joaquin Valley, from Bakersfield to Sacramento.

Saturday mornings, we'd load up a rhythm and blues caravan and take to the road like Gypsies. One of our strongest acts was always Harmonica Fats, the great blues harpist. We also usually had the Olympics, who did their hit tunes like "Western Movies," "Big Boy Pete," and "I Wanna Be a Private Eye." They were a few years removed from their hit-making days, but still just as funny and raucous as ever. Various other soul and rhythm and blues acts from out of Compton and South-Central would go out on these treks with us, too. All it took was a couple of advertisements on XERB to pack the places. We'd do the gig, get people having a good time, grab the cash, and come back home.

I always felt like I was riding into these towns and pulling a bank job. I mean, to me it wasn't work at all. It was having fun in public, like opening up a big window and a microphone on the kind of crazy party I'd want to throw in my own backyard.

The Hollywood makeup job was part of every trip. When I walked into the gig, I did it like Father Divine coming on the scene. We always rented the biggest limousine available in the town we were playing. We drove it up to the entryway and unleashed our own brand of Showtime. First, a couple of shapely young women in tights, stiletto heels, cat-woman makeup, and glittery bra tops would get out, carrying baskets full of rose petals on their arms. A midget would then emerge from the limo, carrying a big cut-glass atomizer and honking on a rubber squeeze ball on the end of a long hose, perfuming the air to make it worthy of the Wolfman's dignified arrival.

Finally, I'd get out of the car real slowly. I'd look around the crowd even more slowly, like I was reading way down into their souls. The midget would begin walking ahead of me, spraying more and more perfume. The women would sprinkle my path with rose petals. I'd hesitate several beats, then begin my regal stroll.

In places like Salinas, San Jose, or Fresno, most people had never seen anything freaky-deaky like this. They would be completely agog. Raising my left hand, which had long false fingernails painted jet black, I would give my blessings and benedictions to the gathered throng. It was like an underworld version of a Cecil B. DeMille epic.

I'd get off on creating this effect like you wouldn't believe. Spinning records on a megawatt border blaster, feeling all those people out there in the darkness getting attuned to the soul and rhythm and blues currents, that was a tremendous experience in itself. But to be off in some town where the day-to-day reality was generally very plain, and to be blowing people's minds with theatrical weirdness, that was the most concentrated, fast-acting fun I ever had in my life. I looked so weird that Lou couldn't stand to walk alongside me. She waited until the crowd was trailing into the place where the show was going to happen, then she followed several yards behind.

After the Olympics did their hits, I'd come out and make a few lascivious wisecracks. I never really had a prepared show. I'd just look into the crowd and say something urbane like, "How *are* all you motherfuckers out there tonight?"

And everybody'd go, "Aaayyy, Wolfmannnn."

"All you motherfuckers give me a big *howl.*"

"Awoooooo . . ."

That was all I knew how to do. But for some reason, the people loved it. Then Harmonica Fats would come on, blowing up a roomful of hoodoo atmosphere on blues harmonica, while I'd lurk over on the corner of the stage, leaning on my cane and bobbing along with the backbeat. Gorgeous women patted my hairy brow with scarves and handed me drinks and the midget sprayed perfume all around my vicinity, so nothing stinky could profane my delicate nostrils.

People would always have a great time at these shows. It was the kind of music they hardly ever got to see live. We always had a beautifully mixed audience, usually equal parts black, white, and Hispanic. Even a few Indians, like Pat and Lolly Vegas, two teenage kids of mixed Shoshone, Yaqui, and Gabrieleno blood who were growing up in Fresno in those days. They came to our shows, and got inspired about breaking into show business. Later on, they put together a band called Redbone and hit it big in the early 1970s with "The Witch Queen of New Orleans" and "Come and Get Your Love."

I still work shows with those guys today, and they're still crazy as hell.

Anyway, there was never any fighting at those shows or even any of that "back off, buddy, before I kick your ass" kind of tension. Even with my being rude and naughty onstage, the spirit was always about fun, like a bunch of kids getting loose because their parents temporarily weren't around.

Since these shows were out away from mainstream show business, I never expected much to come from them. But then one day a booking agent from Las Vegas called up at XERB and said, "I can put you in the Bonanza Hotel for big money. Can you put a show together?"

So I said "Yeah!"

Mo got upset with me. His theory—and, hey, he might have even been right—was that by tripping all over the place to do Wolfman shows, I had less energy left over for taking care of business at the radio station.

The Bonanza Hotel is now the MGM Grand, and everything about it is very Las Vegas–style swank and ritzy. Back then it was a different image: all rough-sawn wood and wagon wheel chandeliers, with barroom gals and checker-shirted cowpokes serving the drinks. It looked like a mutation from the TV show *Bonanza*. You half expected to see Lorne Greene looking over the blackjack dealer's shoulder in one corner, while Hoss rattled the dice up over his head at the craps table and yelled, "C'mon! Baby needs a new pair of horseshoes!"

Going to Vegas meant I had to get my act a little more sophisticated. Now, instead of being kids escaping grown-ups, the audience was going to *be* grown-ups. More or less.

The makeup job used to take an hour. I had to streamline it so I could get ready for the shows quicker. The fake nose went by the wayside. I grew my own beard. I gave up the fingernails and the vampire-style capes for Nehru jackets. I kinda looked like a rounder version of Peter Sellers in *I Love You, Alice B. Toklas*.

There was a terrific, tight, versatile music group that I had worked with in Fresno—Billy and the Good Guys, a bunch of college kids, three of them white and three of them black. I would introduce them, tell a few of the same kind of nasty jokes that I used in the small-town shows, stuff that could make Redd Foxx blush, then I'd go backstage while the band played current hits. Finally I'd come out and sing three or four tunes, "My Girl," "Short Fat Fannie," and some others, and that was the whole forty-five minutes. We did four shows a night. Every one of them was jammed, all the way up to five o'clock in the morning.

The hotel people didn't know what to expect, so they had only booked us into a side lounge on a one-week contract. When they saw people standing around the block trying to get in, we got extended for a whole month. After that, they offered me their big room for $15,000 a night.

During the first week, in that small lounge, we alternated sets with this real clean-cut looking vocal group called the Swinging Lads. We were raw and ragtag; they were the essence of showbiz polish and professionalism. But after we played to boisterous, standing-room-only crowds, they played to empty seats.

The leader of the Swinging Lads was Don Kelley, a guy who looked so much like Paul McCartney that people would spin their heads to stare when he walked by. One afternoon he said to me, "You know, you have the worst show I have ever seen in my life. You've gotta stop using all those profanities."

Kelley had been in show business one way or another ever since he was a kid. He handed me a notepad full of all kinds of ideas and suggestions. "I want you to look at this," he said, "because I really do want to help you. I'd like to manage you. You've got a lot of stage presence. You've got a lot of charisma and everything, but if you want your career to last, you've gotta actually *do* something when you're up onstage. You've got a lot to learn about being an *entertainer*."

I had to admit that he was right. On the other hand, though, I was drawing the big crowds and his only other claim to fame was that he also managed a guy by the name of Joe Gerlach, a sponge diver who dove into a big, wet sponge from a helicopter or a platform or something. Poor Joe had missed a couple of times over the years and had to break the fall with his face, which was compressed into something that looked like the business end of a golf club.

Nevertheless, Don Kelley and I became good friends, and gradually he began to manage me. He sent the Swinging Lads out on tour and stayed behind to coach me and help me grow as a stage performer. When our show went into the big room, he helped me open up the band with a soul horn section and female backup singers.

Bit by bit, I started to become more of a real entertainer. One of the hurdles to get over was that I always used crazy noises and funny sound effects more than actual polished lines and gags. You can do that over the airwaves, where you're usually there to ease people through their workday, their commute, or some quiet hours of relaxing. But when people have dressed up to go out, and paid for a ticket, they come with a whole different attitude. They tend to look at you standing there onstage and say, "Hey, I've paid twenty-five bucks to be entertained. If you don't entertain me twenty-five bucks' worth, I'm gonna be pissed."

We hired writers, so I had great lines to say, and the audience had no trouble getting into the spirit. My singing improved, too.

All along, though, I was concerned about not losing the funky essence of the Wolfman character. I fought the polishing process all the way. I'm willing to work like a mule when it's necessary, but I can be as stubborn as a mule, too. Fortunately, Kelley was a clever kind of muledriver. We worked out our compromises and kept making this Wolfman guy more and more of a substantial, professional show business kind of person. Which is why I eventually got to do my thing for much bigger audiences.

Chapter Twelve

I've often been told that good things arrive in threes. But sometimes, before you can collect on those lucky threes, you get driven down to your knees.

At least, that's how things happened in my world during the pivotal year of 1971: a few months where I came close to hitting bottom, followed by three of the biggest chunks of good luck you can imagine.

During that tough stretch of months, it seemed like — as my old friend the late Albert King said in a song — "If it wasn't for bad luck, I wouldn't have no luck at all."

If I learned anything from this time, it's that you've just got to keep on keeping on. No matter how bad things get. Sooner or later a silver lining is going to come along, with no dark clouds attached.

It was January. Our five-year anniversary of being in charge at XERB was just around the corner. All our expensive renovation of the new offices was freshly finished. Our big sound and video studios were almost complete. We owed maybe $200,000 for the final expenses. Two Ampex sixteen-track machines were all linked up, creating the world's first thirty-two-track studio. They looked like a combination jukebox and robot, and they cost $110,000 just by themselves.

The preachers were bringing in around $80,000 a month, which was 80 percent of all our income. Thanks to them, the financial flow at the station was so phenomenal that we didn't bother spreading out the renovation costs with long-term payments. To save on interest we just paid out cash on the barrelhead for the studio, the equipment, and all the remodeling.

Mid-morning one of those January days, I drove one of my two new Lincolns to XERB and I walked into the reception area. The first person I saw was Lonnie Napier, a bright, eager, nineteen-year-old San Diego kid we had just hired to help out around the studio.

"Something's up," Lonnie said. "Mo's in there with a bunch of bigwigs. They've been here since eight o'clock."

I walked into my office and found Mo looking real upset, surrounded by Teo Bacera, the owner of XERB, and several very dignified-looking Mexican businessmen.

"It's our duty to inform you," they said right out, "that decisions rendered by the government of Mexico forbid you to broadcast any more of this evangelical religious programming, effective immediately. Most of the Mexican public is of the Catholic faith, and these programs have been judged to be detrimental to the youth of Mexico."

That was it. In one stroke, they cleaned out 80 percent of all the money we were expecting to make.

As soon as those guys had gone, Mo looked at me and said, "Bull-fuckin'-shit. This ain't about preachers. It's a squeeze play. Over the past five years, we've bumped our payments up from $30,000 to $55,000 a month, but that's not enough for those greedy bastards! They see we've got a good thing going on here, and they want to take over the action."

"So what do we do, Mo? Offer them more money?"

"Baby, we just ain't got the cake. With all this building and new equipment, we haven't got more money. We've been living today on money we expected to make tomorrow. As of now, that money is not coming in, my friend."

They had us outflanked. We still had to meet our $55,000 monthly payment. Yanking the preachers left us with nothing but the local advertisers. Unfortunately, a lot of them were no-cash, trade-out deals for cars, clothes, and furniture.

Later on, after we finally gave up control of the station, they stepped in and tried to duplicate our formula and our success. They changed the letters to XPRS and programmed soul music, calling themselves "Soul Express." They even put the preachers back on. Somehow, that "government ruling" went by the boards. No matter what they did, they never made a nickel. Eventually they went into the toilet.

Too bad they got so greedy, because when it came to spreading the news about rhythm and blues, the Mighty 1090 was the greatest force ever to hit West Coast airwaves. I would've been happy to stay there, doing my Wolfman thing, forever. While I was getting my memories together for this book, I came across a tape of my last night on XERB. It's still very emotional for me to listen to: telling people that it was my last broadcast after five magnificent years. I didn't get into the dirty details, just told everybody that things had changed and I was going to go out and do my own thing. "And I hope everybody will learn a lesson from the Wolfman right now, that whatever you desire in life, you've got to do your best to make it happen for you. Because if you believe in life, love, and beauty, then you wanta spread the word . . ." Then I played a real tender song, "Darlin' Baby," about yearning for someone you've lost. And that was it.

Mo and I hung on until May, getting deeper in the hole with every month that went by. Neither one of us wanted to give up. Finally, we just didn't send them their monthly check. I started to feel like the radio version of Joe Gerlach, a daredevil who took one high dive too many and got smashed flatter than a pancake.

The debt for everything got up around $600,000. Mo cut out, saying it was a matter of survival. "Bob," he told me as he was clearing out his desk, "the only thing for you to do is declare bankruptcy."

Every lawyer in town was giving me the same advice.

I'm not sure why, but I refused to go that route. I didn't want anybody to get hurt because my deals went south. I got kind of like my old man did when his career tubed out during the Depression: I just dug my heels in as hard as I could.

First I went to the people at the Bank of America, where we owed about $300,000. "Hey," I told them, "you can take my house and all, but if you don't give me a chance to get back on my feet, ain't nobody going to get nothing. I'm gonna pay all these bills off. I don't want to fuck anybody over and I don't wanna go bankrupt. So will you please give me a chance? Loan me just a little more money, enough to keep going. You'll get the whole thing back, principal and interest, too."

Bless their bankerly hearts, they believed in me so much that they went for it. That was the first step in getting back on my feet, but there were lots of dark days still to come.

I need to add a note about now concerning something

powdery that at that time had begun to become a big part of my life: cocaine.

Getting out of the radio booth and onto a stage was a big leap. It was fantastic fun, but it also scared the hell out of me. That's why I needed all my makeup, disguise, and outlandish trappings. Hanging your unprotected ass out there on the stage, doing what you do and care about, giving whole rooms full of people the opportunity to either praise it or put it down—that can make you a nervous wreck. I always did my shows straight, live appearances or radio work, but real often afterward I would blow my brains out with coke.

It's like facing a dragon. Cocaine is a drug that gives you the feeling that you can face any damn dragon.

Or maybe I should say that it *connects* you to that feeling. Because we all have a lot more talent and all-around capability than we give ourselves credit for. I tell that to folks I meet all the time and they look at me blankly, like, "What're you talking about? There's nothing special about me."

But yeah, there is. Everybody is real special and talented. And the more we all remember it, the less time and money we're all gonna waste on chasing after artificial happiness.

The problem is that we've all gotten put down at some time or other—by bigots, or overly harsh parents or hard-nosed teachers, or assholes in general—and we start believing some of what they lay on us. I think everybody's got what it takes to face the dragons in their lives. But it's real hard sometimes. And along comes a drug like cocaine, that charges you up and makes you feel like the way to beat those dragons is by being drug-aided.

I can tell you from experience, you're better off believing in yourself and developing your own powers.

Sooner or later cocaine comes up and demands payment for chasing off all those dragons. Still, even knowing there's a price, it's very seductive to think you can knock all your fears aside with a couple of quick blasts. Your body gets conditioned to that quick hyper-charge of self-confidence. It wants to have that sensation again.

The guy playing Charlie Parker, Forest Whitaker, said it about heroin in Clint Eastwood's movie *Bird:* "They can take it out of your blood, but they can't take it out of your mind."

The first time I ever had cocaine, it was under the direction of a guy who was a connoisseur of wine, food, and drug experiences. He was the leader of a rock 'n' roll band known for one particularly strong and lasting hit. One day he invited me, Lou, and Mo over for an introduction to South America's leading export. After we all took seats, he brought into the room an elaborate box, all covered in intricately hammered metalwork. It looked like an antique from Calcutta or someplace like that. When he opened the lid, there were several well-filled compartments, each one with its own label: grass from Thailand, from the Kona coast, from Maui, coke from Peru, from Colombia, hashish from Turkey, peyote buttons from Mexico, about everything you could imagine—short of heroin.

I'm lucky, compared to a lot of people who got into drugs during the 1960s and 1970s. Something about my constitution allowed me to indulge, then put them aside, without going through any heavy crash. Of course, I'd love to have in my hands today all the money that entered my nose during the 1970s. I'd love to get back the time I could've spent being close with my family. And if I'd known then what I know today, I might've faced my dragons straight up.

In the early 1970s, though, cocaine was becoming "the elite drug" among entertainers. Folks would walk around wearing a gold coke spoon on a gold chain around their neck. People from the record companies, especially, gave out gifts of gold spoons and little bottles of cocaine—"Here, this is for you"—as casually as you would chocolate bars and ice cream cones. You'd be sitting in a posh restaurant, and someone at your table would lay lines down on a pocket mirror and say, "Here, you want a blast?"

There were certain rooms in certain upscale restaurants, usually way in back, that were more or less reserved for cocaine users.

A few months before the XERB situation went sour, we met a doctor who wanted like anything to get tight with show business people. This guy had a chain of abortion clinics going, and later on got himself in some real deep trouble with the law.

As soon as we met him, he started supplying prescriptions for pharmaceutical coke. Totally unadulterated, pure stuff, at just a few pennies per hit.

After that, it was party time all the time. People were over at the house twenty-four hours a day, carrying on like there was no tomorrow.

Grass was available, too, but it was regarded as kind of passé. Something you might do for a giggle, but not the stuff that heavy hitters used.

My trajectory went like this: I got cozy with cocaine when times were good and everything was ascending. Later, when reversals hit, I was still important enough to be getting gifts of the drug. I took them all, because I was in dire need of feeling better. Eventually, I started relying on that chemical lift way too much.

It's like you're *here*, in a place where you don't feel

very confident or happy, and you wanna go *there*, to a place of feeling good about yourself and on top of everything. Cocaine is like a helicopter. It instantly lifts you up and takes you there. Temporarily. But it can never substitute for really believing in yourself. Which can be hard work sometimes, but it pays off much better than any drug.

I've seen a whole lot of people who were close to me get messed up behind cocaine. The drug just takes them away. It's a triple-hard fight to come back, and the people who make it have my deep respect.

The people who *really* buy themselves trouble are the big, big stars who figure out that they can very easily induce doctors to write them prescriptions for the most whacked-out, mind-bending stuff on the planet—the legal drugs. That's the final factor in drug abuse. No law enforcement paranoia, just steady and progressive loss of your humanity. I'm glad to say that for all the nefarious things I've tried at one time or another, I never set foot on that path.

After the collapse of XERB, I really started changing, deep down. Up until 1971, I was a guy with a successful side trip going, based on an invented character. Nobody in the organization actually called me "Wolf." That would've blown my secret identity, made it hard for me to do day-to-day business. Just like Clark Kent didn't want anybody seeing him slip into that handy phone booth and getting down to the blue tights and red cape.

Wolf was the hidden aspect of my personality. But the crisis made me feel like everything I'd aimed for in life was slipping out of my hands, and that feeling sort of broke my heart. In the meantime, it made sense for me to be more public about being Wolfman. Bob Smith's bubble had busted, but Wolfman was still a popular guy who could get gigs.

So Bob Smith, the guy with a million schemes and hustles, went away somewhere, never to be heard from again.

Wolfman Jack, the happy-go-lucky guy whose main concern in life is good times and rockin' music, took over on a twenty four-hour-a-day basis. I became my own invention; my invention became *me*. Just like Samuel Langhorne Clemens gradually became Mark Twain or Robert Zimmerman became Bob Dylan.

You could say that I was escaping reality. And you'd be right. But here's the kicker to this story: as soon as I quit being Bob Smith, things started to pick up. Slowly at first, and then suddenly beyond my wildest, most wolfish dreams.

By now both my Lincolns had been repossessed. Our house payments were way behind. We barely had enough money for groceries. We had to borrow from friends.

The first lucky break came on the night that summer when I attended a benefit screening of *The Concert for Bangladesh*, George Harrison's movie of the big concert he put on in New York with Dylan, Ringo Starr, Eric Clapton, and Ravi Shankar. Out in the parking lot I ran into Bob Wilson, a friendly guy whom I'd met a couple of times before at radio industry gatherings. When we started talking, I found out that he had recently become the program director at KDAY, a 5,000 watt AM station that was playing extended album cuts instead of short pop-radio mixes. There in the early 1970s, music stars were getting more chances to stretch out their artistic identities. KDAY was competing against KHJ, a higher-powered Top 40 station, by going with the longer, hipper versions and by introducing a greater number of new artists.

"You've got a great radio station," I told him. "I listen to it all the time." Which was at least a little bit true.

"Well, why don't you get out of Mexico," Wilson said, "and get on legitimate *United States* radio? Come join us!"

Wilson didn't seem to know that I was down on my luck, but this was exactly the kind of break I needed.

"I'd love to," I said. "Are you serious?"

"Yeah. I'm serious." But he hadn't expected me to jump for his offer.

"Well, okay! Let's work out the details tomorrow!" And we did. They offered me the bargain basement rate of $18,000 a year, less than one tenth of my XERB salary, but all their little station could afford. Even if it wasn't much money, it came at a time when I needed cash something fierce.

KDAY had a peculiar situation. It had started out as a Santa Monica station, but at some point in history the offices and transmitter got moved to downtown L.A., on Alvarado Street. The FCC still wanted them to be a Santa Monica station, so they had to rig their towers to send the signal out westward, in sort of a narrow fan shape. On a good night, KDAY could be heard in Hawaii and in Australia, but it couldn't be picked up ten miles north in Burbank, or forty miles south in Anaheim. Which was part of the hip image of the station. You had to be in the right place to hear it.

I took over KDAY's seven-to-midnight slot, right after a guy named Sam Riddle, a very popular local radio and TV entertainer who eventually went on to produce the TV show *Star Search*.

A huge billboard went up on Sunset Boulevard to announce my new gig, with a picture of me in a red satin cape and furry claws: "Wolfman Jack—Howling, Prowling Rock 'n' Roll."

They also booked me to open for Alice Cooper at the

Hollywood Bowl, which turned out to be the start of a long friendship. Here's another guy who had become his own invention. Alice's real name is Vince, and he isn't really a cross-dressing queen, just a crazy rock 'n' roller from Phoenix who got famous by taking a gender-bender trip to extremes. It worked real good for him. He never had a Top 40 hit, which is the more typical way to strike it rich, but everybody wanted to see his insane act. Plenty of folks bought the albums, too.

On the evening of my first KDAY broadcast, Wilson was waiting impatiently for me when I rolled in at five minutes to air time. "Wolf," he said, "you've never even been in this studio before! Don't you want to know how to run our board? Should I try and get you an engineer for your first night?"

He was in his mid-twenties, straighter than any arrow you've ever seen, had never had a whiff of anything illegal in his life, and dressed himself in three-piece suits every day.

"I don't need an engineer, Bob. Just show me the board."

Wilson went into an explanation of where all the important switches were, how to run the tape cartridges, and so on, all the time looking at me like he expected me to be taking notes. Instead, I reached into my little kit bag, took out a number, and lit it up.

"Oh my God! You can't do that," he yelped. "This isn't Mexico!"

Wilson was almost petrified with fright. He stood in the other room to watch me do my show. With only five minutes' learning time on a new board and all that reefer smoke in my brain, he expected me to bungle the whole gig. But I didn't make a single mistake.

After what I'd been through, I was happy as hell to

sign on with the KDAY crew and become a little worker bee. Every evening around six, I'd head my slightly used Cadillac down the hill, waving to all my movie star and movie producer neighbors, rounding the bend by the famous Pickfair Mansion halfway down, flowing into Sunset Boulevard right by the Beverly Hills Hotel. At my side there was a rumpled brown paper sack holding some fresh sandwiches Lou had made me.

I was one short step from the outhouse, but still acting like I lived in the penthouse. I didn't have much cake, but I could still show some frosting.

Besides the Cadillac, there was a broken-down, ragged old Ford Country Squire station wagon parked in the driveway. Whenever I had to appear at an event, I would roll up in the Caddie and grandly hand the keys to a valet. Meanwhile, my manager and anybody else who had to come along and do behind-the-scenes work, they would park the Country Squire about two blocks away. When the event was over, they'd stand outside and pretend that they were waiting for the valets to fetch their ride—until the coast was clear and they could secretly slink off and walk to the dented-up Ford.

What Bob Wilson was doing at KDAY was new on the scene at that time, but now it's one of the most dominant formats: AOR—album-oriented rock. Instead of individual tunes, we played three or more in a row, making the cuts flow into each other. Sometimes we did an entire side of an LP.

There was such an explosion in new and different music at the time, with weirder, more far-out groups showing up every week. Folks needed a way to sample a lot of music before they could decide what they liked. At KDAY we played lots of Rolling Stones, Beatles, Chicago, and Pink Floyd. It was a real quick education for me in pop music, because I'd always done rhythm and blues up to that point.

The long-play format cut down on my rapping, but I always had plenty of visitors. Lots of people started coming around during my shift. Jerry Wexler, the producer of many of Atlantic Records's classic soul tunes, including most of your favorite Aretha Franklin sides, was one of them. Jerry very recently wrote a terrific book about his own life and times in the music business. It's called *Rhythm and the Blues*.

Another frequent visitor was this weird English guy named John Lennon.

He's been gone for years now, but Lennon remains one of the most intense, amazing cats I've ever met. I thought I had pressure from the banks and all—man, he had the whole Federal Bureau of Investigation breathing down his neck.

John liked to have fun, but he also was the kind of guy who lived a whole lot of the time entirely inside the complicated circuits of his own mind. Or, as he once expressed it to me, "To boogie or not to boogie, *that* is the Christian."

He actually talked like that.

We had a natural rapport because John wanted to get close to everything basic and elemental in black American music, to blend it with his own rock 'n' roll vision. He respected the amount of background I had, and how I'd been tuned in since even before they called it rock 'n' roll. He wanted to hear over and over about the old Alan Freed shows at the Brooklyn Paramount, and the nights I spent tape-recording Dr. Jive and the other great soul jocks. In fact, John said that he and the other Beatles heard me for the first time during their very first tour of the United States, back in early 1964, and they flipped.

They thought they knew all about American rock 'n' roll culture, but the Wolfman was fresh information for their Liverpool ears.

John and Yoko were living at that time in a cottage at the Beverly Hills Hotel, registered under a phony name. Sometimes, after my shift was over, John and Yoko would have their limo driver bring them up to our place on the hill. He and I would do some blow and keep talking music and the American scene until the sun came up.

Yoko and Lou would have their own thing going, talking about mysticism, spiritualism, ghosts who walk among us, the inner meaning of life, and whatever else.

Even if we barely had any money, I still had some decent microphones and tape recording equipment up at the house. We set up a studio there, and started figuring out what to do with all the hundreds of hours of XERB shows that we had on tape.

My manager and I cooked up an idea that, as far as we knew, had never been tried before. Up to that time, disc jockeys were just local guys, well-known wherever their station's signal went, but anonymous everywhere else. But because I'd been on the border blasters, my show had already been heard in several corners of the country.

The plan was to capitalize on that advantage, and all my XERB tapes, by offering prerecorded rock 'n' roll radio shows to stations everywhere.

For a lot less than it cost to get the real thing in person, stations could have a nationally known disc jockey on the air nightly, exclusive in their area. Lonnie Napier got to work, reviewing tapes of old shows and editing out any comments that pinned down a specific time and place. A caller might have originally said, "This is María Pérez from El Monte High School, and I want to dedicate 'Land of a Thousand Dances,' by Cannibal and the Headhunters, to my boyfriend, Chuckie." Lonnie trimmed out the names of the schools, the towns, and any mention of what time of year it was. We recut the old XERB tapes to fit any town in America, at any time. It gave the shows a timeless quality.

Which, as I was soon to learn, was making an impression on *another* very impressionable and creative guy—George Lucas.

At any rate, we called this new radio business "syndication." Not only did it work out well, it caught on with some other radio entrepreneurs, like Casey Kasem. We were the first syndicated rock 'n' roll program that ever went on the air. Casey may be a lot richer than I am, and quite possibly smarter, too, but he didn't get his thing going until about two or three years later.

At first we were on a station in Honolulu, K-POI, and one in Tulsa. The master stroke came when we hooked up with the air force and also with Armed Forces Radio. That's when the syndication really took off.

Bob Wilson, the KDAY program director, joined forces with us as a 50-50 partner. That's how he got the money together to start a publication called *Radio and Records*, which soon became the bible of the radio and records business. He eventually sold *Radio and Records* and became a multimillionaire.

We first set up the syndication business and the publication offices in the same place—an office on Sunset near Vine where a wig company had just gone out of business. The walls were bright orange, the carpets were muddy brown. All along the wall they had these cubicles that the wig heads used to sit in. It was 1970s-style bizarre, but it was cheap.

The insanity of Vietnam was still going on at this time. The men and women who were serving time out there had a profound need for the fun and romance that were waiting for them back home, so *The Wolfman Jack Show* had some value as a soul tonic for all those folks.

In fact, the whole soul music revolution, if you think about it, was about the same time as the Vietnam years.

There were other kinds of songs on the hit parade, too, but during this time of big-time nationwide unhappiness, lots of people opened up to the emotional intensity of soul. It just proves how certain kinds of music can get right into you at the deepest levels and heal what ails you. That's exactly why Aretha Franklin scored nine Top 10 hits between early 1967 and mid-1968, then came back into the Top 10 in 1971 with "Bridge over Troubled Water." About the same time, Sly and the Family Stone were lighting up with "Dance to the Music," "Everyday People," "Stand!," "Hot Fun in the Summertime," "Thank You (Falettinme Be Mice Elf Agin)," and "Family Affair."

This was also about the time that Hendrix burst on the scene and totally tore up people's minds about what an electric guitar could do. And, of course, all the fantastic Motown artists—the Supremes, Marvin Gaye, Smokey Robinson and the Miracles, the Temptations—were having their peak years.

Anyway, one of the things I feel best about, looking back across my career, is giving those overstressed, hard-hit folks serving in Vietnam a sense of happier times to come. Something to get their minds beyond the foxholes, Agent Orange, medevac chopper rides, and all that other *Apocalypse Now* craziness.

While the syndication business slowly built up, a new visitor began showing up at KDAY. Rocco Ubisci would come by, share a joint or two, and talk real excitedly about a brand-new TV show he was helping to produce.

It was called *The Midnight Special*. He told me that Stan Harris, one of the premier TV directors of the day, was directing, and a young, ambitious, creative guy named Burt Sugarman was the executive producer.

The first *Midnight Special* was a get-out-the-vote program on NBC aimed at young people. It aired in August of 1972, while folks were trying to decide between George McGovern and Richard "I Am Not a Crook" Nixon.

That first show had John Denver as the host, with Linda Ronstadt, Mama Cass Elliot, the Everly Brothers, War, Helen Reddy, the Isley Brothers, Harry Chapin, and David Clayton-Thomas. Like most of the shows to come, it was a real diverse bunch of artists.

The election didn't turn out so hot, what with Nixon getting reelected just to be driven out of office a few years later, but *The Midnight Special* itself did just great. NBC liked the ratings so much, it brought the show on a full-time basis in February of 1973.

The first episode or two used Johnny Rivers as the show's host. Johnny has tons of talent—after all, he's sold some twenty-five million records in his time. But he wasn't totally comfortable with the hosting gig. There was the general idea that it would be good to have a co-host, someone a little more used to emceeing, because the show needed continuity.

Most people don't know this, but it was old Alan Freed himself who gave Johnny Rivers his show business name. He was actually born as Johnny Ramistella, a New York City kid who grew up down around Baton Rouge, absorbing all that funky, swamp-style music. Back in 1963, in the early days of the Los Angeles rock 'n' roll scene, he had a band together and they got hired at the Whisky-A-Go-Go. Even though he mostly was playing other people's tunes, Johnny got to be about the most popular act in L.A. The club owners were practically throwing punches at each other to sign him up. He put out his first album in 1964, *Johnny Rivers Live at the Whisky-A-Go-Go*. One of the tracks on that album was "Memphis," a great but at that time not very well known Chuck Berry tune. Even though Chuck's original version hadn't been a hit, musicians dug playing the song because it had this great instrumental hook, a 9th chord that Chuck had sliding up and down the neck of the guitar.

Johnny's version of "Memphis" went to No. 2 on the charts. He became one of the best-selling acts in America. About the time he got on *The Midnight Special*, he'd just been in the Top 10 with his version of the old Huey "Piano" Smith hit "Rockin' Pneumonia."

Johnny used to live near me. Anytime he was going to cut a tune, he'd come over and ask me whether I liked it. So it was Johnny Rivers who first started Rocco Ubisci and the other producers thinking about hiring me for the show.

The day I went to meet Stan Harris, Don Kelley said, "You ought to carry your fangs with you and, when the time feels just right, slip 'em on. That'll really turn those folks on." I walked in very properly dressed, all neat and clean. Stan wasn't a rock 'n' roll era guy, so he didn't know me all that well. "What do you think you can add to the program?" he asked.

Nobody had ever done a program before based totally on live rock 'n' roll performance. Which means that most of the stars of rock 'n' roll at that time had little or no experience with performing for TV cameras. I said, "I can help you a lot with getting the right people, and helping them get a feel for how to deliver the best possible TV performance."

We kept on talking in that vein, and everything was

going well. At a certain moment when Stan was distracted, I slipped in my fangs and just kept talking as if nothing had changed. Half a minute later, Stan began staring at me. Suddenly he jumped up like he was terrified and said, "You're not gonna get hairy or anything, are you now, Wolfman?"

From that time on, we became real great friends.

There were eventually more than four hundred *Midnight Special*s, going all the way up into early 1981, and I was on almost all of them. Just like I predicted, through the whole run of the show I stayed real busy behind the scenes, keeping nerves calmed down and talking people through their stage fright.

The money I was making on *The Midnight Special* was pretty low. I got paid double scale, which only amounted to about $750 per show. And the hours were real long. But I was getting my mug out in front of the nation every week, mixing and mingling with all the greats and near-greats of the era. Eventually, I hung out with about everyone from the Beach Boys to the Reverend Jesse Jackson on that show, not to mention Chuck Berry, Little Richard, Ray Charles, Aretha Franklin, Linda Ronstadt, Bill Cosby, Steve Martin, Steve Miller, Chevy Chase, George Burns, Elvis, John Lee Hooker, Billy Crystal, and, as the advertisements always say, much, much more.

I'll get into some more *Midnight Special* stories a little further on down the road.

While all this radio and TV stuff was going on, I was still connected to this sort of part-time manager guy, who primarily booked my weekend road shows.

One day, Don Kelley saw a crumpled-up old memo sitting on this guy's desk, concerning a phone call from Universal Pictures.

"How come Universal called Wolfman?"

"Aw, those jerks," he said. "I talked to them a couple of weeks ago. They said they might like to hire Wolf for a movie part, but first they wanted to interview him. So I said, 'How much are you gonna pay him to come in?' They said they wouldn't pay for the interview time, so I just blew 'em off."

Kelley stuck the memo in his pocket and decided to check things out for himself. Bless his heart.

This is what he learned: there was a young newcomer, fresh out of USC film school, working with a producer named Gary Kurtz to develop a 1960s-era teenage movie project for Universal. His name was George Lucas.

It was a real low-bucks deal. The principal thing going for Lucas, probably the main reason he had a shot to make any movie at all, was that Francis Ford Coppola, who had just become a super-heavyweight with *The Godfather*, liked Lucas and his ideas.

The buzz on George Lucas had started in film school. Every time they had a showing of newly made student films, his were the ones that got people excited. But, of course, he had never before made a movie for a studio. When you get to the big leagues, it isn't so much whether people say, "My goodness, what an insightful artist!" It's whether you induce them to buy lots and lots of tickets.

Anyway, Kelley got an interview set up. So one hot summer day he and I rode across the Cahuenga Pass, angled down the Lankershim exit, and drove onto the Universal lot.

We asked the guards at the gate where to find George Lucas, but they didn't even know who the hell he was. Eventually, this sweaty guy pushing a cartload of electrical cables and spotlights pointed us in the right direction. We found Lucas in a little house trailer set up on blocks over in a dusty corner of the backlot. There was no air conditioning, so that trailer was a sweat box.

As soon as we arrived, a nice secretary lady said, "Mr. Lucas is running a little late, but he'd like you to look over these for a few minutes before your meeting."

And, with that, she handed us two copies of a script labeled *American Graffiti*. Now, I knew what an American was, but I wasn't too sure where Graffitis came from.

Also, I'd never been around a movie studio before, and I had no idea how they did things. It was new territory for Kelley, too, but he was doing a better job of remaining casual. Personally, I was going crazy.

I flipped my copy open and tried to look real professional as I read the first page. I rifled ahead to a place near the middle, then I jumped around to another spot, and another. On almost every page I kept finding the oddest thing—"Wolfman Jack says this . . . " "Wolfman Jack says that . . . "

It made me very nervous.

"Don," I said, "can we step outside for a minute to talk?" He looked at me and then at the secretary, and she just gave us a honey-sweet smile, as if to say, "You folks do whatever you like. We'll be right here."

Once we got out a little ways from the trailer, I said, "Hey, man, do you see how they got my name all over this script?"

"Yeah! Isn't that great!"

"I don't know, man. I mean, how much money do you think I gotta give them?"

"What do you mean?"

"This is a lot of publicity for me. They must want some money for it, right?"

"I don't believe they want your money, Wolf. I believe what they want is for you to play the role of Wolfman Jack. It looks like you're going to play yourself."

"You mean they want to *pay* me to be in this film?"

221

"I believe that's how it works—if you get past the interview, that is."

So now that I understood the movie business, we went back in to meet our fate.

George Lucas turned out to be one of the easiest people to talk to that I've ever met in my life. He was just twenty-seven years old then, a short, wiry, sort of Scotch-Irish-looking guy, who had grown up in a California Central Valley farm town called Modesto. He'd spent all his teenage years cruising and being zonked out about hot cars, rock 'n' roll music, and curvy teenage girls all at the same time, and now he wanted to make a movie about those coming-of-age nights and torn-up emotions over wondering whether you'd ever get laid and what the hell you were going to do with your life.

To put across such a big spectrum of universal emotions, he was going to need a large number of characters. That meant he had to find a way to tie all the different characters' stories together, into a single, unified package.

His idea was to have a disc jockey who is a shadowy, mysterious figure. Because he came through all their car radios, spouting patter and being kind of the unseen life of the party, the DJ was involved with all the characters in the story. So he wanted me to be the needle and thread that sewed everything together.

George told me that when he was in high school, he and his friends used to cruise the streets, listening to my broadcasts on XERB, and sometimes the signal would go in and out, which gave it a kind of mystical, ethereal quality. Some of the kids thought I was flying around in a plane while I did the show, just staying out of reach of the authorities.

I mentioned before that I had a long span of being

sick, right in the middle of my childhood, and that was my first step in becoming more stuck on radio. Well, George Lucas told us something about himself that was similar but more intense.

It happened right before his high school graduation. He was a marginal student. His head was always someplace else instead of schoolwork. He had this cheesy Fiat coupe that he'd stripped down to make it even lighter and punched up the half-pint engine to its absolute limits for racing.

One afternoon he made a run to the town library from his family's house out in the country. On his way back, just as he was about to turn up the driveway, along came one of his buddies in a big-ass Chevy Impala. George didn't see him coming. He cranked into the turn, and his flyweight little Fiat took the full force of the Chevy. In about half an instant, little George and his little car were both wrapped around a nearby tree.

The smash-up was so gruesome, it made the front page of the next day's *Modesto Bee*. George was a mess. People thought he wasn't going to make it.

Lying in that hospital bed for the next several days made him think real, real hard about what mattered most to him, and what he wanted to do with the rest of his life. Like I had done, in my own kind of juvenile delinquent way, he decided to concentrate on something he loved.

For him it was movies. The wreck where he almost died was the start of his life.

His high school grades were too low to get him into a regular college or university, so he went to Modesto Junior College and eventually blasted his way into the University of Southern California.

While he was there, he got the idea to do a documentary on me. Not because he knew me, which he didn't, but because he was fascinated by the idea of how people can have a relationship with a disc jockey, listening to him at work or after school, day after day, until that DJ becomes part of their life, practically a friend. Sometimes, pretty much their only friend.

This was in 1967, when I'd only been in L.A. for about a year, and he didn't know how to get in touch with me. Or maybe he showed up at the station looking like a teenage fan and "Bob Smith" the station manager chased him off.

At any rate, Lucas hooked up his film instead with a very popular guy, Bob Hudson, whose nickname on the air was "Emperor Hudson." The result was a twenty-minute reel called *The Emperor*. Even though another one of his films, a science fiction movie called *THX 1138: 4EB*, went on to win a prize at the National Student Film Festival, *The Emperor* was overwhelmingly the best-liked film of Lucas's student days.

By the time our interview was over, I had agreed to play myself in *American Graffiti* for $3,000. Which is not exactly Jack Nicholson money, you understand, but it was bread I was extremely glad to get at that hard-pressed time, nonetheless.

Back at KDAY, Bob Wilson was upset that I was going to take a few days off during ratings sweeps week. "This is crazy," he said. "Who the hell is George Lucas? He's a nobody!"

Of course, Wilson cooled out eventually. We always ended up getting along real good. And when the time came, he helped out with promotion for *American Graffiti* in a big way.

As it turned out, I had one other connection to Universal Pictures. Because I was still in a ritzy neighborhood, I lived next door to a guy who was a movie producer.

He happened to be good buddies with Ned Tanen, a very up-and-coming young executive who recently had been named chief of production for Universal.

Tanen had a premiere about to happen, and he desperately wanted a lot of young people to see it, to know if the movie would be successful with a young audience. My neighbor told him to call me at KDAY. A free movie sounded like fun, so, between records, I told my listeners that they could get in on the action if they hurried down. As it turned out, so many kids came flocking to get in that they had to turn hundreds of them away.

Tanen called me up the next day and said, "I sure owe you a favor, Wolf. I never realized so much response could come from a radio announcement."

Meanwhile, *American Graffiti* went into production up in Northern California, a little ways above San Francisco. There wasn't much money. They got a lot of the classic cruising cars for the movie by hooking up with local car clubs. Lucas was such a motorhead, he knew how to talk their talk.

None of the actors were well known at all, so none of them were making any kind of significant salary. There was Ron Howard, who hadn't done much of anything since he'd outgrown the role of Opie on the old *Andy Griffith Show*. There was Harrison Ford, who was a rookie supporting himself around Hollywood by doing carpentry jobs. Richard Dreyfuss was the top-ranked guy because he'd had a bit part in *The Graduate* that you'd need a microscope to find.

Paul LeMat was equally unknown. So were Cindy Williams, Candy Clark, and Suzanne Somers.

It had to be that way. The movie's total budget wasn't enough money to cover Marlon Brando's lunch tab.

Most of my "screen time" in the movie is when my

voice is coming out of dashboard speakers, giving dedications and cueing up essential rock 'n' roll hits like "Ain't That a Shame," "Rock Around the Clock," "Why Do Fools Fall in Love," "Johnny B. Goode," "Get a Job," "Surfin' Safari," and so on.

As a matter of fact, the *American Graffiti* soundtrack album is out on CD now. If you love oldies, it's about as good a collection as you'll find.

Lucas and I spent dozens of hours listening to tapes of my old radio shows, picking out dedication calls and ad-lib bits that he thought were gems, so we could use them on the soundtrack.

It took two days to shoot the scene where Richard Dreyfuss comes out to the lonely radio station and tries to get a message put on the air, to connect him with a mysterious blonde girl he saw riding past in a white Thunderbird.

Dreyfuss's character, Curt, has this belief that the Wolfman has the power to make it happen. But he's taken aback when he discovers the mighty voice of the airwaves is coming from someone who is pretty much just a normal human being.

"Gee," he says, "I've known you all my life, but you're not at all what I expected."

"You'll find that applies to a lot of people," I tell him.

In radio, your performance is mainly just "stand and deliver." You improvise all the time. It was a little unusual for me to be working movie-style, doing the exact same thing over and over again in search of the perfect take. Dreyfuss was more tuned in to it. He kept looking for different little angles to take to put more life into the scene.

One improvised thing I can take credit for out of that whole great picture: the bit where I hand him a melting popsicle and say, "Sticky little mothers, ain't they?"

The rest of the movie belongs to the wizard intelligence of Lucas, and Gloria Katz and Willard Huyck, the folks who conceived and wrote it with him. And the fantastic performances of all those unknowns who went on to be major, major stars and film industry heavyweights. Think for a moment about the kind of money those folks all went on to make, starting with the *Star Wars* series, the *Indiana Jones* pictures, and a few miscellaneous other things like *Parenthood, Close Encounters*, and *The Fugitive*.

Kinda gives you chills, doesn't it?

The great thing about *American Graffiti* is that it didn't just appeal to people who were high schoolers in 1962, the era the picture was set in. If anything, younger people dug it even more. It nailed perfectly the emotions of teenage life—hung up on wanting to be popular, wanting to be loved, and wanting your life to work out in some kind of cool way, different than your parents'.

If you think about it, except for my character, practically all the grown-up characters in the movie were unbelievably dorky. And that's how everybody feels about grown-ups when they're sixteen, seventeen, eighteen years old, isn't it?

The budget was exhausted when the movie was finished, and Lucas himself was totally tapped out. He didn't have enough money in his jeans to throw a set of recapped tires on the beat-up silver Camaro he was driving at that time.

Meanwhile, Universal was real uptight about the movie. Even Dreyfuss admitted he didn't think it'd make a dime.

Folks told me that at the first preview, which they held up in San Francisco, Ned Tanen said he hated the movie. Coppola got so mad at him that he whipped out his checkbook and offered to personally buy it away from the studio.

All in all, Universal was getting pretty sick of the whole deal.

On May 15, 1973, there was a preview in L.A. I got on the air at KDAY and helped them draw a big crowd of young folks. Coppola and Tanen were still fighting, but this was one of the wildest, best-loved movie premieres anybody had ever been to. The young people were absolutely crazy for *American Graffiti*—the cars, the tunes, the look, the emotional pull. Fox and Paramount heard about how it went down and they both told Universal, "If you don't want to release it, we sure do!"

Universal went ahead, kind of reluctantly. But they also told Lucas that they were no longer interested in that idea he'd been pestering them to do next, that far-fetched story about a kid named Luke Skywalker who teams up with a space cowboy named Han Solo and a Princess named Leia to save the galaxy from the bad guys.

And that's how Universal let *Star Wars*—and several billion dollars—slip right out of their fingers.

Anyway, my manager and I dug *American Graffiti*, and we realized that the better the movie did, the more people would see my face on the silver screen. Which had to be great for my career.

Tanen was still a friend. We told him that we wanted to make promotional appearances on behalf of *American Graffiti* at our own expense. He generously gave us boxes of *American Graffiti* record albums and some posters. We mapped out a blitzkrieg tour of ten major market areas, setting up giveaway contests for the albums and other stuff.

Other than what we did, there was practically nothing happening for advance publicity. When the execs at Universal checked ticket sales for the movie's first week, the cities we'd gone to were way ahead of the rest of the country. From that, they started to believe in the movie a little more.

Of course, *American Graffiti* went on to become one of the most successful pictures of all time. And of all the top-grossing pictures in Hollywood history, it's the only one that was made real, real cheap.

It didn't take the country by storm, it just did very good business and kept gradually getting stronger. Then it stayed strong for a very long time. When the 1973 Academy Award nominations came out, it was up for Best Picture, Best Direction, Best Original Screenplay, Best Supporting Actress (Candy Clark), and Best Film Editing. The New York Film Critics gave it their Best Screenplay Award, and it also won a Golden Globe as Best Comedy of the Year.

When things started turning out so great, George Lucas did me one of the greatest favors anybody ever did for me in my life.

Around the time that *American Graffiti* had just made its first $20 million in profits, one day I looked in the afternoon mail and found a letter from George Lucas and Gary Kurtz. In it, they outright gave me the perpetual rights to a small percentage. I just about had a heart attack!

Just two years before, when XERB got pulled out from under me, I felt like no one in history had ever gotten such a raw deal. All of a sudden, Lucas and Kurtz had completely overturned the rules of normalcy in Hollywood and had convinced me nobody had ever gotten such a sweet deal.

The first three checks from *American Graffiti* paid off all my old XERB debts once and for all. Then the checks kept on coming for a long time—about $150,000 to $200,000 every six months.

Believe it or not, it's been over twenty years since that

movie came out. To this day, we still get a lovely little royalty check every once in a while. George and Gary chased the wolf away from the Wolfman's door.

Naturally, my former sort-of manager, the one who originally told the *American Graffiti* people to shove it, was no longer part of the organization. As a sort of going away present, he decided to do a number on me.

For two years, this guy had been driving a Cadillac Eldorado that I owned. He racked up more than a thousand dollars' worth of parking tickets all over town, but he also knew several cops and they kept letting him slide.

One night I had a gig at the Playboy Club down in Orange County. My man called his buddies, who alerted the local cops that some L.A. bastard who wouldn't pay his parking tickets would be leaving the Playboy Club at one o'clock in the morning. Then he parked across the street to enjoy watching the whole thing go down.

That night was the only time I've ever spent in jail— which is remarkable considering some of the stuff I've done in my time. Lou drove down and paid the tickets, but I was cussing up a storm and the longer I ranted, the longer they kept me locked up. Sunrise was peeking through the bars by the time I finally got free.

Of course, if those cops knew how much toot I was doing around that time, I might *still* be a guest of the Orange County criminal justice system.

In the meantime, out in New York City, something nice was happening that I didn't even know about. Don Imus, on a morning-time WNBC radio show, was doing Wolfman Jack bits and also crazy preacher bits. He called me up one day just to say he was a fan. Over the course of a few weeks, we became real good friends over the phone.

WNBC had a problem on its hands. They wanted to have the top-ranked evening-time rock 'n' roll show in the city, and all the fantastic ad revenue that would come from being number one. But there was a guy named Cousin Brucie on WABC that kept beating whoever they put on the air against him.

Imus, who to this day remains one of New York City's favorite radio people, advised the WNBC honchos that they ought to give this wild wolf guy out on the West Coast a try. Mr. Perry Bascomb, a very nice man who didn't deserve the heartaches I was soon going to give him, started calling me up and trying to talk serious business.

All this was real flattering, but I just didn't want to go to New York at that time. My recent success had not only pulled me out of debt, it had given me something known in the show business world as "fuck you money."

A performer might spend years, perhaps even a whole career, desperately taking anything that's offered. Sometimes even stuff they hate. But when you've got your "fuck you money" together, you only have to take jobs that strike you as really desirable.

To stall off WNBC, I said that I would meet with Mr. Bascomb in a beachfront hotel down in San Diego—if they would buy the rooms. When they agreed, I went down there with about six rowdy friends, enough cocaine for everybody, and a disposition to party.

I kept Bascomb sitting around for two days while I was getting high and having a good time. Finally, at three o'clock in the morning, I rang his room and said, "I'm ready now. Meet me out by the swimming pool in fifteen minutes."

The hotel's pool area was deserted. I waited at a table under an umbrella with my vial of cocaine, a mirror, and a straw. When Bascomb sat down, I offered him some. "I don't do that stuff," he said disgustedly.

"You do what you wanna do," I said. "I'm gonna do

this." So this big NBC executive, who had never been high in his life, sat down before a rude, crazy-in-the-head, coke-snorting disc jockey to extend a generous offer. And I was thinking, "I've got the sonovabitch now."

Before long, we'd cut a deal for the most money I had ever made in my radio life: $350,000 a year. That was a pretty good boost from my $18,000 at KDAY.

Plus I would have my own limousine to pick me up, along with a secretary, a personal bodyguard, and my own private, well-ventilated room at Rockefeller Center where I could smoke my grass. Because, Bascomb explained, people came through the building all the time on guided tours, and the radio studio had a big window, right on the hallway where all these folks paraded by. It would be bad for NBC's image for the tourists walking by to see, night after night, a bearded, howling maniac with his eyes lit up by the glow of a smoldering doobie.

Chapter Thirteen

Not long before we went to New York, David Bowie came through L.A. on his premiere American tour. These were his "Ziggy Stardust and His Spiders from Mars" days. His people approached us about hosting a big party in his honor—sort of "old-time rock 'n' roll meets the new kid on the block."

We decided to go all out. The guest list was a hundred-person mix of music stars and TV, radio, record, and movie executives. We rented a coffin, put it by the front door, and hired a guy in a vampire costume to spring out and greet each guest as they arrived. A band was playing in the living room and out in back we were screening *Blacula*, a truly classic bad horror movie that was brand-new at the time. Check it out, 'cause if you like it, there's a sequel that's even worse—*Scream, Blacula, Scream!*

For the first few hours, the biggest hit of the party was a little robot. You could talk to it and it would answer your questions and also serve drinks. A technician was standing by to explain how to talk to the robot. It was a short little machine, so you had to bend over to carry on a conversation with it.

A woman who wrote for *People* magazine just thought that robot was the most marvelous thing she'd ever seen in her life. "Who is the inventor?" she kept asking me. "Is he here tonight? Do you think he'd like to be interviewed for *People?*"

"Geez, I don't know, lady," I said. "Maybe you should ask the robot."

A little later on, she went off to find a bathroom. When she opened the door, there was some guy sitting on the edge of the tub wearing a headset, talking in a science fiction-type robot voice. Suddenly she put it all together: our "technician" who was working with the robot was tipping this guy off, telling him what to say with secret signals. It was all just an elaborate joke.

She got all furious and stormed out. Folks were trailing after her, saying, "It was all in fun," but she never spoke to any of us again.

Too bad for her. She would've found out how David Bowie stayed so thin. The party lasted about twenty-four hours. Different activities were going on at different times, but one thing was constant—a line of women standing in front of the door of a small bathroom near the back of the house. David had disappeared in there, and he spent practically the whole party entertaining those women consecutively on a one-on-one basis. Sometime late the next day I went in there to use the can and found David and a woman curled up in each other's arms, sound asleep.

Somebody told me that he didn't do as well later on, when he went over to Hollywood High in hopes of picking up some younger admirers. The girls there didn't go for him. Maybe they were jealous. The dress David was wearing was so much more chic and expensive than anything they could afford.

Anyway, getting back to WNBC in New York: Have you ever had a part of your life be so overstimulated and overeventful that you can't remember some of the most basic facts about it? Like where it was that you lived?

Lou and I just put our heads together, and it took us fifteen minutes to recall the name of the Long Island suburb we lived in during the frantic year when I did the evening slot on WNBC in New York and also flew back and forth regularly from Los Angeles to tape *The Midnight Special.*

It was Brookville. Only ten or twelve miles from where I grew up, but a thousand times more swanky.

Before we departed L.A., John and Yoko sent us a nice letter that kind of foreshadowed the unusual tone of our upcoming New York adventure.

Dear Wolfman and Wolfwoman, velkomen to n.y. (when you do)! look forward to seeing/hearing you in fun city, you will liven up the air/waves. . . . .

this letter will self explode in 3 yrs, to protect your innocence, in case of failure, smoke it; we can arrange for your place to be bugged before you get here, at NO EXTRA CHARGE, mark a cross in the appropriate spot below.

(yes) . . . .

(no) . . . .

if undecided put a urine specimen in a small box of kornflakes, and mail it to your local

congressmenwomenchilddogcatfleagoat;ETC

yours in heat (n.y. style)

john and yoko (them)

235

ps.what time is it?high over central park!
yours
apparently,
johnyokoonolennonoyokojohnonolennonoyokono
ps. excuse spilling i deaf
pps. anything you think may be taken down and used as
evidence

John stamped the letter repeatedly with "THE GREAT
SEAL of NUTOPIA," which depicted a great seal, of
course, balancing a ball on his nose.

Like I said, John Lennon just loved to go for long rides
down his own brain stem.

Lou and I leased an incredible mansion there in Brookville, a baronial, splendid, sumptuous, walled and gated,
two-story, columned Long Island estate—the multimil-
lion dollar kind you see advertised in breathless terms in
the back pages of *The New York Times Magazine*.

"Casa del Lobo" became its official name—at least for
the duration.

Besides Lou and the kids and myself, and a secretary,
cook, and two maids, Casa del Lobo was populated by
a constantly changing pack of hangers-on. Folks I met in
bars and at parties. Losers, Lou called them, and they
drove her nuts. Sometimes there were fifteen to twenty
of them. Most of them were ripping us off one way or
another, but the work pace was so intense and the money
was coming in so fast that we couldn't keep track of
anything. It was the wackiest, wildest time of my life.

There were two guys around Casa del Lobo, though,
who definitely earned their keep.

Dooger was my bodyguard, a muscular six foot seven
karate expert who could single-handedly take down a
whole gang, but whose mind had stopped maturing
somewhere around the age of fifteen.

You've heard of muttonchop sideburns? Man, these guys had the whole leg of lamb on their faces! This was one of my typical road shows, bringing rhythm and blues to small towns all around California.

Psychedelic Wolf! Two bucks for a night of trippy lights and thumping music. When we arrived, the Lancaster Roller Rink was rockin'.

That's the great Les McCann on the right, enjoying a friendly hug. The little guy in the glasses? A fresh young upstart movie guy named George Lucas. We spent a whole lot of hours picking his favorite "Wolfisms" for *American Grafitti*. *(Jeff Dunas)*

My first acting gig, and I'm paired with an emerging heavyweight like Richa

Dreyfuss. Lucas said, "Just be calm and be yourself," but I was excited all over.

DEWEY HIGH SCHOOL
YEAR BOOK HONOR ROLL

Hang Loose! Your l'ol buddy Big John '60

Roses are Red Violets are Blue Tulips are Yellow Carol

Hey! Hey, don't forget to be bad and take me with you! Falfa

JOHN MILNER '60
Auto Mechanic

CAROL MORRISON '65
Art

BOB FALFA '60
Agriculture

"R.T.O.B. Uncle asked that Curt Sto..."

To a real swell kid Have a nice summer. Always, Laurie

To one of the Best People I'll ever Know! LUCK, Steve

CURTIS HENDERSON '62
Science

LAURIE HENDERSON '63
History
Head Cheer Leader

STEVE BOLANDER '62
English
Class President

Good Luck... from a hot cat to a cool jewel Toad '63 (I hope!)

XOXOXOXO

How's your Boogaloo?

TERRY "TOAD" FIELDS '63
Business

DEBBIE MEDWAY '61
Home Economics

WOLFMAN JACK '51
Finger Popping

I'm not crazy about this Wolfman likeness, but it was pretty cool to be on the same page, and in the same movie, as Dreyfuss, Harrison Ford, Paul LeMat, Candy Clark, Ron Howard, and the rest when they were in the early stages of their fine, fine, superfine careers.

You can't get a more impressive on-air guest than this guy. Dick Clark took over my spot one afternoon. James Brown was another friend who liked to help me out by playing disc jockey for a day. *(Jeff Dunas)*

(top) Murray the K, "the Fifth Beatle," was yet another star disc jockey who came calling at KDAY. Between him, Dick Clark, Don Imus, and Howard Stern, I've rubbed elbows with some of radio's all-time greats. *(Jeff Dunas)* (facing page) John Lennon lived in a very special world. It was like his imagination was an electric guitar, and he played tunes on it all day long.

dear **Wolfman and Wolfwoman**

velkomen to n.y.(when you do)!look forward to seing/hearing you
in fun city.you will liven up the air/waves!dont come via the desert!
the 'thing'might follow you here....we are now ensconced at I.W.72.nd at
apt.72.nynynynynynynyn.TEL.............

        this letter will self explode in 3 yrs,to protect
your innocence.in case of failure,smoke it;!we can arrange for your place
to be bugged before you get here,at NO EXTRA CHARGE.mark a cross in the
appropriate spot below.

        (yes)....................

        (no).........-...........

              •

if undecided put a urine specimen in a small box of kornflakes,and mail it to your
local congressmenwomenchilddogcatfleagoat;ETC

        yours in heat(n.y.style)

      john and yoko(   )
ps.what time is it?high over central park!

      yours

      aparrently,

     johnyokoonolennonoyokojohnonolennonoyokoo

pps.excuse spilling i deaf.

(to boogie or not to boogie,that is the christian...)
pps.anything you think may be taken doen and used in various evidence against the fi

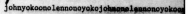

Cousin Brucie was actually a real nice guy, but publicity is vital and the WNBC brass thought this tombstone would land us on the front page. They were right!

Emceeing *The Midnight Special* was a gig that brought me together with all the leading people in music over a multi-year span. If producer Burt Sugarman ever releases the old videotapes, it'll be a great time capsule of '70s music and fashion.

Tony Randall and Jack Klugman were solid pros, but I kept getting distracted by those tasty boogaloo dancers. This, of course, was *The Odd Couple*.

One of my finest TV delights was doing a skit with the late, great
Redd Foxx.

When I was a kid, "a square" was the worst thing you could call somebody. But being a Hollywood Square was something else—and good for exposure, besides.

After brother Brian took a sudden hike, Carl Wilson of the Beach Boys
stepped up into the interview chair.

I've always been honored that black people have accepted me as someone who valued their culture, and took to it with all the heart and soul I had. To be made an honorary Temptation just knocked me out!

Mike Howard was my on-the-air sidekick, a talented young man of a thousand personalities, all of them spectacularly warped.

Every night, as more normal New Yorkers were boarding their buses, trains, subways, and cars, Mike, Dooger, and I would slide into an NBC-chartered Cadillac limo and cruise from Long Island to Rockefeller Center. We'd wave to the family, friends, and what-have-you folks out on the broad lawn as the gates of the mansion closed behind us electronically, then we'd head west on the Long Island Expressway.

Mike and I would share a doobie, usually our only chemical misbehavior of the night, at least until the show was done.

As much as I loved getting my head bent in those days, I was concerned about staying in control enough to do the show. It could be, in fact, that that professionalism policy saved my life. Without it, I might've stayed ripped twenty-four hours a day.

Dooger didn't do any drugs. When he needed to relax, he'd walk out of the studio and go over to Times Square, hoping to find some bad guys hassling good guys. When the opportunity presented itself, Dooger would step in and bust up the nasty people, then he'd come back to WNBC feeling all refreshed.

Sometimes, Mike might have a little bit of a hangover from the previous night. After all, the various treats of Manhattan were very much ours for the taking. And as soon as we went off the air, we generally took what the Big Apple offered.

For whatever reason, some of those nights when we were driving in I'd feel a need to snap him into the present moment, to set a tone for our night's work.

"Mike," I'd say, "do you see all those people headed home in their cars? Do you see all those lights glowing in the towns as we pass by, and in the great city that lies ahead? When you open up that microphone, *all* those people can listen to you. And all of them will want to have fun. They are poor, poor folks who have been having a hard day, carrying around heavy burdens. We must relieve them of their burdens and let them have some peace and happiness and good times."

When the driver had us right on the edge of New York City, I'd tell him to pull over.

"Everybody out of the car," I'd say. Mike, Dooger, the driver, and I would all stand on the side of the road, staring at the cityscape rising before us. I'd raise my hands over my head dramatically, like a Pentecostal preacher. "Before your eyes here we have over ten million people sitting in front of us. They're all going to be in the palms of our hands tonight. They're gonna want to be with us, because we're gonna make 'em happy. Feel 'em, man. Feel 'em! They're out there."

The driver would be embarrassed, but first Mike and then Dooger would raise their hands like supplicants who were about to receive a religious experience. The people driving by would be staring at us. Mike would clap his hands together, gaze to heaven, and start chanting in the high-pitched voice of a Hindu mystic character he'd concocted for the radio show.

"Oh, my God," I'd say, "I feel the spirit coming upon me! Here he is, the exalted Maharishi Yogi of Berra! Greet him, ladies and gentlemen. Bow your heads! Put your knees to the ground!"

"Peace, Wolfman, peace. Tenk you veddy, veddy much."

"I know you have a wonderful philosophical thing to tell us about. What is the answer to the great human dilemma of our times?"

Mike would fake several mouthfuls of authentic-sounding Hindu gibberish, and we'd all crack up and then pile back in the limo and be on our way.

But even though we joked about it, we really could feel a vibration coming back at us. It was the collective psychic hum of Manhattan, something jittering out there, vibrant, like it was ready to be saddled up and taken on most any kind of ride we wanted to imagine.

Me and Mike were the tripmasters. We had at our fingertips the facilities of a radio station that was 50,000 watts, nondirectional, covering all of New York, upstate New York, Long Island, thirty-seven states around that area. There must have been twenty million people that could listen to us.

Anyway, my WNBC format was to be Top 40, the same as Cousin Brucie's. I couldn't dip into my down-in-the-alley, roots-of-rock 'n' roll tunes to establish an exotic atmosphere for the show. Therefore, making people know *The Wolfman Jack Show* was different from Cousin Brucie's required that Mike and me had to be very quick, weird, and funny, thirty hours a week.

There's a big problem with that kind of job description: being crazy isn't something that you can easily switch on and off like an electric appliance. It's more a way of life. And when you live it to the hilt, like we did, it can generate a lot of friction and wear and tear on yourself and all the people around you.

Especially on your spouse and your employers.

Our craziness is what turned otherwise mild-mannered Perry Bascomb into Mr. Vicious, which is the nickname we invented for him. Another long-suffering guy was Pat Whitley, our program director. We called him "Numb," short for "Numb Nuts."

Both of them had good hearts, and they both probably

spent a lot of behind-the-scenes time smoothing over some of my behavior with the people at the top of the organization. Because every once in a while NBC would threaten to sue me for exposing them to possible lawsuits with the things I said or did on the air. I'd have to have my lawyers talk to their lawyers and offer promises that I wouldn't corrupt the morals of New York City.

Finally, everybody would agree to be cool once more and stop rattling legal papers.

The only reason they didn't fire us outright is that Mike and I, within a few weeks, delivered exactly what they wanted—the most popular nighttime show in New York. We hit the top of the ratings. So our craziness was stirring up plenty of positive cash flow.

The price they had to pay was learning how to live with us.

Most of my life, I had either been my own boss, or else I had worked for bandit operations. And, like the Wicked One, Wilson Pickett, it was generally the midnight hour when my love came tumbling down. All of a sudden, here I was carrying prime time on the flagship station of the National Broadcasting Corporation, in the most important city in the world. Which means that, while carrying out my mission of being full-tilt loony, I was surrounded by corporate suits of the highest rank.

Still, the deal I made when Mr. Vicious and I sat out by the pool in San Diego stipulated that the network would accept what Wolfman Jack did and go with it.

Prior to my first night on WNBC, we hired a tombstone company to make up a granite tombstone, and a crew went out that first night and set it in cement in front of ABC's headquarters. It said: "Cousin Brucie's Days Are Numbered—WOLFMAN JACK IS ON THE PROWL."

ABC needed a jackhammer to remove that calling card.

The Temptations dropped by on the first night, along with lots of other music stars. They made me an Honorary Temptation. The only white one in the world, I might add. Aretha sent a telegram saying, "It's good to have soul in the city." Somebody with the name Robert Zimmerman sent the message "It's all over now, Baby Bruce." Lots of other folks sent telegrams, from the Everly Brothers to the Skyliners, Mott the Hoople, Little Richard, Bette Midler, Elton John, and Harold Melvin & the Blue Notes.

Time sent a reporter around to check out the scene. The way the feature came out, I think the guy caught a fever: "Eyes popping, goatee aquiver, paunch abounce, his whole body keeping time with the music, Wolfman Jack seems to live every song as a new experience. . . . He invests radio with almost mystical powers. . . ."

On a typical night, Mike and I would be dragging our mystical powers into the RCA Building at Rockefeller Center just as the weary folks who worked day jobs there were pouring out. We'd go up in the elevators to our floor, step around the corner, and see the news man, Sam Hall, in front of the big glass window where tourists could watch us genuine radio animals in our natural environment.

Sam had one of those impressive radio voices, very sonorous, so the news flowed out like it was being delivered by God's own spokesperson. But in real life Sam was a just slightly reformed hippie.

We entered through a side door and took our seats by a big console, facing a couple of microphones. Our engineer, Bobby, was just a few feet away. Big record bins were within reach of Mike's chair.

Bobby was one of the greatest engineers I'd ever been around. In fact, when I signed on I said that I wanted to have the best engineer on the whole WNBC crew. Well, the union guys took it seriously, and they got together and voted Bobby in. Boy, he was a great pro. You didn't have to worry about anything. He could read your mind, find sound effects to fit right into the bits you were doing, always delivered with fantastic timing.

Sam Hall would be trying to finish the news with dignity and we'd be trying to bust his composure, handing him phony news releases: "FLASH—Four bales of top-grade marijuana washed up on the shores of Long Island this afternoon and were immediately taken to Casa del Lobo for analysis. More on this story as it develops."

It was the tail end of the war in Vietnam. The headlines of the day were all about Watergate and Richard Nixon's and Spiro Agnew's disgraces. A lot of heavy things were happening. A lot of people were in pain. The news would come on and remind everyone. That used to drive us crazy. We'd get 'em up, then the news would bum everybody out.

Sam Hall's news segment would take up five minutes at the top of each hour. Out of the news they would go into a jingle, then right back into music. We'd always open the hour with a hit record. Well, that was a time when lots of hit records ran from four to six minutes long. So there were usually ten or twelve minutes at the top of each hour when Mike and I could sit on the fire escape and watch the cars go by while we plotted out what we were going to do on the show.

We had a whole bank of telephones. Once the show got going, they'd be going like a psychedelic light show. And when you're working in New York, the audience is so diverse. Calls came in from Harlem, from the Upper East Side, from the Jersey Shore. Sooner or later there'd be someone who appealed to Mike's finely honed sense of abnormalcy. His eyes would flash, he'd clap a hand over the mouthpiece and say, "Wolf, we *got one!*"

242

When you talk to, say, a hundred people in a night, you're always going to find at least two or three really strange individuals. Especially in New York. Pound for pound, New Yorkers are about the funniest people in the world.

We would go into anything with these callers. Anybody that was being a smart-ass, I always used it and made it work in reverse, to get them laughing. Sometimes they'd get hot under the collar, but I always smoothed it out in some kind of way.

There was a device on the board that gave us a seven-second delay, in case somebody's language got too salty. One night the device was broken. Halfway through the show some lady called to say, "I don't want to hear any of this vulgar goddamn cursing on the radio." A minute later, somebody else called up and said, "Hey, lady, fuck you. I don't wanna listen to your shit neither."

This is not the kind of content the Federal Communications Commission wants heard over America's airwaves. WNBC fixed the seven-second gizmo first thing next morning.

Of course, the DJs themselves were out of whack a lot more often than the machines. One night I got a real obnoxious caller who inspired me to say, "Sir, I want you to go over and put your radio on the floor."

"Yeah? What do you want me to do that for?"

"I want you to squat on that radio."

"What did you say to me?"

"I want you to stick your radio up your ass. Goodbye!" BANG!

The next day, management handed me another lawsuit. "Did you tell someone to stick the radio up his ass? How can you do that on NBC radio? Are you trying to get our license yanked?"

"Naw, I just got carried away."

243

WNBC was the straightest place I ever worked for, so I must've felt I had to overcompensate with naughtiness. Just like when my folks tried to straighten me out by sending me to the Quaker school, and I disrupted the meditation hour with poo-poo jokes. There was nobody on the border radio stations to censure me, but I actually became the loosest and lewdest ever when I got to the big time. Funny how that works.

Maybe I have an irresistible urge to piss off authority figures. One of my favorite characters on the show was Pervo the Clown, who used to try to get warm and friendly with little boys: "You like clowns, don't you, Johnny? Pervo has a trick that I bet you've never seen before."

A long time later I realized where I got Pervo the Clown from. He was a twisted, disguised memory of that wino priest who once lifted me up on the table and took a pass at my goodies.

Pervo wasn't in the best of taste. Neither were very many of the other fifty-odd characters who "visited" our show. But we used to get calls from people who said they heard some of our routines while they were driving and they started laughing so hard that they had to pull off the road.

All our bits were composed spontaneously. I'd say something like "Mike, you got thirty seconds, man. We're gonna do a Willie D., then go into this other record here."

Willie D. was a black garage attendant who wrote poetry. His versology ran to things like:

> Have you ever seen
> The baddest of the bad,
> The meanest of the mean?
> They eat pizza of the mind

Two bites makes them stand up
And speak from their behind . . .

When it was time to concoct a bit, Mike would run
into the next room for a few seconds and write something
down, and then dash back just in time to deliver it as
the record ended.

We did an episode every night on what was happening
at Casa del Lobo. Real eerie sound effects, like vampires
and werewolves were prowling around there.

I'll admit this: not every show was choice. Some nights
we were as dead as Clancy's nuts. But I'd say 80 percent
were great. We'd get an idea, we'd describe the situation,
then we'd go right into it. Let it flow.

Maybe the humor was a little juvenile, but for the
audience, we were a stand-in for all their desires to be
naughty, and to slip loose from the rules that everybody
has to go by. It was like we were getting away with what
they wanted to get away with. And that's kind of what
people want from a rock 'n' roll disc jockey. They're
stuck in a classroom or an office, or behind a pile of
housework, but their alter ego gets to play loud music
and crack risqué jokes.

The people who tuned in would like to turn around
and just be silly like us. They had to settle for getting
the vicarious feeling of doing what we were doing.

That's why every classroom is going to have a class
clown, to express everybody else's frustration with following the rules. We were the class clowns for a whole
city and parts beyond.

There were always people coming to the studio, wanting to get in on the party. All kinds of illegal stuff would
come walking through the door, and there you'd have
it. It was like someone with a magic wand was making

it all happen. But, like they say, you've got to be careful what you wish for, 'cause you just might get it.

In order to get up and see us, folks had to go through two security guards downstairs. And then they would come through turnstiles and come up the elevator and get off. Walk around a bend, all gray walls. And they would see a big sign that said WNBC. Big glass doors. There was a recording studio for shows and a live studio on the right-hand side. On the left side there were pictures of the jocks and the other people on WNBC.

Just to get up there to look in the window, if they didn't have their name on a list downstairs, they had to have a good hustle going. So they were usually really slick people—pimps and pushers pretty often. Somebody had to go out to the glass doors and let them in.

Of course, New York people are the greatest hustlers in the world. All of a sudden out of nowhere, a naked girl would appear, saying somebody sent her as a token of their friendship. Later on, somebody else would fall by with choice drugs.

During a long record cut, Mike and I would head over to Numb's office, get out on the fire escape and figure out how we'd get rid of all the people in the studio.

One night, a guy who wanted to impress us with his access to the finer things in life showed up in the company of a half dozen ladies of the evening. "Wolf," he said, "how d'ya like these?" The women smiled at me and pirouetted around the broadcast booth, giving me front and back perspectives. It was quality.

"Well, they look very nice."

"Okay, girls. He likes you . . ."

And with that they stripped down and started dancing to the music—Sly and the Family Stone, as I recall—and sitting on our laps and generally being squirmy, lively, and companionable.

The folks who were tuned in to the show heard a lot of giggles and squeals in the spaces between songs, with me saying, "Oh, my gracious, but you won't believe what's goin' on here in the studio. Five or six young ladies here have decided to model their birthday suits for the Wolfman, and every time they start to giggle, they start to jiggle, y'understand?"

We described on the air everything we were doing. And everybody thought it was a fantasy. The girls were moaning and cooing, and I was adding sound effects, too. Any kind of sound you could want, I had on tape. And I had it from different distances, too, so you couldn't tell if we were fooling around live or just punching up cassettes and doing a bit.

NBC brass probably thought it was another Wolfman goof. But this time it was happening for real. And Mr. Vicious wasn't fooled.

Suddenly we got a call from one of the first-floor security guards. Perry Bascomb had come all the way from home to check out our antics. He'd never visited the program before. I guess he knew the sound effects library well enough to be aware that our "fantasy" was for real.

"Grab your clothes, ladies," I said. "You gotta get out of sight right now!"

The women snatched up all the clothes from the floor and split for the nearest broom closet, offices, or whatever nook or cranny they could find. It was a mad scramble, but very exhilarating to watch.

In a couple of minutes they were all out of sight. Two heartbeats later, Mr. Vicious was standing in the studio doorway. From his hand there dangled a skimpy pair of ice-blue panties that he'd found out by the elevator doors. A record was playing, but I had Bobby leave the mike switched on. I pointed to the red warning light that meant "open mike," and put my fingers to my lips. If he

247

had said anything to me, it would've gone out over the airwaves.

His face started getting redder than the warning light. I almost expected steam to vent from each ear, and a sound blast to come out like a factory whistle. He shook a fist at me, then turned around and stormed out, slamming the door.

The hallways at WNBC were very drab and somber-looking. We were always talking about how good it would be to see the place redecorated. One night Mike and I started improvising a bit and I said, "We're painting the studios here while we're doing the show tonight. Look at that wall over there, Mike. Isn't that nice? Kind of a green turquoise look. While I finish another wall, you folks listen to this . . ."

When the next record was over, I hit my right hand back and forth in the palm of my left hand to imitate the sound of a paint brush slapping a wall. "I got this door almost finished here. By the way, if any of you folks out there have any spare paint brushes or extra paint, why not bring 'em up here to the studio? Let's do the whole place!"

Lo and behold, within an hour about twenty or so different guys showed up with real paint cans, drop-cloths, and everything. Real, honest-to-goodness house painters. They had red paint, pink paint, blue, all sorts of leftover colors.

As they began painting, I described it over the air.

"We're out in the hallway now. Lemme speak to this gentleman in the white cap. Good evening, sir. What's your name?"

"Murphy."

"Tell me, Murphy, how ya doin? Think we can freshen up this hallway?"

"Yup. We got lotsa paint, no problem."

"All right, we're gonna play some Creedence Clearwater now, then we'll come back later and see how you're doing."

We kept that bit rolling all night. All the NBC execs out in radioland must've thought it was real comical. Until they came in the next morning and found that our studio and all the adjacent hallway was a mishmash of chartreuse patches, plus orange, cocoa brown, periwinkle blue, and about twenty-five other miscellaneous revolting colors.

That night's work ended up costing me about $28,000. But it forced them to finally redo the studio, just like everybody had always wanted.

Getting reactions from corporate bigwigs always made the crazy moments more delicious.

One afternoon, Mike and I had a luncheon meeting with Vicious and another exec at a restaurant all the way up at the top of Rockefeller Center. We were on the roof, walking near the ledge, when Mike smiled at us all and simply said, "Excuse me, I have another appointment."

With that, he put two hands on the ledge, hopped up on it and began acting like a tightrope walker. He took three steps, grabbed his nose between two fingers, waved, and hopped straight over the side.

The three of us almost had heart attacks. We couldn't bring ourselves to go over to the edge and look, expecting to see Mike's body fluttering down, story after story, headed for the middle of the street like a busted human kite.

We finally got up the nerve to check out what had happened. There was Mike on a ledge just a few feet below, rubbing a sprained ankle and grinning up at us. "Uh, fellas," he said, "can one of you give me a hand?"

We had to do more than just give him a hand. Somebody had to carry the silly sonovabitch all the way back down to the studio.

That was how much we were up all the time.

It's hard to entertain people with zaniness and yet keep it at the right pitch. It's important to keep your metabolism up and your juices flowing. I was acting a part, a happy-go-lucky guy who was the antidote to the overbearing seriousness of life. No matter how I actually felt, I had to get down to the essence of that personality every day for five hours.

That's the hardest part of working full-time in the happiness business. You can never expose your unhappiness to the audience. They're the people who support you. They're the boss. You take care of them, try to make them as happy as you can.

We were truly making folks happy. WNBC was the best happiness business trip I ever had. We would get something really funny going and there was something zapping back and forth between us and our audience that you could feel in the air. Mike Howard just couldn't sit still sometimes. He'd have to be dancing around. The engineer would feel it, too, and sometimes even the news people and the corporate honchos would come in to experience the feeling together with us.

When the show was done, Mike and I would head off for a night on the town. We had an unbelievable time. No matter how much money NBC was laying on us, people in New York practically wouldn't let us spend a dime.

One of our favorite spots, appropriately enough, was a bar known as Doctor Generosity's. It was over on East 73rd and Third. Mike, Dooger, and I would stroll in there after a show, feeling expansive. We'd step up and order drinks for everyone in the place. Later, I'd ask the bartender what I owed the house. "Your money's no good here," he'd say. I'd argue. I'd pull out a roll of money—in those days I always carried at least $5,000 in my pocket—and peel some bills off. He'd keep shaking his head and refusing.

It was like the Band's lyric in "Cripple Creek": "A drunkard's dream if I ever did see one."

I loved it.

We kept running into a certain guy—it would cost me my kneecaps, if not my life, to tell you his name—whose father was high up in the New York Mafia. Every time we met he would slip a tiny baggie of cocaine into my breast pocket, saying, "A friendship gift from me to you."

A lot of times there were New York Knicks basketball games or other sports broadcasts during my show. We'd be responsible for doing a one-hour show, then we'd have the rest of the night off—with full pay. When the Knicks had a home stand, that kind of mini-vacation happened maybe twice a week. And even with that interruption in my situation, I still maintained my position in the ratings. New York was my oyster.

In clothing stores, I'd go in and pick out a beautiful suit. Something in the latest style, with a ticket that said "$1,500." The clerk would start writing up a bill of sale. Before he got done the manager would snatch the paper out of his hands and tear it up. "We're just happy that you've chosen our store, Wolfman," he'd say. "It's on the house."

The same thing happened at restaurants, lunch counters, and trattorias from Little Italy to the Upper East Side.

Where were all these nice, generous people when I was in a deep, dark financial hole, toting brown bag lunches to a low-paying job?

But that's how it works: When you need help, you're

on your own. As soon as you're well off, everything arrives for free.

What a system!

Anyway, during my year in New York, I got to know everyone from movie stars to some of the upper-echelon people who really run the city. And they all treated me very nicely. The contrast was so extreme—down and out one year and lavished with all kinds of attention and goodies the next. A voice in the back of my head kept saying, "Take it now, baby, 'cause it could all disappear in five minutes."

James Caan was a good friend. About every other week we'd be getting together for a party at his place.

I did party hearty, and sometimes I didn't make it home at night. Which cut down on my commute expenses, but was real displeasing to my wife. We started drifting apart. I was working hard, taking drugs too often, and selfishly glomming on to all the free stuff that was offered. Including, selfish bastard that I am, the free-spirited attentions of some lovely women. I should have been grown up enough to turn it down. Unfortunately, when people every day were shoving tasty stuff right at me, I found I wasn't good at refusing. That created hard times between me and Lou.

She forgave me for my transgressions, and we moved on with our lives . . . but she never let me forget. Still hasn't.

Let me explain Lou in one short story: One winter night she and I and my manager were leaving Madison Square Garden after I'd hosted a big concert. For the first and only time in my career, a mob of people actually started ripping my clothes off my body. There I was, down to skivvies and bare kneecaps, freezing. I had to huddle in the parking lot attendant's shack for warmth.

And some big, meaty guy had grabbed the only part of apparel that hadn't been destroyed, a black, flat-brim cowboy hat. Lou caught sight of him getting away, found a stick, chased this huge guy for two blocks in her high heels, and whacked the beejesus out of him. She returned to the parking lot ten minutes later with the hat in her hands.

That's my Lucy. Sweet, loyal, and pretty, too. You just shouldn't ever mess with her.

At any rate, I wasn't the only WNBC jock who was having trouble staying on the straight and narrow. I understand Don Imus has become a model citizen these days. But back then he used to finish his show, get up from his seat, and go immediately down to this Irish bar in the neighborhood and get totally smashed. Then he'd be back in the building, wandering the halls. Any salesmen or executives that walked by, Imus would buttonhole them one by one, saying, "You're out of work. You're finished. Your job is done here. Clean out your desk. You're fired!"

They were all insecure anyway, so that scared the hell out of them.

Late one morning after I'd been on the town all night I caught up to Imus just after he got back from the Irish place. He was drunk as a lord. "Let's grab a cab and go get some lunch," I said.

We hailed a cab and opened the door. Just then, some rickety old lady came along, held us both at bay with a hardwood walking stick, and stepped in to claim the cab for herself. Imus was so wobbly he was about to fall down. He raised the sole of his shoe to the back of her ass and shoved her all the way across the seat.

"Whoops," I thought, "maybe we should retreat."

I hustled him back into the building and stashed the

both of us in the closet of Numb's office until the cops had come and gone.

Imus is probably bigger than ever today. A couple of years ago he hit some serious health problems and went through about five or six long-term nightmares getting to the other side. He's off booze, gone vegetarian, and he switched over from Top 40 to serious talk radio— but always with that unpredictable Don Imus edge. This is a guy who got fired from one of his first jobs at a small-town station by staging an Eldridge Cleaver look-alike contest.

Imus, of course, has an ongoing feud with Howard Stern. They rank on each other pretty regularly. My problem in life is, I like both of them.

For a brief while, toward the end of my run, Howard, Don, and I were all on WNBC together. I didn't have enough time to get to know Howard as well as I know Don, although he put me in his book, *Private Parts*. And once he said on the air that I was the reason he got into radio.

Anyway, I really flipped out during my New York stay. It was overwhelming. Free booze, free drugs, women throwing themselves at me. It got really weird, and sort of swept me away. But that's the way it is when you're on an ego trip: you develop an "I can handle it all" attitude—until something comes along, kicks you in the teeth, and says, "Guess what, buddy: you really can't handle it after all."

Mike hit the wall one night. The next day he told me, "Wolf, I can't be doing this coke anymore. I had a trip last night and I didn't think I was going to come out of it alive."

That was okay for him, I thought. I'm not in any danger. Then Lou finally got fed up enough from my playing around to leave me. She hightailed it to North Carolina. I knew that her main high school sweetheart was still living there, and I imagined her cutting out on me to marry him.

That idea almost killed me. That was my stop light.

Of course, being a perpetual outlaw-child type, I didn't totally stop being out of control. But I at least cut back, veered in the direction of good sense enough to sober up a little bit, and began to consider the possibility that I was destroying myself.

That was progress, but I still had a ways to go.

Chapter Fourteen

Before we get into how I escaped from New York, here's a free tip for you readers. Someday you may plan on leaving town for a long spell and you'll consider renting out your house. Some guy may come along who just left the National Football League, who wants to become a Hollywood actor, and who has the reputation of being a lunatic. My advice is to hold out for a stable tenant just a little longer.

I speak with authority here. While we were in New York, we rented our Beverly Hills house to someone who'd just been cut by the San Diego Chargers and wanted to break into the movies. Before long, we found out that he had funny habits — like eating glass, and also setting himself on fire in our living room. Other times, he got busy with pulling bookshelves off the walls and ripping doors out of their frames. Then he wrote a few bad checks for the rent.

Part of wanting to get away from WNBC was that we wanted to save our house from total destruction.

Mainly, though, it was about wanting to make life easier. The hectic side of New York City life was getting to everyone. Willie D., the garage attendant/poet character who occasionally dropped in on my broadcasts, started getting real antisocial. Like,

> The place I live is crazy
> The folks ain't got much sense
> Some of 'em is lazy
> And most of 'em is dense
> All kinds of fruits and nutcakes
> Are walking down the halls
> If I had me some big-ass boots
> I'd kick 'em in the b-b-backside.

Willie D. was losing his grip, and so was I—from doing a full slate of radio shows, plus occasional promo appearances, plus flying back and forth to L.A. twice a month and taping back-to-back episodes of *The Midnight Special*. A schedule like that can wear a person out pretty quick.

The way I got clear from WNBC for those weekends of television production was by doubling up on Fridays. Mike Howard and I would do two shows in a row. First we'd tape one five-hour show in the afternoon, then take an hour or so to eat dinner, and then go live on the air from seven to midnight.

At midnight, I'd hop in a cab and go straight to the airport. The flight was always in one of those big 747s with a circular staircase leading to an upper deck. The stewardesses got used to my twice-monthly commutes. They would have a place upstairs all set up for me to go to sleep. "Come on, Wolfman. Here's your little bed." By the time I woke up we'd be in L.A.

Close to one year after arriving in New York, my

pathway out of WNBC opened up during a weekend I spent up in Toronto. I was emceeing a concert there that was part of a big annual event. On Saturday afternoon I was signing autographs in a building where a car show was going on. Some Playboy Bunnies were posed around my table. As I inked my scrawl on an eight-by-ten for a patient fan, up came Burton Cummings, the leader of the Guess Who. You know, the guys who had "These Eyes," "Laughing," "No Time," and "American Woman."

Burton stuck out his hand and said, "Hey, Wolfman. I've just written a song about you. We're going into the studio tomorrow to cut it, so why don't you come and be on the record with us?"

"Great," I said. "How about we get some beer and drugs and some other goodies and maybe some of these Bunnies might wanna join us and have a good time?" I smiled at the one nearest me and she smiled right back. Even though I'd made up my mind to be a better-behaved citizen, I wasn't immune to a little backsliding.

Burton gave me the address of a Toronto recording studio and told me what time to drop by. "It's gonna be fantastic," he added as he walked off.

Well, a few Bunnies did join us. And it was fantastic. The song was called "Clap for the Wolfman." From the title, you might think it was about me catching something that it takes penicillin to cure. And as a matter of fact, I actually was running that kind of a risk during the recording sessions. But Burton's song was about a guy who takes his sweetie out for a ride in his car and finds out that she's more interested in the DJ on the radio than the fella beside her:

> Clap for the Wolfman
> He gon' rate your record high,

Clap for the Wolfman
You gon' dig him till the day you die.

All the instrumental tracks were already done. We spent about twenty-four hours in the studio just cutting the lead vocal and adding some party sounds and spoken-word tracks.

I added things like "As long as you got the curves, baby, I got the angles."

It took a long time because there were lots of distractions, including a young woman named Ingrid, who had a very funny laugh, which we decided to record over and over.

"That's great, Ingrid, you do that some more." And you can hear her real good on the record.

Lo and behold, the Guess Who's label decided "Clap for the Wolfman" was an infectious tune—if you'll pardon the pun—so they released it as a single. It charted at No. 6 on July 20, 1974, and stayed in the Top 40 for eleven weeks.

The Guess Who hadn't had a Top 10 hit for about four years, so nothing big had been planned to support this release. But when "Clap for the Wolfman" started climbing the charts in mid-summer, they suddenly pulled a lot of bookings together.

Burton Cummings dropped by at WNBC one evening and said, "Hey, we're gonna do thirty-seven dates in six weeks. If you can come along and perform on 'Clap for the Wolfman,' we'll give you ten grand per show."

I did the math pretty fast in my head: $10,000 x 37 dates = *more money than I made at WNBC in a whole year!* And I'd collect it all in a month and a half.

It was summer, *The Midnight Special* was on hiatus. The only thing standing in the way of this heaven-sent instant cash was my WNBC contract.

I went to Mr. Vicious and laid it on the line: "I don't wanna turn this deal down. Will you guys please let me off the hook?"

"No. We're paying you tremendous money to do a job for us. We're getting real good ratings. We invested a lot to win this ratings battle. You leave, we'll sue."

"Listen," I offered, "how about if I go over to WABC and talk to Cousin Brucie? If you'd pay him the same kind of money you're paying me, maybe he'd come to work here. That way, I could leave and you'd still have the top-rated jock in town."

Vicious liked that. Frankly, I think he was going to be happy to see my backside disappear out the door anyway. The next night I gave Cousin Brucie a call and we met for dinner.

The timing was perfectly amazing: he was just finishing his contract at WABC. They were only paying him about $140,000 at the time, and they were balking at his requests for a raise. Taking my job would boost his income 250 percent.

"You've got a deal," he said, with plenty of conviction.

The next afternoon, Mr. Vicious had Cousin Brucie signed on the line for two years. He looked at me and said, "Good luck, Wolfman. And don't forget to write."

Then his face lit up with the sweetest smile I'd ever seen him produce. At last, I'd found a way to make him really, truly happy. All I had to do was vanish.

The Guess Who and I took to the road with four or five tour buses and a semi. Every night after a show we'd wind up at our hotel with a whole bunch of ladies who were up for doing everybody. We would stay up the whole night and let the bus cart us away when morning came.

Sometimes we had to load out right after the gig, so

we'd do our partying on the bus. We had a great time, and I got to be great friends with Burton and the other guys in the group. But if the tour had lasted any longer, we definitely would've collapsed.

They say the road of excess leads to the palace of wisdom, but for me it just led straight out of New York.

Chapter Fifteen

Burt Sugarman is an amazing TV and movie producer. He's a stealth-type operator, always walking around silently, hardly saying a thing, watching out for ways to make things run a little crisper, a little more efficient. After the first year, he got the procedures on *The Midnight Special* so much smoother that we could tape two shows over a single weekend. Then, when we got ahead of the game, we could take a little time off.

That allowed me to stretch out and do some more rock festivals and other dates. Or just relax at home, where a team of locksmiths and carpenters had successfully fixed all the things that had been destroyed by our jock/actor/head case tenant. The Guess Who tour paid for that work.

The Midnight Special was great for exposure, but not that dynamic for my finances. Everybody got paid pretty much the same. There were no big-money deals happening. But that show gave me a chance to meet and know almost everybody who was doing big things in music.

We always taped at the NBC studios in Burbank.

Around seven in the evening, when rehearsals were finished, they brought the studio audience in. There weren't any chairs. People just sat on big, colorful pillows like they were in some ultra-hip living room, looking up at a stage. There was a guy named Bill who came to every single taping. That's dedication, plus maybe the original Buns of Steel. Some of those beanbag pillows were awful mushy.

Tammy Wynette had a country hit around that time that went "I wanna see Jesus on *The Midnight Special*, I wanna see the Wolfman bring him on." Well, to my knowledge, the Son of God never made a personal appearance for us. But practically everybody else in show business eventually did. Of course, along with the performers who appeared on the show, people like Jim Croce, Waylon Jennings, the Stylistics, José Feliciano, the Pointer Sisters, Melissa Manchester, Chevy Chase, Billy Crystal, and so on, came all their agents, lawyers, spouses, sweethearts, personal managers, and hangers-on.

Mix in all the hair-styling people, the makeup people, and the wardrobe people. Now, picture half the crowd wearing 1970s-era hot-toned polyester outfits with elephant-leg bellbottoms and platform shoes. It was a genuine circus atmosphere.

NBC's hallways are real narrow. You'd have to squeeze between people to make it from one end to the other. The security forces couldn't keep it under control at all.

Several of the acts that came on the show, like Sly and the Family Stone for just one example, were heavy into drugs.

During one of Sly's two appearances, it took eight hours just to get two songs taped. That's four hours per song, folks. Sly was real hot at the time. "Family Affair" had been a No. 1 hit for three consecutive weeks. But he was beginning to get carried away by the drugs. Practically everyone in his group was a maniac. They holed up in the dressing room for hours on end, snorting coke, drinking whiskey, shooting up heroin. And out in the hallways was an entourage of the most outrageous collection of bebop cats and jive bobbies I'd ever seen — several light-years weirder than any congregation that ever hung out at the old Alan Freed shows at the Brooklyn Paramount.

At his peak, Sly was getting fans of every color into soul. He had about the most progressive sound going in the 1970s. If his best stuff was released right now, it would sound more brand-new than most of what's currently out there.

Of course, the really seasoned pros, like Aretha Franklin, Ray Charles, Chuck Berry, and other people like that, they didn't use any drugs. But they were the exceptions.

I don't think Sugarman ever knew quite how much stuff was being smoked, drunk, snorted, and shot up in the various stars' dressing rooms. A clue emerged every now and then, like when Steve Tyler of Aerosmith was jumping around during a taping and a small vial of heroin, the size they call an "8-ball," fell to the stage from where he kept it tucked behind his left ear.

Basically, the drugs were about insecurity. They were like a campfire that some of the performers gathered around, to feel warm and comfortable and to stop thinking about the scary things out there beyond the circle of the firelight.

Though I can't lay claim to being Mr. Clean, I never got messed up before or during the tapings. That's one thing I've always been honorable about. I wouldn't ever get loaded before a show. It would kill me to do that because it's a rule that you just can't break — not without paying a heavy price somewhere down the road.

If they want to last, performers have to have one thing so deep in their character that it's practically written into their DNA. Chuck Berry expressed it to me once in real down-home language, and you can't put it any plainer than he did: "You can fuck anyone else you want to, but you *do* not fuck the public. They *feed* you. You take care of those people and you make them happy, to the best of your ability. And they're gonna love you right back for it."

Let the congregation say: "*A*-men!"

I was more at ease with the rock 'n' roll people than the producers and directors of *The Midnight Special* were, so it became a big part of my job to help those performers become at ease with making a TV appearance. To carry that off, I had to be straight. I would walk into the dressing rooms of some of these guys and they would have their coke stash laid on the table all lined out on mirrors, and their hundred-dollar bills rolled up into snorting tubes. Usually they'd offer me a line. Here's where my oversize frame helped me out. If someone seemed too wasted to watch closely, I'd hunch over the mirror, block their view, and pretend to inhale a line. Other times, when the people offering the cocaine were still pretty coherent, I'd say, "Hey, fine," and scoop some into a little bottle. "I'll save this for later. Thanks, guys."

Remember, this was the first TV show to be almost nothing but live rock 'n' roll performance. The musicians were kind of nervous about how the sound mix would be, whether they'd look as cool in front of a camera as they did on a stadium stage, and all that.

We only taped the music on an eight-track machine. Every one of the groups that came and did the show live brought along their own mixing technician.

If a group muffed the song during the taping, sometimes we'd let them do it over. It was hard to imagine, for example, how the Beach Boys would need seven or eight takes to do "Surfin' Safari" right. They'd been playing it over and over again for more than a decade. One reason why they faltered might've been the fact that Dennis Wilson, their drummer, usually packed a huge orange juice jug that was half filled with vodka.

Stan Harris was a great director. He had directed several Sinatra and Bob Hope specials. He knew how to handle people. His crew of cameramen and sound guys, they were the best. Top-of-the-line pros. There was nothing they couldn't handle.

Except when it came to *The Midnight Special*.

Stan was a real hard-ass. He didn't cut any slack for prima donnas. He wanted every act to come in and perform as if it were a live show. That's why the show came out so good.

Sometimes I had to be the one to break the news to a performer, "Hey, you have two chances to do your song. If you don't get it right on the second take, it's a good bet that they'll fill in with something else."

Some of the acts would really freak out. I'd have to sit down with them and say, "Hey, man, this is for your *career*. If you don't get up there and take care of business, word's gonna get around."

A lot of times I had to hold their heads while they called up their friend Ralph on the porcelain telephone. There were all kinds of nervous trips going on.

Burt Sugarman has all the *Midnight Special* episodes in a time capsule somewhere, and I hope he brings them back real soon, because I think people would flip out to see them again. Remember, the show was on in the days before folks had VCRs, and it aired very late—right after Johnny Carson on Friday nights, from 12:30 to 2:00 in the morning.

Very few fans had the juice to stay up that late after a long work week. You had to really be into it.

The producers had a strategy to keep people holding on. They put the mainstream acts on first. Middle America-type folks who just finished watching Carson might stay tuned for Barry Manilow, the Bee Gees, Johnny Mathis, Don McLean, or Paul Anka. The hard-core folks would have to wait for the last half hour or so of the program before the more *dangerous* acts came on, like the O'Jays, James Brown, the New York Dolls, Buddy Miles, Slade, Steely Dan, Bo Diddley, Muddy Waters, and folks like that.

We'd do different themed shows—all oldies, all country. I usually moved up from co-host to host for those shows.

They used Helen Reddy for about two years as their regular host. "I Am Woman" had been a No. 1 hit in the fall of 1972. The producers figured that, what with the women's movement beginning to gather momentum, Helen would really help draw some high ratings.

And she did. She was a great pro. But even though she was a living symbol of women's liberation, Helen was married to one of the most negative, messed-up, macho creeps in Hollywood. Ironic, ain't it?

Jeff Wald was his name. He did cocaine in those days at an inhuman rate, and he was one of those unfortunate people who got real nasty instead of getting real high. Everything he saw around him looked wrong. He would chew out the cameraman, the set designer, me, the director, practically anybody. He'd fight with Sugarman almost every night.

One time we were in the middle of taping the Bee Gees, literally halfway through their song, everything going perfect. Then Wald walked right out in front of the cameras and yelled, "Hold everything!"

The whole crew stopped in its tracks. It costs hundreds of dollars per minute to tape a big show like that. The first thing anybody in TV or the movies learns is that when the cameras are rolling you don't do the slightest thing to cause a distraction and waste a single precious second. If you've got to cough, hold it back. You might pass out for lack of oxygen, but the medics can jump in and restart your heart as soon as the director says "Cut." When the big red light is on, it's money time. To interrupt is as out of line as yelling "Let's all vote for Commies" at the Republican National Convention.

"Stop the cameras," Wald screamed. "I don't like this set! I don't like what they're doing. I want Helen Reddy sitting over *there*."

Harris was so shocked he looked down at his right side and then his left, as if he wished he had six-guns strapped on and he could blow Wald away.

The producers would do anything to get Wald out of the building when it was time to tape a Helen Reddy segment. They'd send an assistant producer to start an argument with him in the office and keep him distracted until her bit was done.

Eventually, Reddy dumped him. But before she got around to it, the producers had gotten their fill and, reluctantly, had let her go.

But let's talk about some bright spots. The Bee Gees were some of the best people, and always perfectly rehearsed. They'd get things done in the snap of a finger. Their music wasn't exactly back-in-the-alley soulful, but after a while in show business you start to appreciate the folks who are smooth, together, and able to get the job done right on the first take.

Glen Campbell was another totally solid pro. The thing that amazed me the most about Glen was that he'd *never* break a sweat. They'd have him sitting and waiting for long stretches under the hot lights, rehearsing, playing his guitar, dancing around. Not a single bead of sweat would show anywhere.

The first time I met Glen, he told me, "I've got to thank you for saving my life."

"Thanks," I said, feeling a little baffled, "but, y'know, I really can't remember us ever getting together before."

"It was out on the road," he said, "a long time ago. I was playing solos. One night I was driving somewhere across Texas after finishing a gig, listening to the preachers on XERF to stay awake. I started drifting off to sleep. At exactly the same time that one of my wheels went into the gravel on the side of the road, you came on and started your show with a big old howl. That woke me up just in time."

Glen's such a sincere guy that I have to believe him. However, about two years later, Elvis Presley told me the same exact story about himself. Except in his case it was a tour in a bus, and it was the bus driver who woke up just in time. So, he said, not just him but the whole Elvis Presley band and touring crew owed their lives to me.

Which makes a great story—but lately I've started to suspect that at least one of those two great guys was pulling my leg. Maybe both of them. And you know what? I hereby forgive them both.

Apart from No-Sweat Glen, nearly everyone else that came in to tape a *Midnight Special* segment turned into a wreck by the time they got finished. They'd be soaked in perspiration, nervous, ready to grab the closest fifth of whiskey.

Taping a single show took about eight or nine hours. I had to be there for the whole evening, always on and camera-ready, in case they needed me to step into a shot and say, "We'll be right back with more *Midnight Special*."

In between the acts, I'd go out and try to keep the studio audience happy while the crew set up the stage and lighting for the next performance.

That got to be hard work. TV tapings can be like airplane flights, a few exciting parts with lots of boredom in between. It can take a long time to totally change the set, lighting, and camera angles. Folks in the audience would get restless.

Two days in a row of taping got brutal. I'd generally go home at night and drop right into bed. I didn't party much at all. Which was probably real good for my health.

Undoubtedly the strangest *Midnight Special* taping of all was one night when we had Andy Kaufman on.

Andy was known for creating sweet and simple characters, like his Little Foreign Man, who was sort of the basis for his Latka Gravas character on *Taxi*. As a counterpoint, Andy came up with another character, Tony Clifton, who was the most brash, egotistical, overbearing show business asshole imaginable.

I was out doing the interviews. Two guys who worked with me, Frank Cotolo (aka "Mars"), a terrific comedy writer, and Mellow Mike, a great DJ, were in the green room. That was a place, close by the set, where people could talk and relax. All of a sudden, Andy Kaufman came out of a dressing room that had a star and the name "Tony Clifton" on it. He passed by Mellow Mike and said, "Fuck you!" Then he turned to Mars and added, "Fuck you and the horse you rode in on. I gotta groove. Get outta here."

Then he went up on the stage and yelled into the mike, "I'm sorry. Is it just really too much to ask if the lights could be on me? I'm the fucking star!"

The poor soundman brought the level up on his mike and asked, "Is this fine?" Andy—who was obviously wrapped up in being Tony—said, "Do you fucking people know what the fuck you're doing?" He put his hands on his hips and glared at the whole crew. "I can't work with you people," he said finally. "You're just too fucking unprofessional for my taste."

With that, he stormed off the stage and walked back to the Tony Clifton dressing room.

One minute later, he left that room and stepped into the one next door, marked "Andy Kaufman." Then he came back out, as himself, walked back up on the stage and said meekly, "I'm sorry, but I have to apologize for Tony. He hasn't been feeling well lately. I'll really give him a talking to. I'm sure we can work things out."

Mellow Mike looked over at Mars and said, "And I thought *you* were nuts!"

Another time, Mellow was in the green room, munching down on some snacks, when the Beach Boys all walked in from rehearsing their first number. Somebody asked Mellow what he was doing there. "I'm with Wolfman Jack," he explained.

Brian Wilson, who at that time constantly had his live-in psychiatrist, Eugene Landy, by his side, looked up and said, "Wolfman Jack? I've always wanted to meet him!"

Mike brought him over to my dressing room. Brian looked me up and down and said, "Are you really Wolfman Jack?"

"Yeah, sure I am, man," I said, "and I believe we've met before, too."

Then he started hugging me and saying, "I love you, man. I really love you."

I thought everything was cool after this.

We did the show, as much as possible, as if it were live. We tried to keep the thing flowing through the breaks and everything else. The next thing on the shooting schedule was for me to interview Brian. It was something to fit in just before the first Beach Boys song.

It was one of the few interviews I ever got to do on that show, so I was really excited about it. I told him, "Hey, listen, we're gonna do an interview together. We're gonna talk about how you wrote the songs and all that. Is that okay?" Because people were saying that at that time he was a little zippo, having some really extreme mood swings.

"Of course, it's okay, Wolfman. I trust you."

Pretty soon they had the chairs all set up and the cameras ready for our interview. The live audience was out there, sitting on their pillows, watching expectantly.

Brian Wilson came out quietly and sat down next to me. He seemed a little edgy. His eyeballs were going back and forth.

"How're you doin', man?" I asked. "Everything fine?"

"Yeah," he said, but he was breathing real heavy as the technicians pinned little microphones on our shirts.

Then the camera came on. The director, who was upstairs behind a glass wall, cued us to begin.

"I'm so fortunate to have sitting here with me tonight Mr. Brian Wilson from the Beach Boys," I said. "Friends, here he is. The man behind the Surfin' Sound. Say hi to everybody, Brian."

Brian didn't say anything. He stared at the camera like a hoot owl peering into high-beam headlights. His eyes got bigger and bigger. Then, without ever saying a single word, he got up and ran out the door.

The director banged on the glass and said, "What's going on down there? Where did Brian Wilson go?"

Nobody had an answer. He simply disappeared. He didn't even go onstage with the band for their numbers.

Fifteen years later I met Brian at a benefit in Orlando for the Make A Wish Foundation. And dig this. He was now all rehabilitated and looking good. He had lost about a hundred pounds. And he was still hanging out with his psychiatrist.

I hadn't seen Brian since he vanished from that TV soundstage. I took the mike as an opening act was making their exit, and I introduced him: "Here he is, the California genius, Brian Wilson!"

He came out and said, "Oh, Wolfman Jack. Gimme the mike! Gimme the mike!" He took the microphone away, looked at me with a gleam in his eye and sort of a devilish smile on his face, and said, "Rolling Stones!" Then he gave me the mike back.

Does anybody out there understand what that meant? To this day I can't figure it out.

There was one rock 'n' roll guy, at least, who I always could understand. Old Chuck Berry, he can do it for you. All you've got to do is hear the opening bars of "Maybellene," or "Thirty Days," "No Particular Place to Go," or "Havana Moon." Anytime I've ever been on the same stage with him, he has delivered a fantastic show. One time recently, at a big private party I played with him, two strings on his guitar wouldn't stay in tune. Chuck somehow made it *work* for him. He got the weirdest assortment of gronks, groans, and clamtones out of that beast, and the stranger it sounded, the more fun he seemed to be having. The audience was a little baffled, though.

Chuck always travels by himself. He usually carries a shirt with him, his guitar, a change of underwear, and his toiletries. He arrives with all that stuff in a little briefcase, and his electric guitar in the other hand. He never says where he's staying or what flight he's coming in on.

Nobody ever has to pick him up. So everybody always worries about whether he's gonna show up or not. He's been doing business like that for years.

Chuck also has several unique clauses in his contract. There has to be one of his favorite amps on stage, a certain old-style tube model for that primal, funky, dirty-sounding distortion when you crank it up to high volume. If you don't have that amp, he charges an extra grand. He gets paid about as soon as he shows up at the auditorium. He usually goes to his dressing room and he don't bother nobody—and doesn't want nobody else bothering him—until it's time to step out there and rock the audience.

He never does pick out a band. They're always supposed to have a band there for him. And when he goes out there, the band asks, "What're we gonna do, Chuck?"

He says, "We're gonna play Chuck Berry songs."

I've never seen a band yet that wasn't able to follow him. After all, you just can't be a rock 'n' roll musician if you don't know a whole lot of Chuck Berry music by heart. So he never rehearses, and he never does a sound check.

Anyway, on one particular night that he came in to tape a segment for *The Midnight Special*, he was really sick. The first-aid people checked him out and he had a 103 temperature. He was vomiting. He threw up all over the dressing room. He was sweating like a mule, and he was scheduled to go on in about five minutes. The two of us were alone in the dressing room. Chuck looked at me and said, "Wolf, I don't think I can make this gig."

I kneeled down by the couch and looked him in the eye. I said, "Chuck, there's a whole lot of people out there that're just achin' to see you and this is major television. You're a pro, man. I know you can do it."

"All right," he said. "Give me a hand." Me and another guy helped him out into the hallway. As soon as we passed through the door of his dressing room, he pushed us both away and he walked out into the crowd, gripping his cherry red Gibson by the neck, sweat dripping down his face. He took a towel from a wardrobe person and wiped his face off. As soon as he got onstage, the makeup girl came out after him with a few daubs of something to put some life into his skin tones, because he was looking like the victim of a Haitian zombie spell.

As soon as she got through, Chuck slid his guitar strap over his shoulder and yelled, "Hey! I'm gonna do this now, and if you want to shoot this, turn on your cameras."

Everybody was on a break. The camera guys were caught standing around drinking coffee out of Styrofoam cups and chewing on doughnuts. They all had to jump in behind the controls. The instant he saw them jump, Chuck cued the band and did three numbers in a row, with absolutely no pauses, and he was on top of the music all the way. The songs were done perfect, everything on the mark. It was like watching Joe Montana lead a length-of-the-field, fourth-quarter touchdown drive for the win.

Immediately after that, we loaded Chuck into an ambulance that took him straight to the hospital. When they found out he had pneumonia, they made him stay in bed for three days.

The one thing he'd never do was let down the public. I always remember that.

Another guy who's always at the level of perfection — or else so close to it that you can't tell the difference — is Ray Charles. One night on *The Midnight Special* we had Ray and his whole band, and Billy Preston was there to play the Hammond B-3 organ. We also had Aretha Franklin on that night. They all got together and jammed.

It was one of the finest musical adventures that was ever on television.

Like I said, I hope Burt Sugarman gets up off those old tapes sometime real soon. You'll see lots of 1970s clothing styles that'll get you laughing, including the wigged-out stuff I was wearing. But you'll also discover a big supply of musical treasures.

Chapter Sixteen

Thanks to *American Graffiti* and *The Midnight Special*, Columbia Records signed me in 1974 to put out an album.

There was a whole lot of heavy, introspective singer-songwriter stuff on the airwaves then, so I wanted to do something different, really lighthearted, reminiscent of the days when rock 'n' roll was for dancing and falling in love to. Instead of being the soundtrack for carrying the weight of the world on your shoulders.

We called the album *Fun and Romance*.

Besides being fun to do, the album introduced me to one of my favorite musical sidekicks of all time.

John Herron is a can-do-it-all piano player out of Elk City, Oklahoma. I gave him the nickname "Uncle John." He can play any licks you ever heard on any rock 'n' roll record since time began, plus a lot of stuff he made up himself.

When the Electric Prunes, a psychedelic band from Seattle, had their big hit in 1967, "I Had Too Much to Dream (Last Night)," for some reason their manager got rid of all the original guys and hired John and his band to move to L.A. and "become" the Electric Prunes.

He did that for a while, splitting $2,000 among four band members for each concert performance. Then one night he happened to get a look in the manager's files. John learned that their manager was collecting $10,000 for each show. That convinced him to unplug from the Prunes!

After going out on his own, he did tours with the Beach Boys, album dates with the Doobie Brothers, and blues clubs down in Watts, where he was usually the only white face in the whole crowd.

It turned out that John, who'd been playing profession-ally since he was only thirteen, had cultivated his taste in music by tuning in to my show on XERF from Del Rio, Texas. Apparently, a lot of youngsters from around the Southwest were doing the same thing. ZZ Top honored the tradition with a blues-rock number entitled "Heard It on the X."

Anyway, John and I became great buddies. He and some other musicians joined me for some wonderful live shows that we called "Wolfman Jack's Shock and Rock Revue." We did them four years in a row at Knott's Berry Farm for the Halloween season.

There were some other great players in the band, too. Rick Vito, a guitarist, went on to be in Fleetwood Mac. Tom Mooney had been a drummer with my old friend Todd Rundgren. Dr. John, the reigning king of New Orleans piano, came in as a guest artist. So did the Coast-ers and all kinds of other people.

One time, Jr. Walker and the All Stars showed up, unannounced. Their driver was supposed to take them someplace else, but he got mixed up. My manager spotted Junior standing there with his saxophone in hand and his band trailing behind, with everybody looking kind of confused.

"Junior, we're so glad you're here," he said. "Go on out there and tear 'em up."

And so he did. He rocked the crowd with "Shotgun," "How Sweet It Is," "(I'm a) Road Runner," "What Does It Take (To Win Your Love)," and all his other best numbers. Then we paid him, and they all packed up and went home.

Nobody ever told him he was at the wrong place.

The very first Knott's Berry Farm show, in 1974, was designed around a spooky version of a Wild West motif. There were bales of hay and random tumbleweeds all around the stage. We had hawks and owls perched on stumps, secured by a chain. There was an honest-to-God mountain lion, being held on a leash by a professional trainer.

A song called "Fire" by the Ohio Players was going strong then. It eventually reached No.1 in December. We created a big production number around "Fire" to open the show. I had a hawk chained to my wrist. Flash-pots were supposed to go off on the front of the stage, then I'd emerge, introduce the song, and vanish as the band kicked it off.

While they were wailing their way through the song, I was supposed to run backstage and change costumes, then dart through a tunnel so I could come walking up the center aisle from the back with that hawk still proudly perched on my wrist as the band came to the climax of the song.

It was a beautiful piece of carnival-style show business. I was so into it, I did aerobics for three weeks to get ready.

It started out great. Except for one thing. Some overzealous stagehand put way too much explosive powder in the flashpots. One of them caused a hay bale to catch on fire. None of us onstage could see it, because it caught fire in the front.

The audience saw it, but, hey, we were playing "Fire" and it must've seemed like part of the show.

I made my dash. The band got to the turnaround and started the second verse. About that time, the hay bale caught a nearby tumbleweed on fire. Meanwhile, I slipped in the darkness and sprained my ankle so bad I couldn't get up. The hawk chained to my wrist freaked out and started trying to fly away. I yelled for help, but nobody could hear me because of the music. While I was lying back there completely helpless, a gust of wind nudged the burning tumbleweed around. It set fire to another bale of hay, which spread the flames to the left-side curtain.

By now, smoke was beginning to waft across the stage. The mountain lion was straining to get the hell out of there, practically pulling the trainer's arms out of their sockets. The hawks and owls were beating their wings, flying in place sideways because they were chained down, and screeching in panic.

The audience sat there totally transfixed. None of them moved or went berserk. They all took it to be a masterful live display of special effects by confident showbiz professionals.

The band played on. Finally, somebody broke and ran and all the rest of them followed, just as two or three Knott's Berry Farm employees with fire extinguishers scrambled up and hosed the whole stage down.

The people in the audience were beside themselves with happiness. They seemed to think, "Hey, this is a heck of show!"

Backstage, my ankle was swelling up like a Texas grape-fruit. I wanted more than anything to get carted off to a hospital, but someone talked me into getting shot up with painkillers and finishing the show. I had to do it in a wheelchair, but I kept the hawk on my arm until the bitter end.

Afterward, we all sat around and laughed so hard that our eyes filled with tears. For me, the tears came real easy. I couldn't walk right for nearly three weeks.

A year later, we cooked up a stage show inspired by the *Fun and Romance* album. In spring of 1975 we launched one of the most ambitious, wonderful, and yet ill-fated touring rock 'n' roll variety extravaganzas in the history of show business.

It was called "I Saw Radio."

"I Saw Radio" probably never made it to your town. But I think you would've loved it. Enough of it got saved on videotape to later seduce the Canadian Broadcasting Corporation into financing a twenty-six-show package of half-hour rock 'n' roll variety revues.

"I Saw Radio" was a show designed to evoke the old days of dangerous, exciting music that you could only get by tuning in a midnight DJ. There was an incredible stage set for it—a proscenium arch created by two red-lighted radio towers flanking a forty-foot-tall, 1950s-style radio. The show's title was spelled out right over the top. There was a huge knob on each side, and everything in the show unfolded visually as if it were emerging from a big old radio speaker.

In order to take this monster stage setting from town to town, we packed it with excruciating care into a pair of semi trucks. Our troupe of about fifty musicians, singers, dancers, and stagehands traveled in a couple of tour buses.

I had to fly back and forth between dates to tape the last few *Midnight Special* shows of the season.

That was creating some tension between me and the producers, because I wasn't always there when they wanted me. I had to risk it, because the money they were paying wasn't enough to get by on.

We did the final "I Saw Radio" rehearsals at a big hall in Akron to iron out the set-handling procedures, then we staged our first show of the tour there on a Friday night. As soon as it was done, we had to pack everything up the same night and head for Detroit.

Well, that first show went fantastic. We had a full house. The lights went down, then the audience heard a heavy electronic hum sound and red lights on each radio tower lit up. Then they heard a big click, and the giant radio dial lit up, too.

The dial indicator started moving very slowly from left to right, like someone was searching for a good station. In between bursts of static the audience heard the voices of some famous radio personalities, like Art Laboe, Hunter Hancock, Poppa Stoppa, Fat Daddy, Dewey Phillips, and Murray the K, interspersed with the voices of DJs well known there in Akron: "This is Gary Owens . . . brought to you by Findmeister Broadcasting System to make your Furd feel better and your cragmite grow taller."

Finally, the indicator dial got all the way to the end of the dial. Then a half moon lit up above the stage and three long wolf howls came out of the speaker.

A spotlight hit Uncle John at his piano as he belted out "Good, good music on the RADIO, Wolfman Jack on another show!" There was a whole rhythm section around him, and the dial pulsated in time with their beat. Then one more light hit a big horn section. I came on to abuse the piano and sing a string of gut-bucket oldies like "Dr. Feelgood," "Short Fat Fannie," and "Idol with the Golden Head."

Then we treated the audience to some of the late Alan Freed's original rock 'n' roll DJ patter, recorded from one of his old "Moondog Matinee Rock 'n' Roll Party" broadcasts from WJW in nearby Cleveland. The show also included tributes to Little Richard, B.B. King, Muddy Waters, Slim Harpo, John Lee Hooker, and some of the other blues artists who supplied the original heart of rock 'n' roll.

"Oh yeah," I said, "it was the American blues men that inspired all the British rock groups. From the Beatles to the Stones, they all learned from American blues, 'cause they knew the blues would never come to an end. They are the perpetual motion of e-motion. I tell ya, those sounds make my pantyhose stand up all by themselves!"

The production numbers got real crazy. While the band was cooking on "Rock Around the Clock," dancers were rolling across the stage in a make-believe yellow Deuce coupe hotrod that looked just like the one Paul LeMat drove in *American Graffiti*. We had 1950s-style car hops on roller skates, all kinds of lively people jumping around to the music.

By the time the show was over, we'd dipped into doo-wop, the New Orleans sound, one or two dance crazes, and a slew of Elvis hits. It was a good, sweaty workout.

It took some three hours to break down this elaborate set and pack it on the two semis. Luckily, we had a heck of a crew, which was necessary because the loading had to be done just right, or else our stage and equipment wouldn't all fit in.

The tour was under the direction of a guy who everybody called Hoss, because he looked just like the guy on *Bonanza*.

Michael, the road manager, was someone who dealt with the pressures of his job by taking uppers and never sleeping.

When the trucks and the tour bus reached Detroit, they somehow got directed to the wrong Holiday Inn, one that was located in one of the rougher areas of town. The manager of the hotel played along, like he was expecting them and their rooms were all ready. He accepted a big cash deposit and started handing out room keys.

About this time, the stagehands started unloading baggage, costumes, and equipment from the compartments on the sides of the bus. As soon as they finished off-loading one side and turned their attention to the other, neighborhood folks began ripping off anything they could grab, running down the street at top speed with their show business booty.

Somebody who stepped out on the balcony of their room saw all the pilferage going on, and they yelled down to Hoss. Like a defensive lineman in some crazy game of urban football, Hoss roared his big bulk down the street and collared four or five thieves and single-handedly pushed and shoved them all back to the bus.

About that time, someone figured out that we were all at the wrong hotel anyway. So we packed back up, kissing our room deposits goodbye, and got settled in across town, where the crime rate was a little lower.

Of course, all this extra packing and unpacking meant everyone had less rest than usual before we went in to set up the stage for our Detroit show, which was supposed to begin at 7:30.

As soon as our crew got to the theater, they found a ten-man union crew waiting. The local guys said that their regulations prohibited anybody but them from working in this theater. Even if we were the only ones who knew how to make this complicated and wonderful set come together. We stepped aside and let them go to work. Naturally, they started setting the thing up wrong, meanwhile refusing to accept any instructions from our crew.

At this point, Michael had been up four days in a row. He was popping pills, doing toot, whatever it took to stay awake and get the job done.

It got to be 7:15. The big center brace that linked the two towers and formed the top section of the radio was still waiting to be installed. All the other main pieces had to be fastened to that center brace. The union guys hoisted it in place, but they didn't bolt it down right.

All of a sudden, there was a loud cracking noise. One side of the brace broke off and fell down to the stage floor.

At this point, Michael went out of his gourd. He slammed the head of the union crew against the wall repeatedly as he said, "You're . . . going . . . to . . . walk . . . away . . . and . . . let . . . us . . . do . . . this . . . god-damned . . . thing . . . right! RIGHT?"

The rest of the union crew clustered around. Hoss walked up behind them, tapped them on their shoulders, and pointed out the fact that we had them outnumbered two-to-one. Actually, Hoss practically outnumbered them *by himself!*

"That's it," Hoss said. "You're off the stage."

"You can't do this! We're gonna bring the police."

"I don't give a shit what yer gonna do. We've got a job to do, and if you don't like how things are, you can just pucker up while I'm backing up."

By a miracle, the show got started almost on time. Once it was over, we had to hump everything back onto the trucks and start rolling toward Toledo for a Sunday night gig.

Our crew disassembled the stage and carried it out back to load it in the semis. They were met by fifty members of the union, drinking beers and making nasty comments.

Hoss called the theater's security people, who turned out to be three of the wimpiest rent-a-cops this side of a Don Knotts film festival.

It was midnight. By the time half the stuff was loaded into the truck, a major union honcho showed up and their guys began taking action.

"You punks aren't allowed to take anything else out of this auditorium," he said, "and that's it!"

I was resting back at the hotel, not aware of all this drama. Hoss called me, and patched our phone conversation through some loudspeakers out in the truck loading area so the union guys could hear. "This is Wolfman Jack," I said. "Look, nobody wants to have any kind of trouble here. We're all just working guys, trying to give the people a good show and a good time. Tryin' to spread a little happiness. Let's be cool and be good to each other."

But by then, the union guys had mispacked both semis and there was still a whole bunch of stuff waiting out in the cold, with no place to put it.

"Looks like you got some excess baggage," the union leader said. "We'll help you with it."

At his word, they shoved that beautiful Deuce coupe and a bunch of other props and pieces of scenery into a big, tall stack, poured some kerosene over it all and set it off with a Zippo lighter just as a Detroit police squad car came rolling into the alley.

The driver of the cop car stopped. Everyone froze in

place. The flames started licking up the sides of the yellow hotrod. The second cop opened his door a crack, stuck his head out for about ten seconds to get a fix on the crowd. Then he pulled back in. His door closed and the squad car backed quietly away into the night.

In spite of the Detroit police department's hands-off policy with thug-style justice, everybody got out of there alive. But that bonfire was the prelude to the swan song for "I Saw Radio." En route to our next performance, the driver of one of the semis nodded off along an Ohio turnpike just long enough to sail the whole rig into a massive concrete bridge abutment. The driver and his partner were almost killed, and the few pieces of scenery that had survived burning in Detroit were now in a million splinters. We shut the whole thing down and everybody limped home for a long, long sleep.

A few months later, by the time the truckers were getting their bandages and plaster casts removed, we sold the Canadian Broadcasting Corporation on the idea of a Wolfman Jack TV variety show.

The new head of the network was ready to revolutionize their programming, which was pretty stodgy by comparison to the shows people could get from American networks. So he went for the idea of something like *The Midnight Special*, but slightly crazier.

Chuck Hurewitz was representing me in the negotiations. He's one of the top entertainment lawyers in the business and the co-author of the textbook on entertainment law that most universities use. Randy Achee, the same nephew who I used to tuck into bed after scaring him with wolf howls, was also representing me. He'd gotten out of college and become part of my business team then, and was just sort of cutting his teeth at this time. Now, he's a wheeler-dealer with contacts throughout the industry, and he's just started being part of my management again. I tell you, it pays to have smart relatives.

Anyway, after talks had gone on for two or three months, Chuck and Randy decided to bring the two key Canadian executives down to Los Angeles, in hopes that they'd loosen up a little when they got away from the headquarters in Toronto.

It worked better than we could've imagined.

Chuck's office was right in the heart of Beverly Hills, on the corner of Beverly Drive and Wilshire Boulevard. The view from his conference room was northward, into the green and mansion-studded hills of Bel Air. After a morning of talks, we adjourned for lunch. As they strolled down Beverly with Chuck and Randy, one of the Canadians said, "What if we see a star? That would really be something fantastic to tell the folks in Toronto."

As if responding to a command, the doors of a café right ahead of them opened up and out walked Frank Sinatra.

Minutes later, as they'd settled down to their lunches, over in one corner they spotted Lee Majors, who was then starring in *The Six Million Dollar Man*, and Rod Stewart off in the other direction.

They got totally starstruck. From that point on, they were so easy to deal with that we sort of took advantage of them. A couple of months later we all got the guilties and let them renegotiate a few clauses here and there, so that CBC wouldn't lose money.

Speaking of getting starstruck, it happened to me around this time. I got hooked up to do a commercial for a hair products company. Of course, a hair products company is going to have a head guy (get it?), and this one was named Jim Markham, a very casual fellow from

New Mexico who had become very prosperous in L.A. through partnership in a salon. He liked the spot I did, and offered me a free haircut at his place on Fairfax Avenue, just north of Melrose. Since then we've stayed buddies, and he's done stuff like zooming out to the airport to give me a haircut while I'm waiting for a connecting flight. But on that first day in his shop, I had just climbed into the chair and had the sheet pinned around my neck when in walked one of my greatest screen idols—Steve McQueen. He wanted to see if he could get squeezed in. Jim said, "I can do you next, after I finish Wolfman." McQueen gave us both one of those squinty smiles, then sat down and opened a magazine. About the time his butt hit the chair, in walked James Garner. Now, Maverick had been one of the coolest characters ever on TV—like an American-bred Cary Grant, but with six-shooters. And he wants to squeeze in, and I'm feeling unworthy to stand in the way of these two stars getting service pronto. When in walks Lee Marvin. The essence of the ice-in-the-blood badman, Liberty Valance himself. And I was standing between him and a haircut. I half expected that lead was going to start flying.

These guys all came to Jim because he perfected a cutting style that let you have longer hair, but keep it looking sharp without using grease. Before that, most people either had a military-style cut, or else hippie-style shaggy hair. So Jim's shop got all those Western movies guys like McQueen, Garner, and Marvin, plus folks like Robert Redford, Conrad Hilton, Sinatra, Elvis, Peter Lawford, Fabian, Eddie Fisher, John Huston, and Johnny Carson. And I tripped out every time I saw their famous faces.

The CBC pilot was shot in Toronto over about one week. It was a half-hour format, with one main musical guest who would sing their hits and participate in a couple of comedy sketches, too. CBC just loved our pilot, but they decided to replace the free-spending original producer with someone who was known for working magic on a tight budget.

Two or three months later, we began shooting the show in Vancouver. Moving the location was a budget thing—it cost less bread to fly the L.A. talent straight up the coast than it would to take them across the face of the continent to Toronto. But the strangest money-saver of all was how the producer planned ahead all the songs we'd use for all twenty-six episodes, then herded Uncle John and all the other musicians and singers into a studio and kept them working there for seventy-two hours straight.

As Uncle John said afterward, "I love to play music. But even something that's *fun* is gonna wear your ass out if you do it up for three straight days without any rest."

From that point on the only thing that was left was for each week's guest star to sing their vocals on top of the tracks that we'd already recorded. Uncle John and the rest of the band had one hour to rest after that marathon session, between 6 and 7 A.M., and then he was back in front of the camera, pretending to play the piano while the prerecorded tracks rolled out over the speakers. They put a long one-by-four pine board in his piano so it was impossible for the hammers to strike the strings and sound a note. That was another budget-related thing. If a musician actually played a note on camera, the producers would have to pay them more money.

The guests booked for those twenty-six episodes included Jerry Lee Lewis, B.B. King, the Pointer Sisters, Chuck Berry, Chubby Checker, Little Anthony (aka Anthony Gourdine), Little Richard, Johnny Rivers, Bo

Diddley, Wayne Newton, Dionne Warwick, Kenny Rogers, Abba, Tom Jones, Johnny Mathis, and B.J. Thomas. All of these acts did the show for a pretty modest fee— with the exception of the Pointer Sisters.

A visual trademark of the show was that Uncle John, as bandleader, wore a different top hat every week, each one a little more outrageous than the one before. The wildest was when they put him in a topper that featured a birdcage in the crown, filled with live birds. "I don't think I'm getting paid enough for this," he said.

When B.J. Thomas came in to Vancouver, he looked bone-tired. He'd been on the road for several weeks. He came into the dressing room and slumped into a chair. All of a sudden, a beautiful young girl showed up from out of nowhere. She was dark-haired, with blue eyes, wearing a big football shirt with the number 88 on it. She had a build that made those numbers bend over backward.

"Oh, B.J.," she said, "you're here!" She ran up to him and gave him a big hug and kiss, then she pushed those numbers in his face.

I cleared my throat and said, "I'll talk to you later, B.J." Then I left the room.

Half an hour later, B.J. emerged from his dressing room looking like a million dollars. Number 88 had cured all of his ills.

Another time, Gladys Knight and the Pips flew up to do the show. I had become real friendly with those guys earlier, when they were on *The Midnight Special*, so they made me an honorary Pip. So now I'm a Pip, a Temptation, and a Token, too, since all those groups gave me honorary membership. The only thing left is to become an honorary Marvelette, but I'd have to part with a lot more than just my beard.

One of the most talented guests I ever had was Dionne

Warwick. She's also one of the truly sweetest folks who ever came along. She arrived in Vancouver a day prior to taping so she could listen to the prerecorded backing tracks.

"They're just fine," she told Uncle John, "except I don't think these Canadian girls got the backup parts right. Can I go into the studio and cut 'em myself?" So she went in and recorded her own three-part harmonies all by herself, totally on the money, within about twenty minutes of studio time. And they were perfect.

It's customary to take a guest star out for a night on the town after a taping. Usually, when that star is a man, someone makes the effort to be sure a few unattached and attractive women are along in the party. For Dionne, we rounded up some good-looking young men. "Well," she said, looking pleased but a little embarrassed, "nobody's done that for me before."

When we had Tom Jones on, nobody had to worry about rounding up extra women. It was known that we usually went to the same nightclub, and that night there were at least thirty eager young ladies angling to join our dinner party.

It took about three months to shoot all twenty-six episodes of the Canadian show. I had to go back and forth for *Midnight Special* tapings, but Uncle John was there the whole time. If you've never lived in the Pacific Northwest, well, let's say the rainy season is a little more *tenacious* up there than it is most anywhere else in the world. Sometimes for several days all you see is light gray in the daytime and dark gray at night, with the same steady drizzle piddling on the roof no matter what time of day. One day Uncle John got a little stir-crazy and drove a rental car across the border, through Washington and Oregon, all the way to California, refusing to stop the car until he'd seen genuine sunlight.

When Bo Diddley appeared, somebody had told him
that Vancouver wasn't a real promising locality for finding
soul food restaurants. So he packed along some crucial
supplies from his favorite hometown joint. I was walking
backstage between segments on a taping day and I
smelled this mouth-watering smoky, spicy aroma hanging
in the air. It emanated from Bo's dressing room. I walked
over and tapped on the door.

"Who is it?" Bo asked.

"It's me, man."

"Awww, Wolfman, come on in here, baby. You gotta
taste these ribs."

When I went in, there was Bo Diddley, one of the
original architects of rock 'n' roll, bent over a cheap hot
plate. He'd taken some tin foil and folded it over twice
to create a homemade frying pan. Smack in the middle
of it was two racks of pork ribs in a thick, red sauce. It
looked like the whole thing could burst into flames at
any moment. But those ribs were fine, let me tell you.

Kenny Rogers, another guest on the Canadian show,
did a lot of appearances with me in the early 1970s. He
was always willing to come at the drop of a hat—and
for not much money—to do a county fair or some similar
type gig.

He flew up to tape my Canadian show in February of
1977. At that time, he hadn't had a hit in nearly seven
years. But he had just recorded a song down in L.A., and
said he had a lot of hope for it.

"Can you help me promote my new song?" he asked.

"What's it called?"

" 'Lucille.' "

"Well," my manager said, "how big a hit do you want
it to be? If we saw to it that it entered the charts around,
say, number forty with a bullet in its first week, then got

up into the Top 10 right away, would that be all right for you?"

He was pulling Kenny's leg, but did it in such a sincere fashion that it seemed totally believable.

"Man," he said, "that'd be just great!"

Soon after, "Lucille" came onto the charts very close to No. 40. With a bullet. In very short time, it climbed up to No. 5. Kenny never stopped believing that we were somehow behind the song's success.

Trust me, Kenny, you did it on your own. The hit was in the grooves, where it's supposed to be, not in the promotion.

Two years later, when Lou organized a fortieth birthday party for me in a Beverly Hills restaurant, Kenny was already rich from "Lucille" and also on his way to the peak of his career. "The Gambler," "You Decorated My Life," "Coward of the County," "Lady," and a whole bunch of other hits were right around the corner. He gave me a present of a solid gold guitar-shaped lapel pin and said, "Wolfman, I've got to thank you for all those county fair gigs a few years back."

"But Kenny," I said, "we didn't pay you nothing for those shows. All you got was about five hundred dollars!"

"You're forgetting," he said, "that right then I needed that five hundred dollars *real bad.*"

Recently, as I was settling in for a cross-country flight, I saw Dionne Warwick taking a nap in the seat right across the aisle from me. Still a very lovely-looking lady. When she woke up a little bit later, she got a glance of me, rubbed her eyes to be sure she was seeing right, and said, "Oh, my gracious, Wolfman, I remember when we sang a duet together on your show up in Canada."

"Yeah," I said, "wasn't that a long, long time ago?"

Chapter Seventeen

Sometimes I get like Stevie Wonder. You know, "very superstitious . . ." And Lou studies practically anything she can find about the occult. Well, we both have a feeling that the bad luck associated with "I Saw Radio" continued for quite a while.

And did I mention that I turned down a regular part on a new TV show in order to do that "Radio" tour? Yeah. It was something called *Happy Days.*

Anyway, I've got to warn you, before this next story gets started, that it's a weird one. I don't just mean strange. I mean supernatural. You may not want to believe it. That's all right.

But it really happened.

One still-functioning leftover from the "I Saw Radio" tour was a fantastic Dodge camper that had been my tour bus. There were sleeping quarters in the back, a kitchen, and room for a nice table and chairs in the middle, plus an extra bunk up behind the driver's compartment.

In the summer of 1975 we signed on to do a big

outdoor festival in an out-of-the-way place known as Slaughter Gulch, Idaho, in the vicinity of Sun Valley.

I was doing a lot of outdoor festivals around that time; some of them had as many as 250,000 people.

Lou and I packed off for the festival in that camper, along with my bodyguard, Dooger, plus a songwriter named Guy Finley, and a fellow named Dennis Nicholas, who was then handling road manager chores.

We were five people riding in a deluxe camper, with a trailer hitched on back carrying two customized Harley hogs with all the accessories, including tall sissy chrome bars behind the seats. One of the bikes belonged to Dooger and the other to Guy. The bikes faced forward, with their front wheels chained in place, riding kind of high in the air.

We had two days to get where we were going, so we planned a leisurely trip, including recreational stops at casinos along the way. We also brought along fishing poles, and some handguns for target practice in the desert.

We spent the first night in a Las Vegas hotel. Around mid-afternoon of the next day, as we worked our way north, Dooger and Guy got an urge to ride their bikes. We stopped, off-loaded the trailer, and then drove ahead while they roared along, enjoying their Harleys for a few miles. Everybody was in a great mood.

Not long after we'd chained the bikes back on the trailer, someplace far away from any sign of civilization, Dennis said, "Let's stop here and do some shooting."

Lou stayed in the camper, reading a book. The four of us men walked off a distance, feeling like big-time cowboys with our guns on our hips. There was a small hill between us and the road. We set up some Coke bottles on a dried-out log and that became our shooting gallery.

But after about ten rounds apiece, we all stopped shooting. We had all noticed that everything in the vicinity had become totally quiet—no bird sounds, no crickets, absolutely nothing but the sound of the wind blowing. It made a little chill go up the back of my spine.

I said, "Let's get the hell out of here." And nobody disagreed.

When we got back to the camper, Lou took one look at the four of us and said, "What put you boys in such a hissy?"

"Never mind," I said. "Let's just go."

A few miles down the road, we came upon two women hitchhiking. The three single guys all went crazy.

"Pick 'em up," Dooger said. "Who knows how this might turn out."

I didn't like it. First off, we weren't near any kind of crossroads, town, or even a filling station outpost. I wondered where they came from, and why they were in such a forlorn place. Plus, the way they looked gave me the creeps. They were both biker-chick types, both wearing bib overalls and sleeveless T-shirts, and both brunettes. One had nice curves and was basically kind of pretty, except for a ropy-looking scar on her arm, like somebody had burned her with an iron. The other was overweight, with a real tough and hard-bitten expression. The ugly one kind of hovered over the pretty one, very protectively. And she had a scar, too. It went from up high on one side of her face, crossed between her nose and her lips, and ended on the opposite cheek.

These women made a real spooky impression on me. At the time we picked them up, I was sitting at the table in the middle of the camper. Lou had just started giving me a haircut. I tried to start a conversation.

"Where are you ladies from?"

"We're from around here."

"Where are you headed?"

"We're just out to see the world."

No matter what I asked, they wouldn't give out with a straight answer. They didn't get all flustered about being in the car with someone famous, the way most average people tend to do. In fact, they sort of acted like we were real fortunate to have them along.

When my haircut was done, I went in the back to get away from them. Lou followed me.

The guys were so fixated on charming these women out of their overalls, they weren't picking up on the creepy vibe. Finally, though, Dennis came back to check on me.

"Man," I said, "these chicks really bug me. I know you guys want to get laid and everything, but something about them is just too weird."

About an hour down the road, we had a flat tire. The back wheels were doubles, and one of the inside tires had gone down. We all got out while Dennis jacked up the camper and crawled underneath. While he was stretched out beneath the camper, the jack released itself and clicked down several notches. It pinned him down, but stopped short of pressing enough to cause harm.

Dooger reset the jack and we finally got the spare mounted. When we got underway, Lou and I again retreated to the bedroom area.

After another hundred miles or so, the guys had gotten past their horniness enough to agree that we ought to drop these spooky women off. By now we were several miles on the east side of Reno. When we came to the next little town, Dooger pulled over and said, "Thanks for your company, but we want to travel alone from here on."

This made them real mad. "You guys are being real shitty," the ugly one said. But we held firm and, finally, we saw the last of them.

By early evening we arrived in the next small town in our path. It had a couple of restaurants and one big casino, so we stopped there to relax.

After checking that everything was secure, we locked up the camper and went in to enjoy ourselves.

Two or three hours went by before we returned to the camper. Unlocking the door, the first thing we noticed was a burning smell. We rushed inside and found that our map had been lying, folded, on top of the stove. It seemed like the pilot light must've gotten to it a little.

When we opened the map up, there was a scorch mark beginning about where we had picked the hitchhikers up, and ending about where we had left them off. And there was also a scorched circle up ahead, in the direction we were going.

Lou took over the driving so the guys and I could play cards at the table. She got us into mountainous country fairly close to the Idaho border before she finally found a little turnout. We parked, got everything set for the night, and Lou went to the back to turn in. Dooger crawled into the driver's compartment bunk.

The rest of us, Guy, Dennis, and myself, started up the portable generator so we could stay up and play cards.

About fifteen minutes later, all of a sudden we heard a loud bang, like something had collided with the front end of the camper. It was followed by a sound like a bull bellowing, except deeper and longer-lasting than any animal noise I'd ever heard in my life.

We all looked at each other: "What the fuck was that?"

Just then, Dooger jumped out from the driver's compartment shaking his arms and legs.

"Oh my God!" he said. "I just had a dream. A witch had me and she was swinging me around in the air. Then I heard a godawful noise and woke up."

Everybody shut up for a minute and tried to calm down. Lou came up from the back, rubbing her eyes, asking, "What's going on?"

We each got our guns. We eased the camper door open. Couldn't see anything.

Dennis was the most macho guy in the group. He went out first and we followed. It was very quiet out there. A fine drizzle of rain was in the air, barely more than a mist. The moon was just one night away from being full. The landscape around us was lit up with moonlight, but there was a cloud straight above that looked just like a hole in the sky. No moonlight was shining on the camper. And even though it was late summer, it was so cold out there that you could see your breath.

We eventually agreed that some animal must've bumped into us and then run away. Everybody trooped back inside. But when Lou went back to the bedroom, Dennis followed along to check things out. He pulled back the curtain over the rear window and took a look.

"Ho-lee shit!" he exclaimed. "What is this?"

We rushed to the window. Both bikes were standing up on the trailer, where we'd left them. But on Dooger's bike there was a red glow above the seat. It was strong enough that you couldn't see the chrome sissy bar behind it.

·And then, as we all looked at that red glow, the camper immediately started getting really cold in the back. If you took two steps toward the front, you were warm again.

Lou started lighting candles and putting them everywhere there was a ledge big enough to hold them.

"Fuck this," Dennis said, and he jumped behind the

I was going a little crazy in New York. When the Guess Who invited me on a summer tour, it gave me an escape hatch from the asylum.

Clap for the Wolfman

Words and Music by B. CUMMINGS, B. WALLACE, and K. WINTER

Recorded by The Guess Who on RCA Records

$1.50

This was an honor, and it even climbed the charts pretty well. Todd Rundgren, ZZ Top, and Taj Mahal have all thrown references to me—and the days of outlaw border radio—into their songbooks.

(top) "Have You Seen Her" is still one of the crown jewels of soul music. The Chi-Lites, who recorded that great song, came to see me at my home broadcast studio on Ferrari Drive in Beverly Hills. Don Kelley (upper left) was my manager then. Sometimes folks mistook him for Paul McCartney. *(Jeff Dunas)*

(bottom) Tom Jones was one of the most popular guests on the Canadian Broadcasting Company show I did one year out of Vancouver. Dionne Warwick, B.J. Thomas, Little Richard, and Kenny Rogers also went over big.

(top) If you ever heard me say something disgusting, tasteless, or just plain silly over the air, chances are pretty good that one of these three maniacs wrote it. From left to right, Frank "Mars" Cotolo, "Mellow" Mike Walker, and Brad Hammond.

(bottom) A little-known fact about the Jackson Five is that there were really six of them. Honest! They all just danced so fast that you couldn't keep count. Young Michael had to sit on my lap that day to reach the microphone.

(top) Jesse Jackson's People United to Save Humanity brought me in on several benefit gigs. I like music a whole lot more than I like politics, but Jesse is a guy with a powerful vision.
(left) Talking tunes with Elton John. He's not a soul artist, but he's definitely got a huge amount of music in him.

(right) A very silly shot with Alice Cooper, for a magazine layout. You won't see him posing with a can of beer anymore: Alice is living healthy these days. (bottom) Eric Burdon visiting KDAY. The Beatles and Stones went on to greater popularity, but this guy's band, the Animals, was one of the main forces of the British Invasion. "The House of the Rising Sun" was a No. 1 hit in the fall of 1964. "Don't Let Me Be Misunderstood," "We Gotta Get Out of This Place," "See See Rider," and "San Franciscan Nights" were also strong tracks. *(Jeff Dunas)*

Bob Hope was so classy, he made a guest appearance in this 1979 Las Vegas show and overlooked the fact that I was cleaning seeds from my marijuana in the dressing room.

Helen Reddy brought something special to *The Midnight Special*. She also brought her then-husband/manager, whose antics may have cost Helen her job.

(top) Who's the greatest rock 'n' roller ever? For his long string of hits, for influencing the Stones, the Beatles, and practically everyone else, Chuck Berry just might be the champ. If you don't dig Chuck, you're outta luck!
(left) If you called me the Right Reverend Bishop Wolfman Jack, you'd be right! Here I am popping champagne to celebrate Mike Love's wedding in Santa Barbara, which I performed.

(top) Mike and I getting into our outfits.
(bottom) I guess you might say this is my "altar" ego.

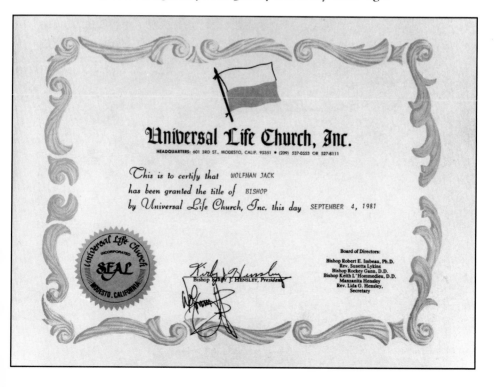

(top) No fooling, though, even a reprobate like me can have a religious side.
"Stoned Out of His Mind" was a hipster version of the David & Goliath tale.
(courtesy Mellow Mike Walker Collection)
(bottom) "I Saw Radio" was a star-crossed experience: some union guys
busted up and burned part of our set, then a truck crash finished it off. But
we had some great music and dancing together. That's Uncle John Herron
on the piano, one of the rockingest, most versatile session cats in L.A. today.

(right) My nephew, Randy Achee, who I chased down the hall when he was a toddler, inventing my Wolf voice as I played at scaring him and his brothers and sisters out of their wits. They loved it. And now Randy is a super-smart entertainment executive. *(Jeff Dunas)*
(bottom) Here's my son, Tod, who looks even more like the young me than I did. He's got a career going with his own artists' booking agency, a pretty wife, and a gorgeous little daughter.

(top) One of my best buddies in rock 'n' roll, Joe Walsh of the Eagles, brought me in as a guest on a video shoot for his tune "How Ya Doin?" The little trolley car pulled him in front of the desk, while I played the part of a disc jockey. The director said I was pretty convincing. *(Nancy Clendaniel)* (bottom) I met Phil Donahue when I did his show in the mid-'70s, then again one very rewarding day at the Kentucky Derby.

As a teenaged music business wannabe, I met Jackie Wilson backstage at Alan Freed's famous shows at the Brooklyn Paramount Theatre. Many years later I introduced him—as well as the Crystals, the Five Satins, Danny and the Juniors, Bo Diddley, and Jerry Lee Lewis—at a big concert in Oklahoma. *(courtesy Mellow Mike Walker Collection)*

Just when you thought your record collection was complete, here's
L'Histoire du Rock and Roll "par Wolfman Jack." I actually blew out speakers
in a Paris radio studio. *(courtesy Mellow Mike Walker Collection)*

the
United States
Air Force
presents

Wolfman Jack

Armed Forces Radio put me on a gazillion stations around the world, broadcasting some much-needed fun to Americans stationed overseas. Fortunately, as you can see, I didn't have to get a military haircut. *(courtesy Mellow Mike Walker Collection)*

And that's just one reason why I still carry on, going slightly insane over the airwaves every chance I get. I never thought my career would last so long. Hell, I never thought I'd live this long. But it's been enormous fun practically all the way. *(Jeff Dunas)*

wheel. As soon as the engine caught, he floored the gas pedal and we shot off in a spray of gravel, ripping down the highway.

The glow over Dooger's Harley began pulsating and getting larger. Every time Dennis threw the camper around a mountain curve, Dooger's bike would lean in the direction of each turn, as if there was a rider on board.

Meanwhile, the cold crept up from the bedroom to the middle of the camper. We all huddled as close as we could get to the driver's compartment. Lou and Guy began sprinkling salt all around the floor. The heater was blasting. All around the driver's seat it was normal, but everything from there to the back of the camper was as cold as a meat locker.

Finally, as we came around a turn, we could see a little town ahead. It was late, and the whole place looked shut down, except for a white church about half a mile ahead, all lit up, with a tall cross on the steeple.

Lou yelled, "Head for the church!"

There were no curbs or sidewalks in that little town, just lawns that came right up to the edge of the road. When we got up to the church Dennis cranked the wheel and we drove straight up on the grass. As soon as we did, there was a loud, electrical-sounding snap, as if a big wire had broken loose from a power pole.

Immediately, everything got peaceful. The temperature in the camper returned to normal.

We came to a full stop right in front of the steps to the church. And when we checked out the back window, the red glow had disappeared from the motorcycle seat. After catching our breath we got out to inspect.

The sides of the camper were so wet from the drizzle that you could run your hand across them and push off a sheet of water. Around back, Dennis's bike was standing upright, sopping wet. On Dooger's bike, the chain securing the front wheel had somehow gotten snapped in half. The tires, the tank, and the fenders were just as wet as everything else, but the seat was totally dry.

We all sat there until sunup, asking each other, "Was this true, or are we crazy, or what?" None of us had ever seen anything like that before. Yet we all experienced it at the same time.

Take this story with a grain of salt, if you want to, but I still get the chilly-willies remembering it now, nearly twenty years later.

Chapter Eighteen

Some wiseguy once said that time was invented so everything wouldn't happen all at once.

Well, in my life sometimes it seems like things are determined to happen all at once anyway. In this chapter, I'm going to share some things that went on concurrently with my *Midnight Special* and Canadian TV show years, and in the years immediately after those two extended gigs.

One night around this time I got dealt one of the biggest ego-crushers of my life. I was driving through Hollywood on Sunset Boulevard when I pulled up at a light on the left-hand side of a Cadillac convertible with four men in it.

"Good-looking car," I thought, glancing at the long lines and the swanky chrome trim. Then I looked up and saw Elvis Presley at the wheel. The other guys must've been part of his Memphis Mafia. I leaned across the seat and rolled my car's passenger window down. The light was just about to change.

"Hey, Elvis," I yelled. "It's me. Wolfman Jack! Hey, how are ya, Elvis?"

He looked my way, but his expression never changed. When the light went green, he barreled off in a cloud of smoking rubber.

I was depressed for the rest of the afternoon.

That's why I was in for such a surprise later on that same year, when I took my two kids, Joy and Tod, to see Elvis do his show at the International Hotel in Las Vegas.

Lou was in North Carolina at the time, visiting one of her sisters. I'd seen Elvis in person before, but I wanted my kids to have a chance to see him, too. I didn't call ahead and try to pull any strings; we just bought tickets like everyone else and ended up with a nice little table near the front. As we enjoyed our dinner before the show, I looked around the room and spotted Clint Eastwood at a table nearby. My kids were a lot more impressed when they saw Carrie Fisher, who they recognized as Princess Leia from *Star Wars.*

Finally, Elvis came on and started rocking the place in his usual heart-stopping style. About halfway through the performance, though, he broke from the choreographed routine and started pacing the stage and talking to the audience. "Y'know," he said, "I've been traveling on the road just about all my life. One of the main people I've always listened to on the radio, and my favorite disc jockey of all time, is Wolfman Jack. And we're very lucky this evening to have him out in the audience.

"Wolfman, don't be shy now. Stand up and say hello to the people." A spotlight hit our table, and I rose up and did just like he asked.

Well, this totally blew my mind. Ever since that three-second heartbreak on Sunset Boulevard, I'd figured that either he didn't know me, or he did know me but hated me like poison.

Then Elvis told the audience a story. Their bus driver

fell asleep one night, out in the middle of nowhere at all. The Wolfman, he claimed, woke him up with a big, crazy howl. They might all be dead if it wasn't for my loud voice.

Of course, it was the same story Glen Campbell had once told me. And chances are it was happy bullshit. But I wasn't about to raise my hand and embarrass the King of Rock 'n' Roll.

Afterward, one of his guys came over and said, "Elvis would like you to come see him backstage after the show. And please bring your kids with you."

Well, I was the proudest papa on the planet that night. Elvis turned out to be the nicest guy imaginable. He talked to each of the kids individually. He gave me his autograph, which I asked for like the unabashed fan that I am. And we talked about the music we both loved for a couple of hours or more.

Elvis knew all about John R. out of WLAC in Nashville, and could recite by heart some of the commercials and raps he used to do. He had an extremely detailed knowledge of southern black music of the late 1940s and early 1950s. He told me about how when he was a teenager he caught "Good Rockin'" Roy Brown's show whenever he could. Which was why "Good Rockin' Tonight," Roy Brown's signature tune, was one of the first songs Elvis ever recorded.

Years later, Roy Brown came to Elvis one night at his home in Graceland. He was down on his luck. He owed the Feds $4,000 in back taxes and they were going to put him in the can the next day. Elvis didn't have his checkbook nearby, so he flattened out a small brown grocery store bag and wrote out a check on it for the full amount. And the bank honored that check the next day, so Roy stayed out of the jug.

From that day on, Brown would tell the story at his

club shows, finishing it by saying, "Elvis was the black man's friend."

I know, because I heard him repeat the tale one night in 1980, performing at the Roxy on Sunset Strip just a year before he died. And when Roy did a show, there really was "good rockin'" that night. He was another of those guys who inspired the first rock 'n' rollers, but somehow never got as much fame and reward as he really deserved.

Anyway, Elvis and I grew to have a very nice friendship. And I learned that he had a phenomenal appetite for beautiful women. Just like they did for him.

Some two or three years after I met Elvis for the first time, Lou and I were asleep in bed one night when the phone rang. Since it was over on her side, Lou picked it up.

"Hello," a voice said. "Is Wolfman there? This is Elvis."

Now, I had a few smart-ass guys on the payroll, like Mars and Mellow Mike, who wrote funny bits for my shows. Lou figured one of them was having some fun with me, because they all knew I was crazy about Elvis.

"Sure," Lou said. "Now tell me who this *really* is."

"This is Elvis. Elvis Presley."

Lou nudged me to roll over and grab the receiver. When I got on the line, the voice said, "Wolf? That you, man? How ya doin'? This is Elvis."

"Elvis?" I sat straight up.

"Yeah. I want you to come over to Las Vegas and be with us a while, man. We're gonna open in a couple of days at the International Hotel and we're partyin' a little bit before it all starts.

"Right about now you should see a limousine pullin' up outside your house. He's gonna take you down to the John Wayne Airport in Orange County. Say the word and I'll send a jet over there to pick you up."

All I could say was "Hold on a minute." Then I shook Lou's shoulder.

"Go out in front, baby. See if there's anything unusual going on."

She came back a minute later.

"There's a white stretch limo out there with the lights on."

"What should I do?" I said. "He wants me to go to Vegas. But he's probably got a bunch of broads there. What do you think I should do, babe?"

Because I was flattered to the point of insanity that Elvis was calling in the middle of the night with an invitation to party, but I didn't want to smoke my marriage because of it.

"You'd better go," she said.

Sometimes you've got to look in people's eyes when they tell you something. Because her lips told me yes, but there was a totally different message coming through her orbs.

"Uh, Elvis," I finally said, with a real regretful note in my voice, "I'd love to, but I don't think I can make it, man."

I don't know for sure what kind of scene I missed out on, but I'm guessing that it was real different from a Cub Scout Jamboree.

Another great performer gave me a hell of a compliment once. That was Freddie King, the great blues man, who passed away back in 1976.

Eric Clapton is just one of several younger guys who learned their guitar chops by copying Freddie's great instrumental, "Hideaway." And, of course, Eric also included Freddie's "Have You Ever Loved a Woman" on his *Layla* album.

Freddie King was a very inventive player, sort of a bridge between the styles of B.B. King (even though they weren't related) and Muddy Waters. He could be real lyrical one moment, then raw, aggressive, and piercing the next. Check out "San-Ho-Zay," "In the Open," or "You've Got to Love Her with a Feeling."

I met Freddie King backstage at a big rock festival in the early 1970s. At that time, Leon Russell was trying to get more of the young white audience hip to Freddie King's music. He helped him put out an album called *Getting Ready*, which had just been released on Shelter Records.

Freddie performed a great-sounding cut from it for the festival audience, a double-time blues shuffle called "Living on the Highway."

I was blown away, because through all the drumbeats and the crowd noises, I made out some phrases that seemed to be about me. "I was about fourteen years old," one verse went, "when I first heard the Wolfman howl." Then there was something about "His heart beat right on time. His hand make two of mine. He taught me how to sing the blues."

"Freddie," I said backstage, almost beside myself, "that song about living on the highway—is that really about me?"

"Yes, indeed, Wolfman. 'Cause you been my inspiration for a long time now." Leon Russell was standing there with us, wearing one of those velvety-looking top hats that were his trademark, with his long hair hanging down to his shoulders from underneath.

"That's right, Wolf," Leon added in his Tulsa drawl. "Me and Freddie wrote that together—with you in mind."

Man, I loved that. The very next day I went out and bought the album. But when I listened to it real close, though, I realized that Freddie—bless him and rest his talented soul—must have been saying that stuff to make me feel good. He was born about four years before I was, so that would've made me just ten years old when he "first heard the Wolfman howl."

That song was really a tribute to somebody who truly did teach a hell of a lot of people how to sing the blues: Chester Arthur Burnett of West Point, Mississippi, better known to the world as Howlin' Wolf.

Now, if you've never heard Howlin' Wolf, put a book marker on this page, set the book aside, and get on down to the nearest record store that sells the blues. Anyone with albums by the Grateful Dead, the Doors, the Yardbirds, Jeff Beck, Cream, Little Feat, or Led Zeppelin in their collection has already heard several Howlin' Wolf tunes. Songs like "Back Door Man," "Wang Dang Doodle," "Spoonful," "Killing Floor," or the all-time hoo-doo classic, "Smokestack Lightning."

My personal favorite is an instrumental called "Houserocker," where each guy in the band stretches out with some hot licks and Howlin' Wolf ad-libs things like "Play that git-tar, Willie Johnson, till it *smoke!*"

Freddie King, Leon Russell, and Howlin' Wolf are just a few of the interesting people I met at one time or another on the festival circuit.

In August of 1974 I was booked into a huge outdoor show near Sedalia, Missouri. That was where I met the great gonzo madman, Ted Nugent, and also my very good friend, Joe Walsh, who was getting ready to join the Eagles.

In all the euphoria after the big success of Woodstock, lots of folks started organizing rock festivals.

My manager and I arrived backstage at the Sedalia show in a helicopter. He scoped out the situation from the air, and it looked extremely unruly. For one thing, out of the forty thousand people there, large swarms of hippies were clambering up these fragile towers near the stage. The towers were just designed to hold one lighting technician and a few small spotlights.

All the noise of the helicopter made it almost impossible for us to hear each other. My manager took a hundred-dollar bill out of his wallet, holding it up for the chopper pilot to see. Then he ripped it neatly through the middle, vertically. "This half is yours to keep," he shouted. "You get the other half if you stay here and make sure that we get out okay."

It was a solid move. When we got to the ground, we learned that the promoters had hired some local Hell's Angels to assist the security forces, and then apparently failed to pay the guys. Which is a very rude move to pull on anybody, especially tattoo-smeared, hog-riding, anarchy-loving folks who wear eye patches, buy Pagan Pink Ripple by the case, and carry chains.

To show their unhappiness, the Angels rounded up the golf carts that had been provided for VIP ground transport and set them all on fire.

This was a more radical version of festival activity than I was prepared for. Also, they didn't have enough water, there weren't enough restrooms, and a huge number of people had crashed the gate.

The stage manager was doing all he could to prevent complete chaos. He begged me to go out and ask the people to climb down off the light towers before somebody got killed.

This put me in a tough spot. I didn't want anyone hurt, but I also didn't come to this gig to become known as a policeman. Most of all, I didn't want those rampaging Angels coming after my ass. But in the meantime, none of the bands wanted to take the stage. It was turning uglier by the minute.

I went out, reluctantly.

I don't know if you've ever looked out across forty thousand heads right at sundown on a hot, humid August day in Missouri, when a light drizzle has begun to fall. Let me tell you, the body heat just *rolls* off of the people. It almost knocks you back.

Steam was rising up off that mass of bodies and into the night air, which made for a real eerie sight. Imagine looking at all those folks, and seeing the flimsy towers swaying over on the side, with dozens of scraggly hippies hanging on to the girders, and off in the distance there's a stack of golf carts giving off some real smelly smoke. This is a scene that would turn anybody's knees into Jell-O.

Ted Nugent saw us headed out there to face the beast. This was when he was still with his band the Amboy Dukes, as I recall.

"If you want," Nugent said, "I'll play some background for you."

This took some *cojones*. The crowd was screaming and yelling in frustration. People had started throwing stuff onstage. One of the towers was starting to rock from side to side.

Suddenly, a guy down in front started screaming up at us. "There's a woman here who's giving birth! Get her a doctor!"

I was overwhelmed. I stepped up to the mike to tell them that we wanted to start the show. Before I could get a word out—*WHAM*—something very solid hit me in the forehead. I looked down and saw a stubby brown beer bottle spinning around down by my feet.

I shook my head. "WE WANT TO START THE SHOW," I said.

I smiled, and gave the crowd a couple of heartbeats to let the words sink in. "We want to start the show,"

I continued, "but first we've got to help out all of these people who are stuck on the towers. They want to get off, but they can't see to do it."

I turned to the stagehands who were out by the front corners of the stage. Each of them had a small spotlight that could be aimed into the crowd. "Could we shine some lights over there, please? 'Cause they're trying to come down from the tower so we can start the show."

A few of the tower climbers started to inch down. It was working!

" 'Cause it's going to fall," I added. And then *all* the people started coming down.

Then I told everyone, "Now we want some peace. A woman is giving birth right down in front here."

Ted Nugent had just had a little kid, and he had written a lullaby. Which is not what you'd expect from the Motor City Madman, but nonetheless he stepped up to the mike and began singing this pretty tune, backing himself with an acoustic guitar. It was the most amazing moment. If he'd done a gospel number instead, I'd have gotten religion right there.

Except for a goofed-up few guys here and there who were just yelling aimlessly, probably because of pills, the whole crowd hushed.

From that point on, the concert went on pretty good and everybody got home safely.

A week later, about the time that our chopper pilot was explaining to his bank teller why he was depositing a C-note held together with cellophane tape, *People* magazine reported that a baby had been born during a rock concert near Sedalia, Missouri.

The proud parents named their boy Wolfman Johnson.

Y'know, besides having to admit that my own kids are grown up and I've become a grandfather, now I have to reflect on the fact that, somewhere out in the great Midwest, a kid named Wolfman Johnson recently became old enough to vote.

As anybody who has spent a good deal of time on the rock 'n' roll trail can tell you, fly-by-night promoters are one of the hazards of the trade. The post–Woodstock era was the worst, but it wasn't the end of the problem.

We were doing an oldies show in Minneapolis only a few years ago. The Shirelles were there, and Freddy Cannon and several other acts. Just before curtain time, we learned that the promoters had disappeared. Nobody was going to get paid. Meanwhile, there was an auditorium out there completely filled with fans. After half an hour of delay, they started going a little nuts. They were stamping their feet, whistling, beginning to yell a few obscenities.

Most of the performers were packing up and getting ready to leave. I hated being in the situation. I mean, no performer likes traveling thousands of miles just to get ripped off. You can stay home, get ripped off right there, and save yourself all the travel expenses, y'know?

But I also really hated the thought of all those pissed-off people in the audience going home with a massive case of the sour grumbles, or maybe even rioting and hurting each other.

Lonnie Napier, the same guy who came to work for me when he was just nineteen and I was running XERB, is now my full-time road manager. He came up and said, "We've got to get out of here while still we can. There's no show."

Freddy Cannon came up at the same time and asked, "What're you guys going to do?"

The Shirelles came over, too. They asked us, "Are you guys going to back out?"

"Folks," I said, "I wanna try something here. But just

to be smart, somebody should go tell the limo driver to be ready. 'Cause this might not work."

I went out onto the stage and started playing the piano. Standing up, in case I had to cut and run.

Now, nobody is going to mistake my keyboard skills for those of a Rock 'n' Roll Hall-of-Famer. But I can pound out "Blueberry Hill" about as good as the star of your neighborhood bar. So I did that old Fats Domino favorite, and the crowd mellowed down a little. Then I went into "Tears on My Pillow." By the time I finished singing "You don't remember me, but I remember you," Freddy Cannon had walked up behind me and tapped me on the shoulder. He took over the next verse—" 'Twas not so long ago, you broke my heart in two . . ." And when we hit the chorus, the Shirelles were right there: "Tears on my pillow, pain in my heart, caused by you-ooo-ooo-ooo, you-ooooooo . . ." Totally unrehearsed, but when one of the Shirelles took the last note of the chorus and sent it soaring, man, the hairs on the back of my neck stood up.

Remember, I said before that Minneapolis is a real hip city. I knew it from the early 1960s, when I managed radio station KUXL. Well, those people in the audience never once complained about the other acts, who were all long gone. They knew they'd caught a very special night. It turned out to be one of the most fun, people-pleasing shows I'd done in a real long time.

My longtime friend Chuck Berry is someone who's developed a bulletproof way of doing business: half the money must be delivered before he even leaves his living room in old Saint Lou. One hour before he takes the stage, the other half must be handed to him in a brown paper bag.

Because he's one of the greatest that ever lived, and

can pack a show all by himself, Chuck gets away with it.

Over the years, I've done more shows with him than I could possibly count. He's always backed by a blue-collar band made up of local musicians or other acts on the same bill, all of them excited to play with the Master. It's a rite of passage. Bruce Springsteen did it on his way up, and so have several hundred others, from big stars to woulda-beens and coulda-beens.

Chuck always shows up real early, even though he's almost always the last act. One time I happened to be walking past the promoter's office door when my man Chuck was receiving the goods.

It was a sight to see. The promoter reached in his desk and pulled out something that looked like a grade-schooler's lunch sack. Chuck fished out a bundle of bills that looked like close to $20,000. He hefted the stack, gauging its weight. He riffled the long edges of the bills like a riverboat gambler checking a deck for markings, then he put the greenbacks up by his right ear and sampled the sound they made when he ran his thumb across the ends.

Then he smiled, shook hands, stuffed everything back into the stack and vanished like a wraith. Didn't even see me as he brushed past.

From that day on, whenever I got paid I'd slap the money by my ears, Berry-style. But I was just goofing, faking it for an effect. Chuck, I believe he could *smell* a stack of bills and tell you how much is there, to the last penny.

Of course, money alone isn't enough for anybody. Ultimately, Chuck wants the world to remember that he's been laying down prime, influential sounds since back in '54.

Very recently I emceed a show that included both him and Johnny Rivers. As you know, Johnny kicked off his career by doing several Chuck Berry tunes.

There's no crime in that. In the first place, Chuck collected a ton of royalties off of Johnny's versions. And second, people who've done Chuck's material include Emmylou Harris, the Stones, the Beatles, the Grateful Dead, Aaron Neville, and probably the guy who sat next to you on the bus Wednesday morning.

However, on this one particular occasion, Chuck Berry was apparently in the mood to let the world know who THE MAN was. As Johnny was getting ready to go on, he walked up to the promoter and said, "I'm gonna go onstage now."

"But you're the headliner."

"Don't worry. I'm gonna go on later, too. But I wanna go on now."

And you don't say no to one of the Founding Fathers, right?

So Chuck took the stage and played "Memphis," "Maybellene," and all the rest of his tunes that Johnny does. Then did all of them a second time, duck-walking up a storm and reeling off all his classic double-string rock guitar riffs—the same ones that you'll hear copied on just about every single Rolling Stones record ever made. Then he told the crowd, "Thank you very much. I'll be back right after Johnny Rivers."

Johnny did his regular set, including "Memphis," "Maybellene," and all the others.

Chuck returned, then played all the same songs again, driving his point home.

Of course, you've got to expect that the big stars have big egos. Jerry Lee Lewis, for example, does what Jerry Lee Lewis wants to do, and everyone else can go to blazes. But he's also got a heart big enough to park a Lincoln Continental inside. He just hasn't got the Lincoln itself. The IRS takes his cars away every few years in their semi-regular raids for back taxes.

I hosted a show with Jerry Lee about two years ago, and it just happened that two of my little grand-nieces were there. He met them backstage, and just before it was his turn to go on he said, "Wolf, I want you to grab that chair over there, bring it out onstage, and let them two little gals sit in your lap and enjoy the show from up close."

We did it, and I bet those girls are going to remember it as long as they live. I sure will.

I wasn't around when Jerry Lee and Chuck had their famous clash at the close of an Alan Freed show at the old Brooklyn Paramount. But it's a story that has traveled the grapevine for three and a half decades, and it's still real funny.

Chuck and Jerry Lee both had million-sellers on the charts at the time. There was a big argument over who should have the honor of being the closing act on the bill. After some wild arguing, Freed finally decided it had to be Chuck, because his song was just a little higher on that week's charts.

Well, Jerry Lee took the stage and pounded out every one of his hit songs with double the usual amount of gospel-tent frenzy and keyboard-ravaging, piano-bench-kicking fury. When he got down with "Whole Lot of Shakin' Going On," he pulled out a can of lighter fluid from his pants pocket and saturated the piano's innards. Then he lit up a whole book of paper matches, tossed it inside, watched the flames and black smoke begin curling up, and marched off the stage. As he passed by Alan Freed, standing there horrified in the wings, Jerry

Lee said, "I'd like to see the motherfucker who can top *that!*"

Another guy who once in a while gets his ego out of joint is the pride of Macon, Georgia, the irrepressible Little Richard. He deserves a big ego, and a cut out of every paycheck that Paul McCartney and Mick Jagger ever picked up, because Little Richard was the first guy who did that ravin', cravin' thing — the rawest, most audacious singing you've ever heard, the brain-melting one-note piano solos, and the unlimited, hands-on-the-hips, audience-taunting showmanship.

Leon Russell wrote a great and very accurate tribute song to Little Richard, "Crystal Closet Queen," and the refrain goes like this: "Tutti-frutti, the Beauty's on duty . . . When the Beauty's on duty, you know we're gonna have a time!"

Anyway, late in the 1970s I was hosting a big show in Long Beach. At that time, my pride and joy was an outrageous bright, tight fluorescent pink leotard outfit that a wonderful black lady costume designer back in L.A. had just stitched up for me in time for this gig. It featured a matching vest and a belt with dozens of small mirrors stitched into them. I also had a customized Fender Stratocaster with a mirror epoxied all across the front.

This was when laser lights were kind of a new thing on the concert circuit, and glitter rock was the hot ticket of the day. I opened my set with Gary Glitter's hit, "Rock and Roll Part Two." Then I did Queen's "We Will Rock You." To excite the crowd, I would aim the guitar to reflect the spotlight back at them.

Whenever I'm going to introduce somebody at a show, I go up beforehand and ask them personally if they have any preferred things they'd like me to say. For example, there's a man you probably know as Little Anthony. And you know by heart all the Little Anthony and the Imperials hits—"Tears on My Pillow," "Shimmy, Shimmy, Ko-Ko-Bop," "Goin' Out of My Head," and a few others. Well, nowadays he wants you to know him by the name he grew up with: Anthony Gourdine. And he's a brother from Brooklyn, so I respect his wishes.

Anyway, I got directions to Little Richard's dressing room and went to ask him how he wanted his introduction done. Also, we were supposed to do a number together near the end of his set, and I wanted to know how I should time my entrance. I walked in to see "The Georgia Peach" dressed in a purple outfit that had a couple of tiny square mirrors on it. He took one look at me and my outer space–style getup, and his face dropped right down to the floor.

"Oh, my God," he said. "I can't go on now. You look *prettier* than I do!"

"Richard," I said, "I had this made specially for your show, just to be with you."

Push come to shove, I had to switch outfits before Little Richard would agree to leave his dressing room.

Of course, I've got an ego, too. And every now and then, somebody comes along and does me a favor by letting a little air out of it.

Recently I was sitting in a coffee shop at the Dallas airport, killing time before a flight back home to North Carolina. I was wearing one of my favorite traveling outfits, a big, black, wide-brimmed cowboy hat, black jeans, and a fancy pair of black cowboy boots.

Suddenly I felt like someone was nearby and I looked up. There was Jacqueline Bisset standing next to my chair, a lady who had been making my pulse race for a long time.

Could it be that she was a Wolfman Jack fan? Well, apparently so.

"I've always been a great fan of yours," she said, with

warmth that reached all the way down to the silver-tipped toes of my boots. "And I just have to tell you, I could not miss this chance to say hello to you. I've thought you were wonderful ever since you started. My kids love you just as much, Mr. Jennings, and we've got all of your records."

Right now, Jacqueline Bisset is probably sitting home in Beverly Hills, sore as hell at Waylon Jennings for sitting there like a bump on a log while she said such nice things to him.

Another time, I was at a big mid-summer benefit at Dodger Stadium, sharing a bill with Sidney Poitier, George Peppard, and lots of other famous folks for Jesse Jackson's organization, PUSH.

The initials stand for "People United to Save Humanity." But we did so many benefits for Jesse in those days that my manager started calling it "Promotions Under Stress and Harassment."

Anyway, a friend and I were down in the ballplayers' locker room, which was the coolest place in the building. We noticed someone on the other side of the room, seated at a folding table and deep in concentration with a pencil and a pad of paper. It was Marlon Brando.

Now, ever since *The Wild One*, *Viva Zapata*, *On the Waterfront*, and *One-Eyed Jacks*, I've been a huge fan of this guy. I mean, who hasn't? I stared at him in silence for the longest time. Finally, I pulled some courage together and went and stood by his table. I could see that he was writing a speech. I could also see that he was purposely ignoring my presence.

I kept hushed until I couldn't stand it any longer. "Mr. Brando," I began. "Marlon . . ."

Brando waited two or three ticks and then he looked up into my face.

"I didn't want to interrupt," I said, "but I also didn't want to miss a chance to say how much I enjoy your work."

He sat there like a sleepy giant tortoise, regarding me warily out of one eye.

Finally I said, "I'm Wolfman Jack."

He scanned me slowly, from my head to my toes and back again, like a movie camera on rusty hinges. Then he leaned back a few inches, cracked about half of a smile and remarked, "The hell you say!"

That was it. I didn't push my luck another inch. I was more delighted than a little kid who'd gotten a personal handshake from Santa Claus. But I also understood that he wanted me to leave him alone, so I did.

I mentioned several pages back that at one time I was the Right Reverend Bishop Wolfman Jack. I got that title in 1982, while doing a favor for Mike Love of the Beach Boys.

Back in the old days, whenever their band did a big show there was always a little silver bowl filled with cocaine backstage, maybe $3,000 worth. Everybody could just dip in and take what they wanted. Before they got onstage, nearly all of it would be gone.

Mike Love and I spent many nights after concerts, getting high and talking. One day I was visiting at his place in Santa Barbara, which has this wonderful view from up on a cliff, overlooking the whole valley below. There's a little guest house right up at the edge of the cliff, with the pool and a steam room right beside it. That's where we were sitting when he told me that he and his sweetheart were planning to get hitched. "I want you to marry us. None of my other four marriages have been successful. I want this one to work and I want you to do it for me."

I said, "I can't, man, I'm not a preacher."

He says, "Don't worry. There's a mail-order church thing, the Universal Life Church Incorporated of Modesto, California. They'll fix you up."

I looked into it. Lots of folks had signed up with this outfit during the Vietnam War, attempting to beat the draft. You could be a plain old preacher, but for about $50 more you could be a bishop.

I figured I might as well go all the way. So pretty soon they sent me a certificate that gave me the legal right to do a marriage.

I got together with my writers and we concocted a marriage service that was heartfelt, but very beboppy. Then somebody went down to a religious supply store and got me a groovy-looking set of robes, with all the flourishes in the right places. *People* magazine was on hand to record the scene, as Mike and his very lovely bride tied the knot in front of about a hundred guests at his big house. One photo opportunity the *People* people missed was my manager rushing down to the county courthouse to personally make sure the marriage certificate got properly registered, just so there was no chance of a lawsuit or something if the marriage went south. And, unfortunately, it did go down the tubes within about six months.

Mike's original plan had been to charter a Concorde and have Bishop Wolfman Jack emcee three Beach Boys concerts in three different countries on two separate continents within twenty-four hours, all on the day of his wedding. For good measure, he wanted to do this on the Fourth of July, with the ceremony taking place somewhere between Paris and Washington, D.C., at supersonic speed.

You've gotta love that kind of ambition.

Of all the music stars I ever met, and got a friendly word from, the most unlikely of all was the undisputed "King of Country Music," Roy Acuff.

For those who only know about rock 'n' roll, Roy Acuff was born way back in 1903 and he grew up to be one of the great stars of the Grand Ole Opry. By the time of World War Two, he was almost equally as popular as Frank Sinatra. In fact, he ran for governor of Tennessee in 1948 and nearly won. A little later on, he joined forces with a songwriter named Fred Rose and created Acuff-Rose music, which soon became the most powerful music publishing business in Nashville history. All the best-known Everly Brothers and Roy Orbison tunes were on Acuff-Rose, just to name a few.

By the time I finally met him in 1979, Acuff had developed a reputation as a crusty old coot. He'd given in to the Nitty Gritty Dirt Band when they pleaded with him to be part of their great *Will the Circle Be Unbroken* album, along with Doc Watson and Mother Maybelle Carter. But he hated hippies, so he walked into the studio and told the band, "They call me 'One-Take Acuff,' boys. Let's git this done and I can go home."

Roy Acuff had a whole lot of respect for the Easter Seals charity. In the late 1970s I did a lot of appearances around the country on behalf of Easter Seals. It happened that 1978 had been a record-breaking year for contributions. Not many people knew that, but old Roy Acuff did. When he found out that I was flying in to Nashville, he drove down and waited for an hour at the airport just to shake my hand.

There was no press there, no hoopla of any kind. So as I walked into the lobby, this hippie-hating, seventy-six-year-old codger who'd built the foundations of country and western music stepped up to me, extended his hand, and said simply, "You wear your legend well."

I thought that was about the best compliment anyone ever gave me.

Speaking of legends, around this same time I did a big charity telethon at the Hollywood Bowl. There were dozens of stars, but, of course, the biggest of all was the main guy behind the whole thing—Bob Hope.

He sent me a very nice letter afterward, mentioning my two kids by name and saying how proud they must be of their old man. Which was a classy PR touch on his part. But the letter was addressed to "Dear Mr. Jack," so I figured he didn't really know me from Adam.

A month later I was sitting in my dressing room with my pal Mars at *The Midnight Special*. With free time on my hands, I was sifting a fresh ounce of marijuana in the lid of a shoe box, using the jack of diamonds to pry seeds loose from the buds.

While I was preoccupied, doing a workmanlike job on my stash, there was a knock at the door. Mars opened it. I heard a sudden catch in his throat as he said, "It's Bob Hope."

I looked up from my handiwork. Mars's eyes were as big around as the planet we named him for. Bob Hope stepped briskly into the room. I froze.

"I heard you were in the building," he said, as I attempted to cover the dope with my hands. "I have to thank you so much for when you came and did my show."

I couldn't get up to shake his hand, and I was incredibly embarrassed. Now, I'm sure Bob Hope has probably seen reefer before. But he's such an icon. I felt like my pants had dropped and I was standing with my weenie exposed in front of the Pope himself.

Two years later, when I was headlining at the Riviera in Las Vegas, someone called my office and said, "This is Bob Hope. When is Wolfman going to have his opening night?"

Everybody figured it was somebody having a laugh on us, but come opening night Bob Hope was right there, in the front row.

Kind words from stars are great, but the really everlasting good feelings come from the things that everyday, down-to-earth people share with me every now and then. One night I introduced Ray Charles's show at Radio City Music Hall. It was a benefit to raise money for blind people. I think he had a big hit record at the time. I asked the crowd to hold up matches and lighters and pay tribute to Ray as he took the stage. When I described the scene, Ray threw both arms around me and rocked us both back and forth in a mighty hug.

Well, the hug thing turned out to be contagious. I walked backstage and began making my way toward the exit, thinking about the plane I had to catch to get myself back home. Before I got to the door, three big, burly guys descended on me. Two were black and one was white.

Now, I'm pretty big, but these fellows picked me up and passed me from one to the other like a little girl's doll baby. Between the three of them, they just about hugged the breath out of me.

It turned out that these guys were all Vietnam vets.

When my syndication activity was at a peak, and I was on the Armed Forces Network, I was on some 1,400 radio stations worldwide. That included Vietnam, of course.

These guys told me that through all the slogging in the mud, seeing their buddies die, and wondering whether they'd get back home in one piece, or at all, the main thing they had to look forward to from day to day to was the great rhythm and blues music and the jokes and wisecracks on my show. By doing my thing in a Hollywood studio, I was helping them keep it together. And they made it out the other end of a pretty hellish experience.

I never talked about the misery of the war on those Armed Forces shows. I figured they needed to be taken to a happy zone.

"We goin' into the Wolfman's Happy House now," I would say. "We goin' to put down our heavy burden. We gonna get down, baby. Come on in here, Little Richard, and tell the people all about that gal from back home, that ol' 'Long Tall Sally.'" Then I'd hit 'em with sexy love ballads in between the rockers and the funky R&B.

As you probably know by now, black folks did a very heavy percentage of the most dangerous work in that particular misadventure. A great book called *Bloods* paints a real convincing picture of what they went through.

Anyway, I ended up canceling my flight and spending the rest of the night with those guys in a Manhattan saloon.

A few years later, I got hired for $10,000 to come in and play records in some big hotel lobby in Washington, the night before the dedication ceremonies for the Vietnam Memorial Wall. In honor of Chuck Berry, I got the money up front.

The lobby was set up to hold about three thousand people, and I was perched in a DJ booth that looked out over everybody's heads. The place was filled beyond capacity and everyone was having such a good time, I lifted my $10,000 in cash over my head and yelled, "C'mere and get this money. Let's get us something to drink!"

They came at me in waves and I just flung hundred-dollar bills at them. The whole wad went in a couple of minutes. They went out and bought cases of beer and cases of Jack Daniel's and we kept that party going all night long.

The next morning it came time for the march down the boulevard to the Memorial. A bunch of those guys lifted me on their shoulders and carried me all the way to the dedication.

A lot of guys still come up to me now after shows and say, "Wolfman, remember the night you spent all your money?"

I sure do, and it was more than worth it. That was one of the finest times I ever had in my life.

Another time when I had a huge helping of fun was the year I worked for the Kentucky Derby. I was traveling with my nephew Randy. The same lad who used to make me bribe him with quarters so I could get time alone with my girlfriends. There was a week-long series of events scheduled, including big concerts with Dolly Parton, Kenny Rogers, and Bob Seger.

On our way into Louisville, it just happened that the food on the airplane was really, really bad. I love to eat, but this stuff was so bad that I sent it back and just did without.

A southern guy named Trig Black was in charge of most of the major events surrounding Derby Week. He'd outbid the regular guy and it was his first time to handle such a big ball of wax. When we got off the plane, just about every stretch limo available in the states of Kentucky and Tennessee was waiting out by the curb. The one Trig had for us was the biggest one of them all, a dark blue Lincoln.

Our driver, a very calm and professional type guy who happened to be black, introduced himself as John R.

"That's funny," I said. "When I was a kid, a guy named John R. did a rhythm and blues show out of Nashville. He was my disc jockey idol."

"That's who my folks named me after," John R. said.

To me, this was a *sign*.

We were on a tight, tight schedule that first day, and I knew that Trig was expecting us right away at a local radio station to plug the Seger show. But my stomach was growling like a grizzly bear, and I said to John R., "Now, John, I know you're the kind of person who'll know where the best ribs in all the South is. I mean, here in Louisville anyway."

"Well," he said, "there's a great place on the outside of town. But if we go out there, we're likely to be late."

"That's okay," I said. "Take us, please."

Randy was freaking out. It was his job to get me to the gig on time. But occasionally I just get fixated. And John R. up there in the driver's seat kept describing exactly how good these ribs were going to be.

"This is true, down-home barbecue," he said, "real smoky and real spicy," and by then I didn't care if I had to kill somebody to get those ribs in my hands.

Finally we pulled up in a shantytown area outside the city, a community where there was more cardboard than wood in the shacks. Next to one extremely humble place there were three fifty-five-gallon drums that had been cut in half and put on stands of crisscrossed two-by-fours. The other halves were mounted on hinges, so they could be closed up to trap the smoke. Iron bars were rigged across the drums to make a grate, holes were poked in the sides, and all three barbecue smokers were going full tilt as we drove up.

As soon as I stepped out of the limo, the guy running the barbecue stand recognized me and went nuts. He said he always used to listen to me on that crazy Mexican station. For $10, he laid enough barbecue on us to feed a small army. I took one taste, wiped a tear from my eye as the chili sauce hit home, and handed him a C-note. "Baby," I said, "this is worth every damn penny!"

Finally, I was ready to let John R. drive us to that radio station, where we arrived a half hour late.

Trig, one of those rare southern guys who talks faster than any New Yorker ever born, ran out to the parking lot as our Lincoln rolled in. "Wolfwherehaveyoubeen?" he said. "We'reabouttogoontheair!" He sounded like an auctioneer on little white pills.

That was the first time I'd ever seen the guy. And the first thing I noticed was that he was about five and a half feet tall, and also five and a half feet around.

I knew what to do next. While he kept talking a mile a minute, I said, " 'Scuse me a second, Trig." Then I reached into the car and brought out some ribs dripping in sauce. "I have a feeling that this here's something you're going to enjoy mightily."

He caught a whiff of that hardwood-smoked aroma and in that instant, all the stress was forgotten. Everything was cool. Trig hunkered down in a corner and gnawed those ribs until his teeth were clacking on the bones. I almost couldn't hear to do my thing for the radio people.

I ain't finished with this Kentucky Derby story yet, but I wish I could take a break and go get another serving from that same fantastic Louisville barbecue man. I can taste those ribs right now. Have mercy!

This was the year that Seattle Slew ended up winning the Derby. ABC had hired me to attend and say things on camera like, "Hey, we're having a good time here at the Kentucky Derby! Come on down! This is old Ralph over here. Hello, Ralph. Look at the terrific horses he's got."

In between those few spots, we had a lot of free time.

Louisville, during Derby Week, is all kinds of fun. Everybody is in a party mood, from the old-money set to the poor folks on the fringe of town.

Thanks to ABC, Randy and I had fantastic access to every layer of Louisville society. At the track, we could go up to the main echelon, where the rich had their own little private enclave.

"Hey, man," I said to Randy, "the people who *own* these horses are sitting around us. Let's split up and start getting friendly with these folks. We might learn something valuable."

He began working one side of the room while I did the other. We shook hands with everybody. And we started getting tips from these people, really getting into the underground inside of what was happening.

Thanks to our new friends, we began winning money on one race after the other. I'd come in with $500, but by the time I went to my hotel that night I was able to hand $20,000 to the concierge and say, "Do me a favor, good man, and stash this loot in your safe."

Anyway, after a little while we knew everybody in those luxury boxes. They were loving us to death and we were having mint juleps with 'em, rubbing elbows with the landed gentry of Kentucky.

These were country gentlemen and gentlewomen, baby, like you might see in the movies. Starched white linen and high collars. The whole routine.

We walked out for a while to confer with the ABC people. Up walked Phil Donahue and Marlo Thomas, and we all started chatting.

"Listen, man," I told Phil, "in the next race you've gotta bet on Satan's Thunder."

This was a horse that was quite a long shot. But I had just been talking with some blueblood type guy who had

330

been drinking pretty heavily, and bragging about inside information. And I had kept saying, "Hey, tell me a little more. It sounds good."

"I've been told," he said through a mint-julep-induced fog, "that someone gave that horse a little something to make him real happy . . . You know what I mean, Wolfman?"

Phil kind of laughed and chuckled as I related all this. I could see that he wasn't taking any of it seriously. You hear all kinds of supposedly inside bullshit at the racetrack. It gets pretty comical at times. But when Randy and I went down to watch the horses being led up to the starting gates, Satan's Thunder was stomping and sweating and foaming, looking like he was going to jump right out of his own genuine horsehide skin.

"This son of a bitch is gonna win, man," I told Randy. "Run back and put another thousand on for me. Here, put a hundred on for yourself, too."

Randy laid down the extra money, which was nearly everything I was carrying at that point. He and I got up to the blueblood boxes just in time to see the horses go charging out of the gates to start the race. We kind of muscled our way into one of those little wooden boxes where the most sedate, polished families sit during Derby Week, where everybody you see around you probably inherited their tickets from their fathers and grandfathers before them.

It was a mile-and-a-quarter race. Satan's Thunder started way in the back. By the halfway point, though, he'd advanced to midway in the pack.

As they came around the last turn, all of a sudden he kicked out to the side and ran like someone had stuck a hot poker up his ass. It looked like all the other horses were standing still.

Randy and I were losing our minds. We were both screaming at the tops of our lungs, "Whooooooooo! Come on!" By this time, all these elite-type people were staring at us instead of the race. They hadn't expected this outbreak of Brooklyn-style behavior in their well-mannered midst.

I got so excited I was waving my arms and saying to this lady beside me, "Jesus, lady, you got to yell for this horse." As the words came out of my mouth, my arm flailed through the air. I knocked her mint julep out of her hands and all over her starched white linen dress.

Satan's Thunder was up to third place. It got down to the last eighth-mile when I yelled at the top of my professionally trained voice, *"GO, YOU MOTHER-FUCKER, GO!"*

The lady looked at me like I had just caused an avalanche of turds to fall in her lap.

"I *beg* your pardon!"

The race ended in a dead heat. While we sat there waiting for the results of the photo finish, I suddenly remembered myself. "Oh, my God," I said to the lady and to her husband, who looked like someone that might have a derringer hidden in his gold-tipped cane. "I'm so sorry. I had two thousand bucks riding on that horse. Please, let me buy you dinner. Let me buy you a brand-new dress."

"You won't buy me *anything*," she said. "There's *nothing* you could buy me to make up for this!"

Well, what else could I do? Satan's Thunder was declared the winner and I just had to collect my winnings.

When we walked over to the windows, Phil Donahue came striding up to us.

"Goddamn it, Wolf!" he said. "Son of a bitch! That

332

horse won! Who'd you get that tip from?" He was dying to learn if there was a long shot he should bet on in the next race, which was the Main Event. But, as fate had it, the winner was the favorite—Seattle Slew.

That's okay. I won money on him, too.

Chapter Nineteen

When enough people had gotten over being scared by the Grateful Dead's outlaw-hippie image, and they were starting to enjoy greater-than-ever fan loyalty and record sales, Jerry Garcia said something like "Even if you were the town whore, stick around long enough and sooner or later you become respectable."

And I guess that's what my trip is. I started out as an opportunistic renegade. By now, I've lasted long enough to become sort of an American Original Respectable Renegade. And a link to the Golden Age of Rock 'n' Roll.

But I still love the idea of being some kind of pirate. That's why I jumped with both feet on an opportunity that came along about 1981, when some folks from England contacted me about participating in a revival of Radio Caroline.

When rock 'n' roll was in its formative years, England and the European continent didn't have a wealth of radio stations. There were very few channels, and each of them was under tight government control. But sailors and merchant marine type folks would return from

America to places like London or Liverpool with hot records they'd picked up Stateside. Thanks to disreputable groups like the Beatles and the Rolling Stones, who copied songs off these records, there came to be a big demand for blues and rock 'n' roll. However, the conservative folks who called the shots at the British Broadcasting Corporation were reluctant to put this music on the air.

That's why pirate radio blossomed. One operation was Radio Luxembourg, which ran a transmitter from a ship out in the English Channel. Another was Radio Caroline, which beamed into England from a ship in the North Sea. These stations played the hip, subversive, outside, *exciting* stuff that caught the ears of young would-be musicians.

The government eventually saw to it that these stimulating stations got shut down.

Lots of people were aware that plans were afoot to restart Radio Caroline, so it had to be done with a little secrecy. You could be arrested while you were going out to a pirate radio ship. So my cohorts and I went to Europe under the guise of promoting a compilation record package.

The plan was to do radio guest shots and other dates around the Continent, then one day secretly hop on a seaworthy craft that would deliver me to the new broadcast ship's secret location, somewhere in the North Sea. Then Radio Caroline would ride again, inaugurated with the Wolfman's howl and a mighty blast of rhythm and blues.

Illegal, perhaps, but definitely irresistible.

This was to be the trip of all trips. Unfortunately, in the renegade business you often have big plans that come within half an inch of going all the way, looming briefly on the precipice of greatness, only to fall over the cliff instead.

The rebirth of Radio Caroline was one of them.

"This is really going to open up the other side of the world to us," one of my pals enthused as we got off our plane at Heathrow Airport outside London. Actually, I already had quite a few fans on that side of the Atlantic. There was a guy in England who did a very open imitation of me (but didn't do it very well). Despite the popularity of *American Graffiti*, though, there weren't many people in England who recognized me. It was actually pretty nice to go walking down the street and not hear anyone yell "Hey, Wolfman!"

We had spent a lot of time in America making up special Radio Caroline broadcast tapes. My writers consulted with some British folks, to figure out how effectively my kinds of jokes and remarks would translate, going from American English to English English. The people putting money into the project were worried that my humor, or "humour" as they spelled it, might not go over with the British.

We got so thorough in our preparations that we even bought patches to stick on behind our ears for preventing seasickness. The North Sea develops a pretty mean chop in a storm.

After initial meetings in London, we went to Paris and promoted records. We were doing interviews left and right.

Meanwhile, I never got to meet the guy, this sort of English Donald Trump type financier, who was putting it together. He kept stalling. Strange things seemed to be going on behind our backs, but we had no idea what they were.

Over in Paris, I did a show in French that was sort of

a history of rock 'n' roll. There are some French people who have a deep love affair with images of 1950s and 1960s America. I heard of one group there that collects old records, goes around in black leather jackets, and calls themselves the Dixie-Fried Hellcats.

Of course, I don't speak any French. So to do that show I had to sit at a table facing a French guy who would recite two or three syllables in a row. I repeated them as closely as I could, then my man Lonnie got busy with a razor blade and spliced all the syllables into complete sentences. We hammered out thirty separate half-hour shows like that.

I'd done much the same thing before in Germany and Japan. In fact, my fake Japanese was smooth enough to earn me the title of "The Emperor of Pleasing Graciousness" in that country. And some German magazine gave me the title of "The Laughing Chancellor of Comedy." That's okay, though, you can keep on calling me Wolf.

However, if you're more comfortable with "Pardon me, my your Gracious Emperor-ness," stick with whatever feels natural.

While I was in Paris there was a guest radio shot on Europe One. When I was ready to go on the air live, I asked the engineers for some telephone books, which puzzled their French brows.

Long ago, though, I picked up a trick from Alan Freed's broadcasts. He used to thump on a phone book in time with the beat of the records he was playing and shout along, either joining the singer in a chorus or just improvising something between the lines.

This time, I handed the phone books to my buddy Mars. They put on a record and he started beating the Paris phone directory while I began screaming wild exhortations.

I could see the engineers going nuts. The meters on their boards were dancing maniacally. They'd never heard anything so loud in their lives. In fact, Mars and I blew their studio speakers right out. They went off the air, saying all kinds of things in French that we couldn't understand, and probably wouldn't want to.

I loved it. My feeling is, "I do what I do." If you hire the Wolfman, you get a Wolfman performance.

As you know from what I said earlier about Marlon Brando and George Lucas, I'm nuts about movie people. I did a few movie and TV things after *Graffiti*—some *Battlestar Galactica* episodes, and a bit as a crooked preacher in a funny but gruesome picture called *Motel Hell*. I've always wanted to expand on that side of things.

Toward the end of our European stay, my manager and I were in the café of our Paris hotel one morning. He was talking with a press agent who was supposed to be a real important guy around there, but I more or less tuned out of the conversation and focused on the big, buttery croissants in front of me.

At some point, a fat guy with a beard came over to our table. The French guy introduced him to me, but I had kind of lost interest in deciphering foreign accents, so I didn't catch the name. I was homesick for America anyway.

Well, this new guy at the table was very pleasant with me, and he seemed to be a fan.

"I always thought you were really a character," he said.

"Thank you."

"Maybe we could sometime get together. I'd like to talk to you."

"Yeah. Let's do that sometime."

Shortly after that he left. A couple of minutes later the

French press agent said, "It appears that Sergio Leone thinks quite highly of you."

"*What?* Wait a minute! That man was Sergio Leone?"

I had just been talking to the creator of *A Fistful of Dollars, For a Few Dollars More, The Good, the Bad, and the Ugly, Once Upon a Time in the West,* and *A Fistful of Dynamite.* This was the guy who kicked Clint Eastwood's career into high gear and totally inspired his style as a director.

"Yes."

"Why didn't anybody tell me?"

"Ah, but we did."

I went running out of the café, croissant flakes flying off my jacket all the way, through the hotel lobby, and out into the street.

No luck. I never saw Sergio Leone again.

Luck ran out on Radio Caroline, too. We got word while we were still in Paris.

There were three versions of the story going around: one, there never was a boat; two, the boat was in bad shape and it sank; three (and this is the one I like to believe), the government sabotaged the boat to keep Radio Caroline off the air.

Speaking of shows in different nations, the years I was on the Armed Forces Radio Network did a lot to make folks in the Land of the Rising Sun a little bit Wolfman Jack conscious.

One time I had to quickly catch a flight to Japan after spending a day hosting a car show at the Los Angeles Convention Center. Because we'd been selling autographed photos at the car show, my manager was carrying about $3,000 in cash, almost all of it in one-dollar bills.

Just after arriving at the Tokyo airport, we were walking along a balcony area. There was a bit of a crowd gathering down below, maybe 150 people. I didn't know what was happening, but it appeared that a Japanese celebrity was somewhere among the crowd.

"Don," I said, "do you still have that cash in your carry-on bag?"

"Yeah. Why?"

"Hand it to me, okay?"

I opened the bag and took out two fistfuls of dollar bills. I stepped up to the edge of the balcony, gave out a wolf howl—"Awoooooo . . ."—and said, "Have mercy! The Wolfman wanna thank all his fans for comin' out to welcome him!"

Maybe twenty or so of the people down below looked up. I sent some greenbacks fluttering through the air. As soon as those bills began landing on everybody's shoe-tops, the whole crowd was looking my way. I showered them with more. People started swarming in, doubling and tripling the size of the crowd. It takes a while to get rid of three thousand singles. By the time I'd gotten done with dispensing paper money and Wolf-style benedictions, the scene was turning into bedlam.

There've been a bunch of times when I've been waiting at a red light, people have noticed me and begun trying to make contact and I've thrown money out of my car windows for them. It's always a kick. But this must've been the only time in Tokyo history that some fool played Instant Cash in public. The wire services picked it up, but somehow they got the story confused, so they reported that it was hundred-dollar bills that old Wolfman Jack was throwing around.

One time I did a live TV show that was being beamed to Germany for the Armed Forces Radio and Television Service, but was shot live at the Palladium, a big theater two blocks east of Sunset and Vine in Hollywood.

The host of the show was Johnny Grant, the honorary "Mayor of Hollywood." He's the guy who's always grand marshal of the Hollywood Christmas parade, which they televise just about the time you're trying to recover from eating too much Thanksgiving turkey. If you've seen footage on TV news when somebody is getting a star with their name on it on the Hollywood Walk of Fame, Grant is the little round gnome of a guy who's standing on the side, smiling like it's the greatest day of his life. He takes his honorary mayordom real seriously.

My road manager was going to play his electric guitar and Mars was going to play piano while Les Brown and his Band of Renown backed up my vocals on the Big Joe Turner classic, "Shake, Rattle and Roll."

We were waiting backstage for Johnny Grant to introduce us. "I can't just go on *normally*," I said. "We've got to do something funny."

Mars used to do a weird character called Hoppy, based on Dennis Hopper in *Apocalypse Now*—a whacked-out, hopped-up photographer in a grimy army fatigue jacket. Except, where Dennis Hopper's character had an overwhelming awe for Marlon Brando's character, Hoppy was nutty and obsessed over Wolfman Jack. He was always saying, "He's like, he's like *too much*, man."

I handed Mars a Polaroid camera.

"When Grant introduces me," I said, "you go out there and be Hoppy. Shoot pictures of the audience. This will be great 'cause they don't expect it. Then you'll introduce me and I'll come out."

"All right," Mars said, "but the cameras are rolling, so everything we do is gonna go out on the air."

"Aw, come on. Let's do it!"

As Grant introduced me, Mars came running out in his fatigues with a ropy bandanna around his head, looking like he just crawled out from under a sheet of cardboard in a back alley. He looked out feverishly over the audience and said, "Hey, wait a minute, man! Stop the applause! Wolfman will be right out, but he wants me to take a picture of the audience. You're always taking taking taking pictures of him. He's gotta, he's gotta have a picture of *you*."

Johnny Grant knew nothing of this. He instantly decided Hoppy was actually some genuine lunatic off the street. Which is a great compliment to Mars's acting ability. Although if you knew Mars you might say, "Naw, not that much of a stretch."

Anyway, little Johnny Grant ran across the stage from the wings, grabbed Hoppy, and tried to wrestle him off the stage. Meanwhile, the camera kept rolling. Mars had a live mike in his hands. He was trying to do the bit and also trying to tell Grant out of one side of his mouth, "Johnny, stop! It's part of the act! Leave me alone!"

Meantime, he kept talking to the audience, "Hey, man, you're gonna see the Wolfman . . ."

Grant wouldn't give up. He threw everything he had into the struggle, yelling, "Hey, Security! Get this guy out of here!"

Eventually I walked up to him and said, "Hey, Johnny, how ya doin', man? This guy's my piano player."

Grant looked like someone who'd been served with a subpoena. He went limp. Mars ran to the piano and we did the song just right. I was so happy. I'd taken a straight program and dented it completely.

Later on, Grant got real faint and had to be taken to the hospital.

He never said so, but I think the misadventure with Hoppy put him there.

Anyone who wants a star on the Hollywood Walk of Fame has to send an application through Johnny Grant and his official committee.

My guess is that I'll need to wait a long, long time.

Chapter Twenty

In 1974 I was scheduled to emcee a show somewhere in between Washington and Baltimore. Ticket sales had been a little slow, so the promoters wanted to stage something dramatic at the last minute.

It so happened that a new wildlife park was scheduled to open somewhere in the vicinity in that same week. And this park had a huge display of wolves.

Somebody got the bright idea to call up the managers of the new park and say, "Hey, here's something that's sure to get good PR for both of us. Let's tape a local TV interview with Wolfman Jack, and have him surrounded by all of your wild wolves."

Within a couple of hours we were out there, standing on the outside of the wolf enclosure while a TV crew set up their cameras. The wolves were huddled far away, under trees. The park provided five guys in "Great White Hunter" khaki safari outfits, complete with long metal-tipped poles for controlling the wolves.

"We'll bring the wolves over close to the fence," the foreman of the wolf wranglers said. "Wolfman can go in there and stand in front of them. We'll be protecting him from just out of camera range."

They drove their jeep around and herded the pack over, then motioned me to come into the enclosure. I walked through the gate and came within about six or seven yards of the wolf pack before turning to face the camera. As soon as my back was turned, one of those wolves lunged for the back of my right foot and got a solid grip with his teeth just above the ankle. A couple of others circled around in front, in position to spring for my throat if I toppled to the ground. They were trying to bring me down for the kill just like they'd do it to a caribou up in the wild north woods.

The animal handler guys in their picture-perfect outfits froze in place. Fortunately, I had my favorite high-heeled, silver-tipped cowboy boots on. I shook my leg loose from the teeth of the wolf in back and kicked it in the direction of the front wolves. As the wolves took a half step back, the handlers finally snapped into action and kept them at bay until I could hustle my ass back through the fence.

The park people insisted on loading me into an ambulance and taking me to a nearby hospital. They put me in a bed in the emergency ward and said, "Don't worry about a thing. We insist on paying for any treatment you need." What they really meant was, "Please, please, don't sue our brand-new pants off."

Thanks to my cowboy boots, I wasn't hurt in the slightest. There was a bruise around my ankle, but the skin wasn't even broken.

"Get me my clothes," I told my manager. "I wanna get dressed and go back to the hotel."

"No," he said. "This is too good to waste. Think of the headlines: *Wolfman Jack Attacked By Wolves! Beloved*

Entertainer Battles Death Following Freak Attack. We can get this story going worldwide!"

He rushed down to the hospital's pharmacy and rustled up a pocketful of quarters, then got on the phone to all the news services and major papers. It was a Saturday, but he still managed to reach a few people.

Pretty soon, phone calls start coming back, seeking confirmation. But by then I actually was beginning to get sick. Not from what happened to me, but from all the people in the emergency ward who had blood and vomit all over themselves and who were flocking around my bed because they've never met anybody famous before.

I believe in being good to the fans, and I usually carry through on that belief, but I was starting to freak out. I grabbed my stuff and got the hell out of that hospital before we could get the wire services cooking on all that great free publicity.

Not long after we got back to L.A., I got hired to help promote Jesse Colin Young's version of the 1959 Johnny Preston hit, "Running Bear." The gig was to go to various L.A. stations in a limousine with a real, live bear. So there I was, tooling down Sunset Boulevard in the back seat of a limo, with the bear sitting right next to me and the trainer facing him, giving him two or three jellybeans every so often to keep him happy. This was the same bear that was in the TV show *Gentle Ben*. The trainer said, "Wolf, you wanna feed him?"

"Sure. How do you do it?"

"Just keep your hand flat like this. See? And he licks them right off your palm."

I gave it a try, but I must've held my fingers wrong, because the next thing I knew, old Gentle Ben had closed his teeth around my wrist. With my free hand, I rattled the bag of jelly beans and he let go. I fed him the whole bag at once, out of gratitude.

Once I got over the shock, we had a lot of fun. We had lunch at Tail of the Pup, a famous hot dog stand shaped like a giant hot dog. It was situated then on a busy street, about where the Beverly Center is today, and the people driving by almost wrecked their cars at the sight of Gentle Ben on his hind legs, scarfing frankfurters under the L.A. sun. Then we went to the Century Plaza Hotel in Century City for an unannounced visit to some record company executives attending a serious conference. My guess is, some of those guys had to send their suit pants out for emergency dry cleaning after we left.

There was another time, about 1986, when I got into what looked like real danger. This was the one and only time in my entire life that I ever copped an attitude and walked off a gig. The folks I offended taught me a lesson real fast.

The Wolfman Jack Show used to run in the Virgin Islands, on WJKC, a St. Croix radio station. A local promoter down there figured we'd do well with a few personal appearances on the more remote islands.

For a smaller situation like these, I usually travel light — just me and Lonnie and the basic, no-frills package: some tapes of vintage blues, R&B, and rock 'n' roll oldies, which I introduce and kind of improvise on in Wolfman fashion. It's just enough of a show to get the people up and dancing and having a good time. The clubs are supposed to provide a sound system, and any additional live entertainment. So we packed up for a good time in some of the islands' local joints, also working in some higher-paying jobs at big tourist clubs.

One of the first things you learn about in those parts is the phenomenon they call "island time." Folks down there don't have a lot of money, but they've got a beautiful place to live and nature is real generous with fish and coconuts, so people mostly move at a relaxed pace. We landed on the island of Tortola late at night. The guy who met us at the plane pointed to a van and said, "Go ahead and get in." We did, expecting that at any moment a driver would jump behind the wheel. Even with the sun down, it was steaming hot. After sitting in the van for about twenty minutes and seeing nothing happen, we stuck our heads out the window. We saw eight or nine local guys standing around in a circle.

"Hey, what's going on?" I said. "Can't we get going to our hotel?"

"Just a minute, mon," one of the guys said. He stepped back from the circle to show that they were huddled around a little transistor radio on top of a fifty-five-gallon oil drum.

"Dodger game," he added. And nobody moved until the last out in the bottom of the ninth.

After Tortola, we were off to Virgin Gorda in a single-engine plane. The pilot was so huge, maybe four hundred pounds, that I couldn't see where the plane was going. His head and shoulders blocked the windows. After buzzing over a few miles of open ocean, he said we were approaching Virgin Gorda. By the time that I was able to see anything, we seemed to be heading right for the bottom of a mountain.

"Where's the freakin' runway?" I yelled. But as the plane got up closer, a dirt runway appeared, crossways at the base of the mountain. He banked us into a sharp right and landed us BOOM right on the dirt, alongside a rust-streaked Quonset hut that was the airport.

A driver in a jeep pulled up to deliver us to the hotel, pausing every so often for goats to cross the road.

The hotel itself was straight out of *Casablanca*—lazy overhead fans and everything. Wind off the ocean supplied the air conditioning. It was beautiful, but primitive.

We arrived at the gig to find about five hundred people in the club. This was obviously one of the biggest events of the season on Virgin Gorda.

The high humidity in those islands isn't good for electronic equipment. A band was just finishing a set of calypso and reggae-type music. Halfway through their last song, their PA blew out.

"Don't worry," the club owner said. "I got my own sound system." We took a look. It was real cheesy and outdated. Then we took a look at the owner. He was bigger than the pilot who'd brought us in. And—as we would soon learn—he was also the ranking chief of the biggest local clan and a voodoo priest, to boot.

The club was laid out in an L shape, with the stage at the short end and the bar at the long end. When I got onstage, I could only see about two dozen of the people I was supposed to entertain.

Lonnie took the mike and kicked off my set with "Ladies and gentlemen, here he is—Wolfman Jack!"

That was what he said. But what came out was something like, "Hey, gottrurrurr-roogax rurrrr erkump!" The sound system was worse than it looked. It sounded like a live microphone lashed to a TV antenna during a thunderstorm.

"It's like dis sometimes, mon," the club's owner told Lonnie, "just go ahead wit your show."

"Hey, man," I told him, "I just came in from L.A. We don't have stuff like this. We usually have our thing together."

He shot me an ugly glare. "Mon, dis ain't L.A. You better do the show right wit what you got!"

I tried my best. "C'mon over here and dance!" I said, but all that came through the speakers was "Graxx ugger gurks-grubb ack!"

"Listen, Wolf," Lonnie warned, "these people are getting pissed. Let's mellow out and just get through this."

But I just couldn't take the frustration. I let the mike drop to the floor and walked out the back.

Lonnie grabbed up all our tapes and hurried along in the dark to catch up with me.

Through the haze of my anger, I started to remember that we were on an island. A very little one. Filled with people who were probably real loyal to the clan chief. I couldn't exactly grab a cab and disappear to Greenwich Village.

Nearing the hotel, we had to walk through some trees. We began to hear a crunching sound behind us. Some heavy feet were snapping dry limbs on the ground.

"This is it, man," I told Lonnie. "They're gonna come at us with machetes."

The sound moved up alongside. We froze in our tracks and prepared to meet our fate. As soon as we got ourselves ready to die, a cow cut across the pathway right in front of us, stepping double-time, even more scared of us than we were of it.

We wiped some nervous sweat from our foreheads and laughed at ourselves as we walked back up to the rooms. Then we saw that each of our doors had a freshly de-headed white chicken strung upside down from the doorknob, flailing and twitching around, spatter-painting the woodwork with blood.

We both stayed awake all night long, absolutely sure that a gang of natives with long knives would come crashing through our door any minute. I started wishing that I hadn't watched *Curse of the Zombie* so many times in my earlier life.

The next morning, at the Quonset hut airport, the people in charge of the flights kept bumping us from one flight to the next all day long. Obviously, the big chief wanted to make sure we stayed long enough to squirm in our fear. And his tactic was working. Late that afternoon we were finally allowed to board a plane, and I never in my whole life felt better about getting airborne than I did that day.

Fortunately, times like that are the exception. The adventure I get to live out most of the time is the best kind of adventure of all: getting to meet thousands and thousands of people, and have good times with them, relating to each other through music. Like when the Eagles had their "Hell Freezes Over" reunion tour in '94 and I was backstage visiting my old friend Joe Walsh. The Eagles practically never bring nonband members onstage at their show, but Joe told me, "Wolf, I won't go out tonight unless you come out, too." I did it. Walking out there in front of a stadium audience, I collected a wonderful cheer, and all the other guys in the band were totally nice about it. And also in '94 I began doing a live show every weekend in Washington, D.C., from Planet Hollywood for a station called XTRA-104.

Well, if there's any folks who need their minds liberated by music whenever possible, it's the people who run the government, right?

As of right now, my D.C. show is going like gangbusters. We've got the biggest audience of listeners age twenty-five to forty-five, we're playing a lot of what I call "closet classics"—which are great songs that are usually overlooked by oldies stations, like "Something You Got," "Hello My Lover," or the original Shorty Long version of "Devil with a Blue Dress On."

Pretty soon we hope to have this show going out to other major cities. Keep your fingers crossed for the Wolfman, folks.

For my money, music is the greatest medium of communication going. It reflects what people are experiencing, helps them get through difficulties, and teaches them how to celebrate life and be joyful.

I've lived during a time in music for humanity that was unbelievable. It's like they keep playing Bach and Beethoven and Mozart. That music never disappeared. It's stayed fresh to this day. Well, some of this music that we had in the 1950s and 1960s and 1970s will endure forever. I don't think it's ever going to go away. And there's nothing happening today that's going to compete with it. Most of the rappers, they're just trying to pull naughty stunts. There's a rap record for just about any kind of sex you want to get into. Some real raunchy shit. Kids are collecting that and they're giggling and they think that's great. It doesn't work for me. And then there's that poor Seattle guy that blew his brains out with a shotgun. I'm sorry, but for my ears, his music was just as depressing as the way he went out.

Maybe I'm gettin' old, but I don't understand a lot of the culture today. It seems like we're laying stuff on kids before they're really ready to handle it.

I meet a lot of very young kids at my gigs that are into vintage rock 'n' roll. They get shaky when they want to ask for an autograph. Blows my mind every time it happens. I really think that there isn't anything out there that's as exciting for these kids as there was back in the 1950s, 1960s, and 1970s.

The 1980s was kind of like a drop-off point. It got weaker each ten-year period. And now we're in the 1990s and there's next to nothing.

Maybe I shouldn't sound so dire. There's lots of artists, both old and new, doing soulful, make-ya-feel-good stuff that I go for. Like Lyle Lovett, with his great songwriting and arrangements for big bands, or Bonnie Raitt, whose stuff really rings true, or Lenny Kravitz, who is a great, soulful artist. And Ray Charles has recut a lot of his classic sides live onstage. Some of them are a lot hotter than the great originals. And it makes me wonder why we don't hear much Ray Charles on the radio.

One of my problems is, I don't listen to the pop stations. I try to, and I tune in MTV to sample what's happening, but I find that I just can't keep my attention on it.

I don't think it's about being old. I think it's about *not being moved*. Back when Elvis was at his peak, when rock 'n' roll was really hot, even the adults would be into his latest hit tune, whistling along whenever it came over the radio. When the Beatles or the Stones had a great record in the 1960s, the fifty-year-olds were gettin' down to it, too.

Now I meet kids in their teens or early twenties who have a big fixation on rockabilly, or the Doors, the Grateful Dead, Bob Marley, Eric Clapton, the British Invasion, practically anything except what's new today. It's almost like they wish they'd been living in an earlier time.

Part of the problem is radio itself. I still love the medium, but nowadays a new artist has to practically go through a computer bank just to get on the air. They've gotta have a perfect video, and have sex appeal written on their face in big letters. They've got to be a whole lot like what's already popular, so program directors won't be scared to play their records.

In the old days, someone who had a band together in a little town or medium-sized city could go in the studio and press a record of their two best tunes. If the local disc jockeys liked it, they'd get behind it. Just like Dewey Phillips down in Memphis got on the horn for Elvis Presley's first record on the local Sun label.

If those DJs got some request calls in, record stores would pick up on the vibe and stock the record. And if they sold quite a few, the big labels would zero in. Pretty soon they'd extend that band a nationwide deal.

That's why so much great rock 'n' roll came from different pockets of the country, exposing the best regional styles. That stuff had some *flavor* to it. Buddy Holly out of Lubbock, Texas. Fats Domino and Lloyd Price out of New Orleans. Gary "U.S." Bonds out of Newport News. And so on.

Even if I wish there was more adventurous spirit in today's playlists, radio still has a magic to it that no other medium has. To be good in radio is really a very tough thing to do. The only thing you can do is to give them a voice and a personality. They've gotta picture what you look like and where you're sitting and what your situation is like. You've got to be sensitive enough that the people out there feel you, right away, and know you're for real.

On radio, you've got to immediately put your ass on the line. To be a disc jockey today, when the music is so controlled, is harder than it was in my early days. You can't express your feeling for music, like the old-time disc jockeys used to do. You could feel their personalities through the style of music that they played. They knew how to put records together to give you a boost.

That's the thing I studied when I was a kid, when I used to listen to people like John R. and Jocko Henderson and all the others I've praised in this book. I studied their styles because they all made me feel so good. I wanted to be *with* them.

So you might call me a dinosaur, but I'm one of the last people who know how to do that thing, and how to do an improvised disc jockey show. I know how to put records together so over, say, fifteen minutes I've built the audience up to a certain peak. Then I play something to trigger their memory banks and their imaginations and take 'em to ecstasy.

When you hear a guy on the air and you know he knows what he's doing, it's a pleasure to listen to somebody like that.

You can't really learn it in a broadcasting school. You can learn the fundamentals and the rules—how far you can stretch here and how far you can stretch there. But the style of your presentation is something that's got to come from you. It's got to *be* you. And it's got to be hip and be something that everybody digs. Come to think of it, that's what you should aim to bring to whatever you do in life, whether you're a dentist, a cowboy, or a clerk in a store at the mall.

Because it's so *me*, I absolutely love doing my radio show. I get shaky inside. It's an immediate high. I get to lay all my problems aside. They don't even enter my mind.

Speaking of problems, every now and then you've got to stop and admit that everybody on the planet has got their share. Sometimes those problems get people kind of twisted up inside. They get nervous, or shy, or they start acting bad. Anything to get a wall up so other people won't hurt them.

It took me lots of trial and error to figure this out, but I believe *everybody* I meet is really a loving human being. I love them all. I always find something within them that's good.

Sometimes it really pisses me off when people hide that essential goodness behind insecurities and creepy, antisocial behavior. Because I always see talent in there. I see talent in a lot of different people. They don't even know they've got it. They've got to get past their ego trips and their feeling that they're bigger, or they're smaller, than everybody else.

We're all here, we're on the same level, man, and whatever we've got to contribute, that's what we've got to do. Because it's not enough to have talent. That's just the starting point on your journey. You've got to *work* that talent, too. Put it out there, light it up, so it can entertain people, or inspire them.

I always feel it's special to be in anybody's presence. To have people love you and respect you is a real important thing for a human being. The reason my life has been such a terrific adventure is because lots of people have given me that love and respect along the way. I want to use these stories out of my life as way of returning the gift.

I suppose I feel that especially strongly because I'm lucky to be here. My life has been threatened a bunch of times. I think the Good Lord's lookin' out for me. There must be more purpose for me. Otherwise, I wouldn't be sitting here. I've been crazy enough in my life. And I've definitely stepped beyond the boundaries that sensible people would never cross, taken some stupid chances, and come back to talk about it.

I still like to take chances, to bend things in an unexpected direction or two. But in my fifties I've also started to appreciate what calmness is all about.

There came a time, late in the 1980s, that my family and I felt ready to leave Los Angeles and Beverly Hills in the hands of folks who enjoyed big-city life more than we did. Nowadays, when I'm not on the road, my days are spent on the grounds of a very old plantation house in a quiet part of North Carolina, around where Lou grew up. In fact, it's a house that her ancestors built.

There's a lot of history around here. Several different

Indian tribes used to be in this territory, just living off the rich land, the many rivers, and the nearby ocean. The first English colony in the New World was not far from my home. If you listen right, you can still kind of hear an Elizabethan English accent mixed in with the southern-style way people talk around here.

Kitty Hawk, where the Wright Brothers flew the first plane, is also close by. The pirate Bluebeard had a house on one of the rivers around here. Catfish Hunter, the great big-league pitcher, comes from just down the road.

It's hurricane country, too. A year ago, one of the storms lifted a big, old tree right out of our side yard. Recently, a frisky lightning bolt dug a pit in our lawn the size of a big doghouse.

Lou's family history traces back across three hundred years in these parts, to three brothers who came over from England and established plantations. Around that time, Quakers were being slaughtered up in the state of Virginia. The brother who built the house we now live in would go up there and smuggle folks down to safety. He built them a church, and he also built a shipyard in the back of our property, to do repairs on ships that came up the river after sailing all the way from England.

You can still find remnants of that boatyard in the tall grass. And the river still flows through the property. There's some pretty good bass fishing, too.

Overall, we've got about 160 acres. My two children live nearby, and my granddaughter, and a big number of Lou's relatives as well. I'm surrounded by family. That includes Lonnie, who's been with me since the age of nineteen, and his own growing family. They live next door to Tod, his wife, and their baby. Other folks that were part of my scene are off in different parts of the country, doing their own thing. But there's still a strong bond of good feelings between me and Mars, Mellow Mike, Bob Wilson, Don Kelley, Mario Alfaro, Mo Burton, Joe Walsh, John Herron, Mike Howard, and dozens of other folks who've weaved their way in and out of my life's story.

In a sense, we're all family.

The main thing I wanted since I was a young kid was to have a real family. I've achieved my goal. I'm the happiest I've ever been in a long time, here in North Carolina, being with everybody that loves me. Lou and I, through a lot of ups and downs, have stayed married for more than three decades. Not many folks end up married that long, especially when they're involved in show business, the rock 'n' roll end of it in particular. So we're proud of ourselves.

We went through the whole thing together. And that was the fun part of it. Now we can flash back on all the bad times, and all the mistakes we made, all the frivolous bullshit we went through, and realize that we not only made it, we got stronger along the way.

The Wolfman is supposed to be a wild character. But now that you've read my book, I'm pretty sure you've caught on to my scam. You know I'm a nice person, and you know I make you feel good. And I find very fine qualities in you. You're also a gentle person, you're a good person. There's no evil in you. Y'know what I mean?

If everybody was feeling like this, there wouldn't be nobody ripping each other off. What a world it would be if everybody held on to that attitude.

There are certain things that are almost impossible to teach to people, and yet people can learn them. What I hope you've learned out of my life story is the fact that life is a great party, going on all around you, and you're invited. Hey, you might even be tonight's guest of honor!

Jump into that party with everything you've got, smiling until you inspire the folks around you to smile right
back. You've got something special to offer the party.
Let everyone know that you believe it, too. Because time
is just too precious to spend any other way.

I hope the adventures in my life inspire you to follow
your own dreams, too. If you need any more inspiration,
just turn on some of the music we've been talking about
in this book. I promise it'll move you.

Epilogue

Now, I said in the Introduction that the whole world is dying to have soul, and I promised that this book would show you how. In case the answer has eluded you up to now, I'll spell it out real plainly in these closing words.

The quickest, most surefire way to acquire some soul is through entering the happiness business.

I found my way into the happiness business via becoming lovestruck with black music, but there are lots of other avenues.

It's the greatest business of all. You don't need a lot of bread. The inventory is all inside you. And the more competition there is, the more everybody involved comes out winners. You can break in by spending your energy, big-time, in doing nice things for people, whenever you can.

Concentrate on lifting somebody's spirits, at least one time every day. Slip a couple of bucks into that down-and-out guy's hand. Tell somebody you work with how much you appreciate the great job they're doing. Anytime somebody makes you feel good, let them know it.

Amplify those good feelings. Do the kinds of things that will make your family strong and together. Lay out some real good loving touches. Let your hands express what your heart is feeling inside.

That's what being in the happiness business is all about. That's what I try to bring to whatever scene I'm in. Because it's truly a privilege to be in another human being's company—whether in person, over the airwaves, or even through the pages of a book. Beneath our different skins and colors and cultures, we're all connected to the same big heartbeat. When you're hearing that heartbeat, you've got soul.

And now you're ready to get on up to the advanced levels of soulfulness. Here it comes . . .

In my life, I've gone way overboard now and then, in a whole lot of different ways. But I always had this one valuable idea in my head: "When you do right, you're gonna come out right." And sooner or later, no matter how bad I messed up, I remembered that idea, and got back to doing right with the people around me.

Whenever I've gotten lost, that's the beacon that's guided me back home. That's why it don't matter what it is you do in life. You don't have to be a hipster, you don't have to blow tenor sax, you don't have to sing like Otis Redding. Just do right by all the people you meet along the way. Not only because it makes for harmony, but also because it's gonna make *you* come out all right in the end.

Whenever the Wolfman broadcasts, I'm having a nice party in that studio—even if it's all in my head. And no matter if you're feeling happy or depressed, come on in here, man. We're gonna fill you with a little goodness. Maybe you're under a dark cloud. Well, there's a bright sunshiny day over here. We're gonna hip-hop around and play the everlasting great sounds of B.B. King, Rufus Thomas, Elvis, the Shirelles, Jerry Lee Lewis, and all the other soul-shakin', captivatin' masters of music that gets you where you live. We're gonna cook a big pot of that Memphis Soul Stew until we do a total re-do on your boogaloo situation. We're gonna have a good time and say, "Have mercy, baby," and it's gonna make you feel better.

Being the Wolfman is more than just spinning records and making a funky, beastly sound of joy come out of a human throat. It's being a mouthpiece for the possibility of happiness, it's about the great connection to humanity that you can find in just spreading love around and being your own true self.

When enough people find it, we'll all get so inspired in our hearts that all our hang-ups and intolerance trips will get laid aside for good and *we'll all HAVE MERCY on each other*, all the time.

Let the congregation say *"A-men!"*

Byron Laursen wrote two previous national bestsellers, *Show Time* and *The Winner Within*—both with all-time great NBA coach Pat Riley. While researching for *Have Mercy!*, he shared juicy North Carolina barbecue, soulful conversations, and lazy fishing trips with the Wolfman.

Following the Wolf's trail also led him backstage at many concerts, where he met Chuck Berry, the Coasters, and several other lifelong rock 'n' roll idols.

If this book is a monster success, Wolfman Jack has promised to buy him the biggest, nastiest motorcycle in the world.

The Wolfman Jack Fan Club can be reached by writing to Wolfman Jack, P.O. Box 38, Belvidere, North Carolina 27919.

DATE			